INDIE **FONTS 2**

A Compendium of Digital Type from Independent Foundries

INDIE **FONTS 2**

A Compendium of Digital Type from Independent Foundries

Richard Kegler
James Grieshaber
Tamye Riggs
Editors

P-Type Publications
Buffalo, New York
2003

Library of Congress Control Number: 2002117837

ISBN: 0963108239

First Edition.
First Printing: June 2003.

Published by:
P-Type Publications
PO Box 770
Buffalo, NY 14213

Designed in the USA.
Printed and bound in Hong Kong.

Contents

Introduction

Considering the firmly physical origins of type (thank you, Mr. Gutenberg), it's a bit ironic that the internet is now the primary vehicle for buying and selling typefaces. And why not? It's much cheaper to design and build a website, even one with a robust ecommerce system, than it is to continually design, produce, and deliver printed catalogs to potential customers.

What's more, personal computing and the net have contributed to a literal explosion in the number of available typefaces. These days, anyone with a computer and the right software can create fonts. It still takes years of study and practice (and talent, creativity, and dedication) to design quality typefaces—that will never change. But more people are making faces than ever before, and the number of fonts available to computer users continues to grow exponentially.

The inevitable questions come to mind: "Does the world really need more fonts? Hasn't everything already been done? Can't we just use what we already have?" It's only the alphabet, after all…

Let's put to rest right now the notion that we don't need new fonts. If designers had stopped making new fonts, we wouldn't have the exquisite *Dotic*, Miguel Hernández' bitmap fraktur designed for the screen. What would the world be like if František Štorm hadn't drawn his own version of the glorious *Baskerville*, and created its companion grotesk, *John Sans*? These are but a few examples of innovation in contemporary type design—the possibilities are virtually limitless.

In the fall of 2002, the first volume of *Indie Fonts* was published, show-casing nearly 2,000 fonts from 18 independent digital type foundries. Less than a year later, we're pleased to bring you *Indie Fonts 2*, featuring the creations of 19 additional foundries. These type makers range from those who've been around since the days of hot metal to others who opened up shop just this year.

Regardless of the length of time they've been producing type, these foundries share a common goal—they are dedicated to making original digital fonts imbued with a love of the craft, and are committed to bringing their creations to the people that need them.

Although most of the typefaces presented in the *Indie Fonts* series are available for review and purchase on the web, the participating foundries elected to show their designs in the media that type was invented for: print. Ink on paper is still the best way to display a typeface, and there are few things as delicious as the anticipation of turning the pages of a brand new book.

Enjoy the view.

The Editors

Font Style Index

Serif		
655 1722 Roman	692 *Baskerville Ten Bold Italic*	606 Duffy's Tavern NF
655 *1722 Italic*	692 BASKERVILLE TEN SC BOLD	606 Erehwon Roman NF
653 Albion	692 *BASKERVILLE TEN SC B.ITALI*	534 Faber Drei Normal
653 *Albion Italic*	606 Bergling Fantasia NF	534 *Faber Drei Kursiv*
754 Anarcharsis Basic LF Regular 0123	606 Bergling Fantasia Bold NF	534 Faber Drei Kräftig
754 Anarcharsis Basic HF Regular 0123	696 Biblon ITC	565 MVB Fantabular Regular
754 ANARCHARSIS SMALL CAPS REG	696 *Biblon ITC Italic*	565 *MVB Fantabular Italic*
754 Anarcharsis Basic LF Bold 0123	696 *Biblon ITC Swash Italic*	565 **MVB Fantabular Medium**
754 Anarcharsis Basic HF Bold 0123	696 BIBLON ITC SMALL CAPS	565 *MVB Fantabular Med Ital*
754 ANARCHARSIS SMALL CAPS BOLD	696 **Biblon ITC Bold**	565 **MVB Fantabular Bold**
754 Anarcharsis unicase	696 ***Biblon ITC Bold Italic***	565 ***MVB Fantabular Bold Ita***
689 Antique Ancienne	696 **BIBLON ITC SMALL CAPS BOL**	623 Floridium
689 *Antique Ancienne Italiqu*	604 Bo Diddlioni Stencil NF	623 *Floridium Italic*
689 Antique Moderne	549 Cavetto JF-Roman	623 **Floridium Bold**
689 *Antique Moderne Italique*	548 *Cavetto JF-Italic*	606 Gasoline Alley NF
689 Antique Regent	548 *Cavetto JF-Italic Alternate*	487 **Geis**
689 *Antique Regent Italique*	573 MVB Celestia Antiqua Roman	673 Goldenbook Light
475 Bartholeme Regular	573 *MVB Celestia Antiqua Italic*	673 Goldenbook Regular
475 *Bartholeme Italic*	573 MVB CELESTIA ANTIQUA SC	673 **Goldenbook Bold**
475 Bartholeme Medium	573 **MVB Celestia Antiqua Semi**	573 MVB Gryphius Roman
475 *Bartholeme Medium Italic*	573 **MVB Celestia Antiqua Bd**	573 *MVB Gryphius Italic*
475 **Bartholeme Bold**	573 MVB Celestia Antiqua Inline	573 MVB GRYPHIUS SMALL CAPS
475 ***Bartholeme Bold Italic***	573 **MVB Celestia Antiqua Ad**	607 Heberling Casual NF
475 **Bartholeme Extra Bold**	528 Charpentier Classicistique	607 Heberling Casual Bold NF
474 Bartholeme Open	528 *Charpentier Classic. Italique*	690 Jannon Antiqua
474 BARTHOLEME SMALL CAP OPEN	528 Charpentier Baroque	690 *Jannon Antiqua Italic*
692 Baskerville Ten Plain	528 Charpentier Renaissance	690 Jannon Ant. Medium
692 *Baskerville Ten Italic*	725 Dolly Roman	690 *Jannon Ant. Medium Italic*
692 BASKERVILLE TEN SC	725 *Dolly Italic*	690 **Jannon Ant. Bold**
692 *BASKERVILLE TEN SC ITALIC*	725 DOLLY SMALLCAPS	690 ***Jannon Ant. Bold Italic***
692 **Baskerville Ten Bold**	725 fb fh **fk** Dolly Ligatures	690 Jannon T Moderne Plain
	725 **Dolly Bold**	690 *Jannon T Moderne Italic*

690	*Jannon T Moderne Swash Ital*	703	***Juvenis Book Bold Ital.***	656	Mercian
690	JANNON T MOD. SC PLAIN	703	**Juvenis Medium Bold**	458	FTF Merlo Roman
690	*JANNON T MOD. SC ITALIC*	703	***Juvenis Med. Bold Ita***	458	*FTF Merlo Italic*
690	**Jannon T Moderne Bold**	703	Juvenis Text	458	FTF MERLO CAPS
690	***Jannon T Mod. Bold Italic***	703	*Juvenis Text Italic*	458	*FTF MERLO CAPS ITALIC*
690	**JANNON T MOD. SC BOLD**	703	**Juvenis Text Bold**	607	Mrs Bathhurst FGC
690	***JANNON T MOD. SC B.ITAL***	703	***Juvenis T. Bold Ital.***	628	MS KITTY
690	Jannon Text Plain	680	Kandal Book	628	MS KITTY BOLD
690	*Jannon Text Italic*	680	*Kandal Book Italic*	618	ITC Oldrichium Light
690	Jannon Text Medium	680	**Kandal Medium**	618	*ITC Oldrichium Light Italic*
690	*Jannon Text Med. Italic*	680	*Kandal Medium Italic*	618	ITC Oldrichium Regular
690	JANNON TEXT MED SC	681	**Kandal Bold**	618	*ITC Oldrichium Italic*
690	*JANNON TEXT MED SC ITAL.*	681	***Kandal Bold Italic***	618	ITC Oldrichium Demi
690	**Jannon Text Bold**	681	**Kandal Black**	618	*ITC Oldrichium Demi Italic*
690	***Jannon Text Bold Italic***	681	***Kandal Black Italic***	618	**ITC Oldrichium Bold**
693	John Baskerville Plain	612	Laguna Madre WBW	618	ITC Oldrichium Engraved
693	*John Baskerville Italic*	657	Latimer	629	ParmaType
693	JOHN BASKERVILLE CAPS	657	LINDUM	629	*ParmaType Italic*
693	*JOHN BASKERVILLE CAPS ITALIC*	603	Londonderry Air NF	629	**ParmaType Bold**
693	John Baskerville Medium	654	Mayflower	629	***ParmaType ItalicBold***
693	*John Baskerville Medium Itali*	654	*Mayflower Italic*	603	QUADRIVIUM NF
693	**John Baskerville Bold**	611	McKenna Handletter NF	710	Rawlinson Regular
693	***John Baskerville Bold Italic***	611	*McKenna Handletter Italic NF*	710	*Rawlinson Italic*
693	JOHN BASKERVILLE CAPS BOLD	611	**McKenna Handletter Bold NF**	710	Rawlinson Medium
693	*JOHN BASKERVILLE CAPS B.ITALI*	476	McLemore Light	710	*Rawlinson Medium Italic*
538	Josefov Leicht	476	*McLemore Light Italic*	711	**Rawlinson Bold**
538	**Josefov Normal**	476	McLemore Regular	711	***Rawlinson Bold Italic***
703	Juvenis Light	476	*McLemore Italic*	711	**Rawlinson Heavy**
703	*Juvenis Light Italic*	476	**McLemore Bold**	711	***Rawlinson Heavy Italic***
703	Juvenis Book	476	***McLemore Bold Italic***	712	Rawlinson Cond Regular
703	*Juvenis Book Italic*	476	**McLemore Black**	712	*Rawlinson Cond Italic*
703	**Juvenis Book Bold**	476	***McLemore Black Italic***	712	Rawlinson Cond Medium

712	*Rawlinson Cond Medium Italic*	603	**Slam Bang Theater NF**
713	**Rawlinson Cond Bold**	660	*Sparrow*
713	***Rawlinson Cond Bold Italic***	607	Speedball No. 1 NF
713	**Rawlinson Cond Heavy**	468	FTF Stella Regular
713	***Rawlinson Cond Heavy Italic***	468	FTF STELLA EXPERT
601	Risky Business Square Light NF	468	*FTF Stella Italic*
601	Risky Business Square Medium NF	468	*FTF STELLA EXPERT ITALIC*
601	**Risky Business Square Bold NF**	468	**FTF Stella Bold**
601	**Risky Business Round Bold NF**	468	**FTF STELLA EXPERT BOLD**
601	Risky Business Oldstyle NF	468	***FTF Stella Bold Italic***
466	FTF Rongel Roman	468	***FTF STELLA EXP BD TALIC***
466	*FTF Rongel Italic*	607	Strongs Draughtsman NF
466	FTF RONGEL EXPERT	664	Tyndale
466	*FTF RONGEL EXP ITALIC*	563	MVB Verdigris Roman
603	**Saturday Morning Toast NF**	563	MVB *Verdigris Italic*
697	Serapion II	563	MVB VERDIGRIS SMALL CAPS
697	*Serapion II Italic*	694	Walbaum Text
697	SERAPION II SC	694	*Walbaum Text Italic*
697	**SERAPION II SC BOLD**	694	WALBAUM TEXT SC
697	**Serapion II Bold**	694	*WALBAUM TEXT SC ITALIC*
697	***SERAPION II SC B.ITALIC***	694	**Walbaum Text Bold**
697	**SERAPION II SC BOLD**	694	***Walbaum Text B. Italic***
697	***SERAPION II SC B.ITALIC***	694	**WALBAUM TEXT SC BOLD**
659	Sherwood	694	***WALBAUM TEXT SC B. ITA***
567	MVB Sirenne Six Roman	608	WHG Simpatico NF
567	MVB *Sirenne Six Italic*	523	WIRED Serif
567	MVB SIRENNE SIX SC	523	*WIRED Serif Italic*
567	MVB Sirenne Text Roman		
567	MVB *Sirenne Text Italic*		
567	MVB SIRENNE TEXT SC		
567	**MVB Sirenne Text Bold**		
567	***MVB Sirenne Text Bold Ital***		

	Sans Serif	617	*Claudium Italic*	716	**ClearviewOne Blk CN**
509	21st Super Fine	617	**Claudium Bold**	717	***ClearviewOne Blk CN Italic***
509	*21st Super Fine Italic*	714	ClearviewOne Extra Thin	718	ClearviewOne Extra Thin CN
509	21st Fine	715	*ClearviewOne Extra Thin Italic*	719	*ClearviewOne Extra Thin CN Italic*
509	*21st Fine Italic*	714	ClearviewOne Thin	718	ClearviewOne Thin CP
509	21st Regular	715	*ClearviewOne Thin Italic*	719	*ClearviewOne Thin CP Italic*
509	*21st Regular Italic*	714	ClearviewOne Light	718	ClearviewOne Light CP
509	**21st Bold**	715	*ClearviewOne Light Italic*	719	*ClearviewOne Light CP Italic*
509	***21st Bold Italic***	714	ClearviewOne Book	718	ClearviewOne Book CP
509	**21st Black**	715	*ClearviewOne Book Italic*	719	*ClearviewOne Book CP Italic*
509	***21st Black Italic***	714	**ClearviewOne Medium**	718	ClearviewOne Med CP
509	**21st Round Black**	715	***ClearviewOne Med Italic***	719	*ClearviewOne Med CP Italic*
509	***21st Round Black Italic***	714	**ClearviewOne Bold**	718	**ClearviewOne Bold CP**
509	**21st Outline**	715	***ClearviewOne Bold Italic***	719	***ClearviewOne Bold CP Italic***
509	***21st Outline Italic***	714	**ClearviewOne Heavy**	718	**ClearviewOne Hvy CP**
683	Anonymous	715	***ClearviewOne Hvy Italic***	719	***ClearviewOne Hvy CP Italic***
599	Astoria Titling NF	714	**ClearviewOne Black**	718	**ClearviewOne Blk CP**
510	ATTAC Regular	715	***ClearviewOne Blk Italic***	719	***ClearviewOne Blk CP Italic***
510	*ATTAC Regular Italic*	716	ClearviewOne Extra Thin CN	720	CLEARVIEWONE EXTRA THIN SC
510	ATTAC Semi Bold	717	*ClearviewOne Extra Thin CN Italic*	720	CLEARVIEWONE THIN SC
510	*ATTAC Semi Bold Italic*	716	ClearviewOne Thin CN	720	CLEARVIEWONE LIGHT SC
510	**ATTAC Bold**	717	*ClearviewOne Thin CN Italic*	720	CLEARVIEWONE BOOK SC
510	***ATTAC Bold Italic***	716	ClearviewOne Light CN	720	CLEARVIEWONE MED SC
510	**ATTAC Black**	717	*ClearviewOne Light CN Italic*	720	**CLEARVIEWONE BOLD SC**
510	***ATTAC Black Italic***	716	ClearviewOne Book CN	720	**CLEARVIEWONE HVY SC**
599	BIG TENT PLAYERS NF	717	*ClearviewOne Book CN Italic*	720	**CLEARVIEWONE BLK SC**
486	BISCO CONDENSED	716	ClearviewOne Med CN	721	ClearviewHwy 6-B
671	BLAKELY LIGHT	717	*ClearviewOne Med CN Italic*	721	ClearviewHwy 6-W
671	**BLAKELY BOLD**	716	**ClearviewOne Bold CN**	721	ClearviewHwy 5-B
671	**BLAKELY BLACK**	717	***ClearviewOne Bold CN Italic***	721	ClearviewHwy 5-W
749	Charifa Sans	716	**ClearviewOne Hvy CN**	721	ClearviewHwy 4-B
617	*Claudium*	717	***ClearviewOne Hvy CP Italic***	721	ClearviewHwy 4-W

721 ClearviewHwy 3-B
721 ClearviewHwy 3-W
721 ClearviewHwy 2-B
721 ClearviewHwy 2-W
721 ClearviewHwy 1-B
721 ClearviewHwy 1-W
752 Cosmotron
752 **Cosmotron Bold**
480 Culpepper Light
480 CULPEPPER LIGHT SMALL CAP
480 Culpepper Regular
480 CULPEPPER SMALL CAP
480 **Culpepper Extra Bold**
480 **CULPEPPER EXTRA BOLD SC**
529 DeFonte Léger
529 DeFonte Normale
529 **DeFonte DemiGras**
529 **DeFonte Gros**
755 DignaSans Thin
755 DignaSans Regular
755 *DignaSans Italic*
755 **DignaSans Heavy**
512 DISTILLA Light
512 *DISTILLA Light Italic*
512 DISTILLA Regular
512 *DISTILLA Regular Italic*
512 **DISTILLA Bold**
512 ***DISTILLA Bold Italic***
700 DynaGrotesk LXE Plain
700 *DynaGrotesk LXE Italic*
700 DynaGrotesk RXE Plain
700 *DynaGrotesk RXE Italic*

700 **DynaGrotesk DXE Plain**
700 ***DynaGrotesk DXE Italic***
700 **DynaGrotesk LXE Bold**
700 ***DynaGrotesk LXE Bold It***
700 **DynaGrotesk RXE Bold**
700 ***DynaGrotesk RXE Bold I***
700 **DynaGrotesk DXE Bold**
700 ***DynaGrotesk DXE Bold I***
700 DynaGrotesk LE Plain
700 *DynaGrotesk LE Italic*
700 DynaGrotesk RE Plain
700 *DynaGrotesk RE Italic*
700 DynaGrotesk DE Plain
700 *DynaGrotesk DE Italic*
700 **DynaGrotesk LE Bold**
700 ***DynaGrotesk LE Bold Italic***
700 **DynaGrotesk RE Bold**
700 ***DynaGrotesk RE Bold Italic***
700 **DynaGrotesk DE Bold**
700 ***DynaGrotesk DE Bold Italic***
700 DynaGrotesk L Plain
700 *DynaGrotesk L Italic*
700 DynaGrotesk R Plain
700 *DynaGrotesk R Italic*
700 DynaGrotesk D Plain
700 *DynaGrotesk D Italic*
700 DynaGrotesk L Bold
700 *DynaGrotesk L Bold Italic*
700 **DynaGrotesk R Bold**
700 ***DynaGrotesk R Bold Italic***
700 **DynaGrotesk D Bold**
700 ***DynaGrotesk D Bold Italic***

700 DynaGrotesk LM Plain
700 *DynaGrotesk LM Italic*
700 DynaGrotesk RM Plain
700 *DynaGrotesk RM Italic*
700 DynaGrotesk DM Plain
700 *DynaGrotesk DM Italic*
700 DynaGrotesk LM Bold
700 *DynaGrotesk LM Bold Italic*
700 **DynaGrotesk RM Bold**
700 ***DynaGrotesk RM Bold Italic***
700 **DynaGrotesk DM Bold**
700 ***DynaGrotesk DM Bold Italic***
700 DynaGrotesk LC Plain
700 *DynaGrotesk LC Italic*
700 DynaGrotesk RC Plain
700 *DynaGrotesk RC Italic*
700 DynaGrotesk DC Plain
700 *DynaGrotesk DC Italic*
700 DynaGrotesk LC Bold
700 *DynaGrotesk LC Bold Italic*
700 **DynaGrotesk RC Bold**
700 ***DynaGrotesk RC Bold Italic***
700 **DynaGrotesk DC Bold**
700 ***DynaGrotesk DC Bold Italic***
700 DynaGrotesk LXC Plain
700 *DynaGrotesk LXC Italic*
700 DynaGrotesk RXC Plain
700 *DynaGrotesk RXC Italic*
700 DynaGrotesk DXC Plain
700 *DynaGrotesk DXC Italic*
700 DynaGrotesk LXC Bold
700 *DynaGrotesk LXC Bold Italic*

700	DynaGrotesk RXC Bold
700	DynaGrotesk RXC Bold Italic
700	DynaGrotesk DXC Bold
700	DynaGrotesk DXC Bold Italic
606	East Coast Frolics NF
752	EPOCH
482	Ersatz
482	Ersatz Bold
630	Estiennium Regular
630	Estiennium Italique
630	Estiennium Demi
630	Estiennium Demi Italique
630	Estiennium Bold
630	Estiennium Bold Italique
630	Estiennium Extra
630	Estiennium Extra Italiqu
630	Estiennium Black
630	Estiennium Black Italiqu
750	Ether Normal
750	Ether Normal Slant
750	Ether Bold
750	Ether Bold Slant
750	Ether Connected Normal
750	Ether Connected Normal Slant
750	Ether Connected Bold
750	Ether Connected Bold Slant
677	euforia Light
677	euforia Regular
677	euforia Bold
677	euforia inline
677	euforia stencil
481	Extreme Sans

481	Extreme Sans Oblique
481	Extreme Sans Heavy
481	Extreme Sans Heavy Oblique
533	Faber Eins/Zwei Normal
533	Faber Eins Normal Kursiv
533	Faber Eins/Zwei Breit Normal
533	Faber Eins/Zwei Schmal Normal
533	Faber Eins/Zwei Kräftig
533	Faber Eins/Zwei Halbfett
533	Faber Eins/Zwei Fett
564	MVB Fantabular Sans Reg
565	MVB Fantabular Sans Ital
565	MVB Fantabular Sans Med
565	MVB Fantabular Sans Med It
565	MVB Fantabular Sans Bold
565	MVB Fantabular Sans Bd It
599	Fifth Avenue Salon NF
590	Fontana ND Aa OsF Light
590	Fontana ND Aa OsF Light Italic
590	FONTANA ND AA SC LIGHT
590	Fontana ND Aa OsF (Regular)
590	Fontana ND Aa OsF Italic
590	FONTANA ND AA SC (REGULAR)
590	Fontana ND Cc OsF Light
591	FONTANA ND CC SC LIGHT
591	Fontana ND Cc OsF (Regular)
591	FONTANA ND CC SC (REGULAR)
591	Fontana ND Cc OsF Semibold
591	Fontana ND Cc OsF Semibold Italic
591	FONTANA ND CC SC SEMIBOLD
590	Fontana ND Ee OsF Light
592	FONTANA ND EE SC LIGHT

592	Fontana ND Ee OsF (Regular)
592	FONTANA ND EE SC (REGULAR)
592	Fontana ND Ee OsF Semibold
592	FONTANA ND EE SC SEMIBOLD
592	Fontana ND Ee OsF Bold
591	Fontana ND Ee OsF Bold Italic
592	FONTANA ND EE SC BOLD
581	Futura ND Light
581	Futura ND Light Oblique
582	Futura ND Book
581	Futura ND Book Oblique
582	Futura ND Medium
582	Futura ND Medium Oblique
583	Futura ND Demibold
583	Futura ND Demibold Oblique
584	Futura ND Bold
583	Futura ND Bold Oblique
584	Futura ND Extrabold
584	Futura ND Extrabd Obl
585	FUTURA ND SCOsF LIGHT
585	FUTURA ND SCOsF LIGHT OBLIQ
585	FUTURA ND SCOsF BOOK
585	FUTURA ND SCOsF BOOK OBLIQ
585	FUTURA ND SCOsF MEDIUM
585	FUTURA ND SCOsF MEDIUM OBI
585	FUTURA ND SCOsF BOLD
585	FUTURA ND SCOsF BLD OBL
586	Futura ND Cn Light
586	Futura ND Cn Light Oblique
586	Futura ND Cn Medium
586	Futura ND Cn Medium Oblique
586	Futura ND Cn Bold

462	**FTF MORGAN SN CP BOLD**	516	*PLOTTA Light Italic*	517	*REACTION Fine Italic*
462	***FTF MORGAN SN CP BD OBLIQU***	516	PLOTTA Regular	517	REACTION Regular
463	FTF Morgan Sn Cn Regular	516	*PLOTTA Regular Italic*	517	*REACTION Regular Italic*
463	*FTF Morgan Sn Cn Oblique*	516	PLOTTA Bold	517	REACTION Bold
463	**FTF Morgan Sn Cn Bold**	516	*PLOTTA Bold Italic*	517	*REACTION Bold Italic*
463	***FTF Morgan Sn Cn Bd Oblique***	516	PODIUM Fine	517	**REACTION Ultra**
463	FTF MORGAN SN CN CP	516	*PODIUM Fine Italic*	517	***REACTION Ultra Italic***
463	*FTF MORGAN SN CN CP OBLIQUE*	516	PODIUM Regular	517	**REACTION Heavy**
674	MOSTRA LIGHT	516	*PODIUM Regular Italic*	517	***REACTION Heavy Italic***
674	MOSTRA REGULAR	516	**PODIUM Bold**	676	Refrigerator Light
674	**MOSTRA BOLD**	516	***PODIUM Bold Italic***	676	**Refrigerator Bold**
675	**MOSTRA HEAVY**	594	Pragma ND Light	676	**Refrigerator Heavy**
675	**MOSTRA BLACK**	594	*Pragma ND Light Italic*	518	REVALO CLASSIC Thin
601	NEW DEAL DECO NF	594	Pragma ND (Regular)	518	*REVALO CLASSIC Thin Italic*
601	NEW DEAL DECO NF	594	*Pragma ND Italic*	518	REVALO CLASSIC Light
770	Pakt_Regular	594	**Pragma ND Bold**	518	*REVALO CLASSIC Light Italic*
770	Pakt_SemiBold	594	***Pragma ND Bold Italic***	518	REVALO CLASSIC Regular
770	Pakt_Bold	595	PRAGMA ND SCOsF LIGHT	518	*REVALO CLASSIC Regular Italic*
770	Pakt_ExtraBold	595	*PRAGMA ND SCOsF LIGHT ITALIC*	518	**REVALO CLASSIC Bold**
770	Pakt_Black	595	PRAGMA ND SCOsF (REGULAR)	518	***REVALO CLASSIC Bold Italic***
769	Pakt_Condensed	595	*PRAGMA ND SCOsF ITALIC*	518	**REVALO CLASSIC Black**
769	Pakt_SemiBoldCondensed	595	**PRAGMA ND SCOsF BOLD**	518	***REVALO CLASSIC Black Italic***
769	Pakt_BoldCondensed	595	***PRAGMA ND SCOsF BOLD ITALI(***	518	REVALO MODERN Thin
769	Pakt_ExtraBoldCondensed	483	PropTen	518	*REVALO MODERN Thin Italic*
769	Pakt_BlackCondensed	483	**PropTen Bold**	518	REVALO MODERN Light
603	PERSEPHONE NF	682	Proxima Sans	518	*REVALO MODERN Light Italic*
514	PHAT Light	683	*Proxima Sans Oblique*	518	REVALO MODERN Regular
514	*PHAT Light Italic*	683	**Proxima Sans Medium**	518	*REVALO MODERN Regular Italic*
514	PHAT Regular	682	***Proxima Sans Med. Obl.***	518	REVALO MODERN Bold
514	*PHAT Regular Italic*	682	**Proxima Sans Black**	518	*REVALO MODERN Bold Italic*
514	**PHAT Bold**	682	***Proxima Sans Black Obl***	518	REVALO MODERN Black
516	PLOTTA Light	517	REACTION Fine	518	*REVALO MODERN Black Italic*

677	SANCTUARY REGULAR	620	*Tinman Bold Italic*	541	*Wendelin Normal Kursiv*
677	**SANCTUARY BOLD**	521	TRAK Fine	541	WENDELIN NORMAL KAPITÄLCH
519	SEIZE Light	521	*TRAK Fine Italic*	541	Wendelin Kräftig
519	*SEIZE Light Italic*	521	TRAK Regular	541	*Wendelin Halbfett Kursiv*
519	SEIZE Regular	521	*TRAK Regular Italic*	541	**Wendelin Breitfett**
519	*SEIZE Regular Italic*	521	**TRAK Semi-bold**	541	**Wendelin Fett**
519	**SEIZE Bold**	521	***TRAK Semi-bold Italic***	541	***Wendelin Fett Kursiv***
519	***SEIZE Bold Italic***	521	**TRAK Bold**	523	WIRED Light
519	SEIZE Open	521	***TRAK Bold Italic***	523	*WIRED Light Italic*
519	*SEIZE Open Italic*	521	**TRAK Black**	523	WIRED Regular
678	Sharktooth Regular	521	***TRAK Black Italic***	523	*WIRED Regular Italic*
678	**Sharktooth Bold**	773	Ultramagnetic_Light	523	WIRED Black
678	**Sharktooth Heavy**	774	*Ultramagnetic_LightOblique*	523	*WIRED Black Italic*
622	SleepTickets	773	**Ultramagnetic_Regular**	756	Yumi UltraLight
622	**SleepTickets Bold**	774	*Ultramagnetic_Oblique*	756	Yumi Light
557	Spaulding Sans JF-Regular	773	**Ultramagnetic_Bold**	756	Yumi Normal
557	*Spaulding Sans JF-Italic*	774	***Ultramagnetic_BoldOblique***	756	Yumi Medium
753	squirrel regular	773	**Ultramagnetic_ExtraBold**	756	Yumi Bold
753	*squirrel italic*	774	***Ultramagnetic_ExtraBoldObliqu***		
753	**squirrel bold**	774	**Ultramagnetic_Black**		
753	***squirrel bolditalic***	774	***Ultramagnetic_BlackOblique***		
521	STAK Light	775	unisect_light		
521	*STAK Light Italic*	775	*unisect_lightoblique*		
521	STAK Regular	775	unisect_Regular		
521	*STAK Regular Italic*	775	*unisect_oblique*		
521	**STAK Bold**	775	**unisect_Bold**		
521	***STAK Bold Italic***	775	***unisect_boldoblique***		
620	Tinman	775	**unisect_ExtraBold**		
620	*Tinman Italic*	775	***unisect_extraboldoblique***		
620	**Tinman DemiBold**	775	**unisect_black**		
620	***Tinman DemiBold Italic***	775	***unisect_blackoblique***		
620	**Tinman Bold**	541	Wendelin Normal		

01341 1569 5535

425

766	Formation_ExtraLigh
766	Formation_UltraLigh
766	Formation_Light
766	Formation_Regular
766	Formation_SemiBold
766	Formation_DemiBold
766	Formation_Bold
766	Formation_ExtraBold
766	Formation_UltraBold
659	Founders
649	FRESNO
550	FRiKi TiKi JF
745	Furby Light
745	Furby Regular
745	Furby Bold
587	Futura ND Black
587	Futura ND Display
589	Gaudi ND
600	GOTHAM RAIL CO NF
571	MVB Grenadine Regular
571	MVB Grenadine Italic
571	MVB Grenadine Medium
571	MVB Grenadine Med Italic
571	MVB Grenadine Bold
571	MVB Grenadine Bold Italic
571	MVB Grenadine Xtra Bd
571	MVB Grenadine Xtra Bd It
571	MVB Grenadine Black
571	MVB Grenadine Black It
571	MVB Grenadine Ultra
571	MVB Grenadine Ultra It
612	GULLY WASHER WBW

550	Gypsy Switch JF
744	HEADROOM REGULAR
744	HEADROOM BOLD
744	HEADROOM HARD
744	HEADROOM HARD BOLD
551	Holiday Times JF
649	HOTEL
574	MVB Hotsy Totsy Roman
574	MVB Hotsy Totsy Semibold
574	MVB Hotsy Totsy Bold
574	MVB Hotsy Totsy Ultra
574	MVB Hotsy Totsy Rocksie
574	MVB Hotsy Totsy HiLite
513	ID01Left
513	ID01Right
589	Ilerda ND
496	Interlace Single
496	Interlace Double
747	Ixtan Light
747	Ixtan Light Italic
747	Ixtan Medium
747	Ixtan Medium Italic
747	Ixtan Bold
747	Ixtan Bold Italic
612	JEFFERSON PILOT WBW
600	J..ST A GIG.L. NF
484	JORGE REGULAR
484	JORGE OUTLINE
484	JORGE DROP SHADOW
484	JORGE OUTLINE DROP SHADOW
767	Jute_Regular
767	Jute_SemiBold

767	Jute_Bold
749	Kanister Regular
749	Kanister Oblique
513	KNEEON Light
513	KNEEON Light Italic
513	KNEEON Regular
513	KNEEON Regular Italic
513	KNEEON Bold
513	KNEEON Bold Italic
513	KNEEON Square
513	KNEEON Square Italic
455	Bs-Kombat
455	Bs-Kombat Alternate
551	KON TiKi JF-ALOHA
551	KON TiKi JF-ALOHA LiGATURES
552	Kon Tiki JF-Enchanted
552	KON TIKI JF-HULA
552	Kon Tiki JF-Kona
552	KON TIKI JF-LANAI
553	Kon Tiki JF-Trader
600	La Moda NF
600	LANCE CORPORAL NF
456	BS-LOOPER AG STENCIL
456	BS-LOOPER BK STENCIL
767	Maetl_Light
767	Maetl_LightOblique
767	Maetl_Regular
767	Maetl_Oblique
767	Maetl_Bold
767	Maetl_BoldOblique
767	Maetl_ExtraBold
767	Maetl_ExBldOblique

607	**Magic Lantern SW**
743	Magma Light
743	Magma Regular
743	**Magma Bold**
743	Magma Light Condensed
743	Magma Condensed
743	**Magma Bold Condensed**
572	**MVB MAGNESIUM REGULAR**
572	**MVB MAGNESIUM CONDENSED**
539	Maier's Nr. 8 Mager
539	**Maier's Nr. 8 Halbfett**
539	Maier's Nr. 21 Normal
539	Maier's Nr. 21 Mager
604	**MARRAKESH EXPRESS NF**
491	MaxMix One
751	Memory 4SK
751	Memory 12SK
600	MESA VERDE NF
604	Metro Retro Redux NF
600	**MODERN ART NF**
642	MODESTO LITE EXP
643	**MODESTO EXPANDED**
643	MODESTO LITE REGULAR
642	**MODESTO REGULAR**
642	MODESTO LITE CONDENSED
642	**MODESTO CONDENSED**
643	**MODESTO INLINI**
702	Monarchia
702	Monarchia Text
702	Monarchia Swash
702	Monarchia Bold
600	**MONTE CASINO NF**

460	FTF MORGAN BIG 1
460	FTF MORGAN BIG 1 OBL
460	**FTF MORGAN BIG 1 BOLD**
460	**FTF MORGAN BIG 1 BD OBL**
460	FTF MORGAN BIG 2
460	FTF MORGAN BIG 2 OBL
460	**FTF MORGAN BIG 2 BOLD**
460	**FTF MORGAN BIG 2 BD OBL**
460	**FTF MORGAN BIG 3**
460	**FTF MORGAN BIG 3 OBL**
460	**FTF MORGAN BIG 3 BOLD**
460	**FTF MORGAN BIG 3 BD OBL**
461	FTF MORGAN POSTER REGULAR
461	FTF MORGAN POSTER OBLIQUE
461	**FTF MORGAN POSTER BOLD**
461	**FTF MORGAN POSTER BOLD OBLIQUE**
461	**FTF MORGAN POSTER BLACK**
461	**FTF MORGAN POSTER BLACK OBLIQUE**
464	FTF MORGAN TOWER 1
464	FTF MORGAN TOWER 2
464	FTF MORGAN TOWER 3
464	FTF MORGAN TOWER 4
701	Mramor Light
701	Mramor Light Italic
701	Mramor Book
701	Mramor Book Italic
701	Mramor Medium
701	Mramor Medium Italic
701	**Mramor Bold**
701	**Mramor Bold Italic**
701	**Mramor Black**
701	**Mramor Black Italic**

701	Mramor Text
701	Mramor Text Italic
701	**Mramor Text Bold**
701	**Mramor Text Bold Italic**
494	**MUNDENGE ROCK**
757	**NEW AMSTERDAM REGULAR**
755	**New Normal**
755	**New Normal Script**
755	New Outline
755	New Outline
768	**NOVUM_LIGHT**
768	**NOVUM_REGULAR**
768	**NOVUM_BOLD**
768	**NOVUM_EXTRABOLD**
757	OKTOBER
757	OKTOBER SLANT
604	OLBRICH DISPLAY NF
768	OneCross_Light
768	OneCross_Regular
768	OneCross_SemiBold
768	OneCross_Bold
768	OneCross_ExtraBold
768	**OneCross_Black**
768	**OneCross_Black**
514	ORBITA Light
514	ORBITA Light Italic
514	ORBITA Regular
514	ORBITA Regular Italic
514	ORBITA Heavy
514	ORBITA Heavy Italic
613	**OUACHITA WAY WBW**
769	OneCross_ExtraLight

771	REVERSION_EXE	730	Sauna Italic Swash	613	SPINDLETOP WBW
771	REVERSION_TE	730	Qu Ch Ct ffi ft Tt Sw Lig	497	Submarine Extra Light
771	REVERSION_BL	730	SAUNA SMALLCAPS	497	Submarine Light
771	REVERSION_LBI	730	**Sauna Bold**	497	Submarine Regular
771	REVERSION_RB	730	**Sauna Bold Italic**	497	**Submarine Bold**
771	REVERSION_SBI	730	**Sauna Bold Italic Swash**	497	**Submarine Extra Bold**
645	Richmond Light	730	**Sh kk ffl zz Bld Tt Sw Lig**	604	SUPER BOB TRILINE NF
645	Richmond Light Italic	730	**Sauna Black**	640	Sutro Light
645	Richmond Medium	730	**Sauna Black Italic**	640	Sutro Medium
645	Richmond Medium Italic	730	**Sauna Black Italic Sw**	640	**Sutro Bold**
645	**Richmond Bold**	730	**Ck ff ll St Blk Tt Sw Lig**	640	**Sutro Extra Bold**
645	**Richmond Bold Italic**	540	Schwabacher Deutsche Reichsbahn	641	**SUTRO BLACK**
645	Richmond Light Condensed	772	Selector_Light	641	**SUTRO SHADED**
645	Richmond Medium Condensed	772	Selector_Regular	745	Swingo Regular
645	**Richmond Bold Condensed**	772	**Selector_Bold**	745	**Swingo Bold**
645	**Richmond Extra Bold Condensed**	772	**Selector_ExtraBold**	751	Systemez Extra Light
645	RICHMOND INITIALS	520	SHARP Light	751	Systemez Light
613	**Rio Grande WBW**	520	SHARP Light Italic	751	Systemez Regular
604	ROBOT MONSTER NF	520	SHARP Regular	751	**Systemez Bold**
519	ROBUSTIK Light	520	SHARP Regular Italic	751	Systemez Extra Light Force
519	ROBUSTIK Light Obliq	520	**SHARP Bold**	751	Systemez Light Force
519	ROBUSTIK Regular	520	**SHARP Bold Italic**	751	Systemez Force
519	ROBUSTIK Reg Obliq	520	**SHARP Ultra**	751	**Systemez Bold Force**
519	**ROBUSTIK Bold**	520	**SHARP Ultra Italic**	751	**Systemez Extra Bold Force**
519	**ROBUSTIK Bld Oblique**	568	MVB Sirenne Eighteen Roman	702	Teuton Weiss
473	**Robusto Black**	568	MVB Sirenne Eighteen Italic	702	Teuton Hell
602	Rocketman XV-7 NF	568	MVB SIRENNE EIGHTEEN SC	702	Teuton Mager
607	**Roman Holiday NF**	569	MVB Sirenne Seventy-Two Roman	702	**Teuton Mager Bold**
602	**SABRINA ZAFTIG NF**	569	MVB Sirenne Seventy-Two Italic	702	Teuton Normal
556	SAHARAN JF	569	MVB SIRENNE SEVENTY-Two SC	702	**Teuton Normal Bold**
730	Sauna Roman	557	Southland JF	702	**Teuton Fett Bold**
730	Sauna Italic	613	**Spaghetti Western WBW**	609	Thai Foon HB

Script

545	Acroterion JF
545	Adage Script JF
662	Afton
545	**Alpengeist JF**
545	Annabelle JF
609	Artemisia NF
663	Avocet Light
548	**Boxer Script JF**
575	MVB Café Mimi Regular
575	**MVB Café Mimi Bold**
589	CarloMagno ND
573	MVB Chanson d'Amour
549	Charade JF
745	Chube Thin
745	Chube Thin Italic
745	Chube Tubby
745	Chube Tubby Italic
745	**Chube Fat**
745	**Chube Fat Italic**
764	Cinahand_Light
764	Cinahand LightAlternate
764	Cinahand_Regular
764	Cinahand Alternate
672	Coquette Light
672	Coquette Regular
672	**Coquette Bold**
549	Debonair JF
531	Deutsche Schrift Lattwang
624	DogButter Extra Light
624	DogButter Regular
624	DogButter Medium

624	DogButter DemiBold
624	DogButter Bold
658	Elven
575	MVB Emmascript Regular
575	**MVB Emmascript Bold**
679	Felt Tip Roman
679	**Felt Tip Roman Bold**
679	**Felt Tip Roman Heavy**
679	Felt Tip Senior
679	Felt Tip Woman
679	**Felt Tip Woman Bold**
550	**Fenway Park JF**
536	FXGUM
575	MVB Greymantle Regular
551	Jeffriana JF
538	**KLEX**
552	Kon Tiki JF-Enchanted
553	Kon Tiki JF-Lounge
553	**Manual Script JF**
609	Margarita Ville NF
553	Mary Helen JF
609	Monte Carlo Script NF
554	Opulence JF
554	Peregroy JF
660	Plymouth
554	Primrose JF
554	Rambler Script JF
555	Retro Repro JF
661	Roanoke Script
556	Scriptorama JF-Hostess
556	**SCRIPTORAMA JF-MARKDOWN**
556	**Scriptorama JF-Tradeshow**

557	Shirley Script JF
558	Stanzie JF
662	Symphony
589	UNCIAL ROMANA ND
558	Valentina JF
558	Varsity Script JF
558	Viceroy JF
559	**Wonderboy JF**

Non-latin

448	Megalon	モイキチリラ三
450	Noir Braille	

Ornaments

588	Arabescos	
438	Biology	
547	Blairesque JF-Happy Grams	
573	MVB Celestia Antiqua Ornaments	
764	Cinahand Extras	
752	Dark Morsels	
575	MVB Greymantle Extras	
444	Kare Dingbats	
449	MiniFood	
577	MVB Pedestria Pict	
746	RubiasMorenasPelirojas	
732	Sauna Dingbats Solo	
739	Sauna Dingbats Outline	
739	Sauna Dingbats Background	
665	Tyndale Xtras	
503	Xbats	

ATOMIC MEDIA

Jaggies are good.

Retro-future fonts from Atomic Media are the comfort food for twenty-first century design. Great for on-screen and print use, these fonts and icons by Matthew Bardram, Susan Kare, and Miguel Hernández run the gamut of hardcore bitmap design from the past 20 years to the next 20 years to come. Cut the future, paste the past.

Arachnid

Matthew Bardram
1998

Regular

A quick black spider spins the lazy dog in silk

abcdefghijklmnopqrstuvwxyz
ABCDEFGHIJKLMNOPQRSTUVWXYZ

Don't be fooled by the tiny size

{ [(1 2 3 4 5 6 7 8 9 0)] }

Small Caps

CRAZY CAPPED SPIDER DANCES WITH PUZZLED FOX

AaBbCcDdE

ABCDEFGHIJKLMNOPQRSTUVWXYZ
ABCDEFGHIJKLMNOPQRSTUVWXYZ

FULL CHARACTER SET INCLUDED.

{ [(1 2 3 4 5 6 7 8 9 0)] }

Atomic

Matthew Bardram
1996

Inline

How I Learned To Stop

abcdefghijklmnopqrstuvwxyz 12345
ABCDEFGHIJKLMNOPQRSTUVWX

Outline

Worrying And Love The

abcdefghijklmnopqrstuvwxyz 12345
ABCDEFGHIJKLMNOPQRSTUVWX

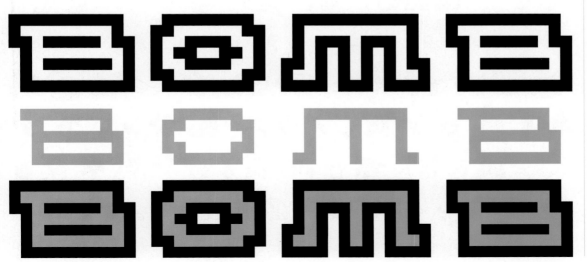

Combine Inline and Outline
styles for overlay effect.

Susan Kare
2001

Pixel illustrations for bullets,
dividers, watermarks, or borders.

fonts@atomicmedia.net

Regular

When we go back to Juarez, Mexico, do we fly

AaBbDdEeF abcdefghijklmnopqrstuvwxyz Don't be fooled by the tiny size
ABCDEFGHIJKLMNOPQRSTUVWXYZ { [(1 2 3 4 5 6 7 8 9 0)] }

Black

Over picturesque little Tucson, Arizona?

AaBbDdE abcdefghijklmnopqrstuv Full character set included
ABCDEFGHIJKLMNOPQRSTUV { [(1 2 3 4 5 6 7 8 9 0)] }

Regular

An inspired calligrapher can create pages

abcdefghijklmnopqrstuvwxyzABCDEFGHIJKLMNOPQRS Don't be fooled by tiny size
TUVWXYZ!@#$z^+*œéáóüàñîÉÁÓÜÂÎ ço≈---:+\I/·.,~´≥≤«» { [(1 2 3 4 5 6 7 8 9 0)] }

Bold

Of beauty using stick, ink, quill, brush

abcdefghijklmnopqrstuvwxyzABCDEFGHIJKLMNOPQRS All characters included
TUVWXYZ!@#$z^+*œéáóüàñîÉÁÓÜÂÎço ---:+\I/·.,~´≥≤«» { [(1 2 3 4 5 6 7 8 9 0)] }

Just yesterday Matthew Carter and I were out back referencing your Egyptian bowls. Ever since Seybold '84, there's been a trend towards pirating display ascenders. · · · Who knew that I would be considered a typographic genius simply by cutting recycled specimen books? · · · I'm teaching a course about reinventing disproportional ears.

Small Caps

Pick-axe, buzz saw, baked ham, or strawberry jam

abcdefghijklmnopqrstuvwxyzABCDEFGHIJKLMNOPQRS Don't be fooled by the tiny size
TUVWXYZ!@#$z^+*œéáóüàñîÉÁÓÜÂÎço ---:+\I/·.,~´≥≤«» { [(1 2 3 4 5 6 7 8 9 0)] }

Small Caps Bold

All a digital designer needs is this font

abcdefghijklmnopqrstuvwxyzABCDEF GHIJKLMNOPQRS All characters are included
TUVWXYZ!@#$z^+*œéáóüàñîÉÁÓÜÂÎço ---:+\I/·.,~´≥≤«» { [(1 2 3 4 5 6 7 8 9 0)] }

Regular

Forsaking monastic tradition, twelve jovial friars gave up their

abcdefghijklmnopqrstuvwxyzABCDEFGHIJKLMNOPQRS Don't be fooled by this font's tiny size

TUVWXYZ!@#$%^&*œéáóüãñîÉÁÓÜÃÎçø ---=+\¡/··.,"'¿¿«» ‹‹ [[1 2 3 4 5 6 7 8 9 0]] ›

Bold

Vocation for a questionable move to flying trapeze

abcdefghijklmnopqrstuvwxyzABCDEFGHIJKLMNOPQRS A full character set is included

TUVWXYZ!@#$%^&*œéáóüãñîÉÁÓÜÃÎçø ---=+\¡/··.,"'¿¿«» ‹‹ [[1 2 3 4 5 6 7 8 9 0]] ›

Sans Bold

Lazy movers quit hard-packing of papier-mâché

abcdefghijklmnopqrstuvwxyzABCDEFGHIJKLMNOPQRS Yes, this font can speak French

TUVWXYZ!@#$%^&*œéáóüãñîÉÁÓÜÃÎçø ---=+\¡/··.,"'¿¿«» ‹‹ [[1 2 3 4 5 6 7 8 9 0]] ›

DON'T FORGET TO READ THE

Small Print

Tall

Forsaking monastic tradition, twelve jovial friars gave up their

abcdefghijklmnopqrstuvwxyzABCDEFGHIJKLMNOPQRS Don't be fooled by this font's tiny size

TUVWXYZ!@#$%^&*œéáóüãñîÉÁÓÜÃÎçø ---=+\¡/··.,"'¿¿«» ‹‹ [[1 2 3 4 5 6 7 8 9 0]] ›

Bold

Vocation for a questionable move to flying trapeze

abcdefghijklmnopqrstuvwxyzABCDEFGHIJKLMNOPQRS A full character set is included

TUVWXYZ!@#$%^&*œéáóüãñîÉÁÓÜÃÎçø ---=+\¡/··.,"'¿¿«» ‹‹ [[1 2 3 4 5 6 7 8 9 0]] ›

Sans Bold

Lazy movers quit hard-packing of papier-mâché

abcdefghijklmnopqrstuvwxyzABCDEFGHIJKLMNOPQRS Yes, this font can speak French

TUVWXYZ!@#$%^&*œéáóüãñîÉÁÓÜÃÎçø ---=+\¡/··.,"'¿¿«» ‹‹ [[1 2 3 4 5 6 7 8 9 0]] ›

¡A NEW DISPLAY PIXEL FONT!
AS PRESENTED BY THE INTERNACIONALLY ACCLAIMED AND
MOST RENOWNED AUTHORITHY
TYPOGRAPHER
ON EARTH
KNOWN FAR & WIDE AS THE GREAT
CIRCA
A CURIOUS BITMAP WONDER
BE AMUSED!
ABCDEFGHIJKLMNOPQRSTUVWXYZ
{[1234567890]}
¿¡?!@&& ÆŒ/%.,:;[¢¢¥$]
ÁÀÂÄÃÅÇĐÉÈÊËÌÍÎÏÑÒÓÔÖÕ ØÚÙÛÜÝŽ
1977-2003

Dotic

The New Dot Times

AaBbCcDdEe

a b c d e f g h i j k l m n o p q r s t u v w x y z
ABCDEFGHIJKLMNOPQRSTUVWXYZ

A collector of books ran into an acquaintance who told him he had just thrown away an old Bible that he found in a dusty, old box. He happened to mention that "Guten-somebody-or-other" had printed it. "Not 'Gutenberg'?" gasped the collector. "Yes, that was it!" said the acquaintance. "You idiot!" yelled the collector. "You've thrown away one of the first books ever printed. A copy recently sold at auction for half a million dollars!" "Oh, I don't think this book would have been worth anything close to that much," replied the man. "It was scribbled all over in the margins by some dude named Martin Luther."

{ Ä Ç Đ É Ü Ô Ñ ä ç đ é ü ô ñ Æ œ Œ ∞ fi fl @ & ¢ ¢ £ ¥ € }

EVERETT QUICKLY VEXED BOLD ZEPHYRS

AaBbCcDdEeFfGgHhIiJjKkLlMmNnOoPpQqRrSsTtUuVvWwXxYyZz$1234567890!

WITH MOXIE AND IMPUNITY

THE FIVE FOXY GENE WIZARDS SPLICE QUICKLY

Regular

ABCDEFGHIJKLMNOPQRSTUVWXYZ$1234567890!+ɑÑÉÁÇÜÄ
GENETICA SPEAKS FRENCH, SPANISH, GERMAN & PORTUGUESE

Bold

ABCDEFGHIJKLMNOPQRS
TUVWXYZ$1234567890!

Matthew Bardram
2001

Square

ABCDEFGHIJKLMNOPQRSTUVWXYZ
abcdefghijklmnopqrstuvwxyz[([1234567890)]]
@#$%`´€¢ŸŒÉÁÓÚÅÑÍÇØ––=+\|/–·¸'""''°º«»‹›ß™¿¡!?

Square Core

ABCDEFGHIJKLMNOPQRSTUVWXYZ
abcdefghijklmnopqrstuvwxyz[([1234567890)]]
@#$%`´€¢ŸŒÉÁÓÚÅÑÍÇØ––=+\|/–·¸'""''°º«»‹›ß™¿¡!?

Square Hollow

ABCDEFGHIJKLMNOPQRSTUVWXYZ
abcdefghijklmnopqrstuvwxyz[([1234567890)]]
@#$%`´€¢ŸŒÉÁÓÚÅÑÍÇØ––=+\|/–·¸'""''°º«»‹›ß™¿¡!?

Crossed

ABCDEFGHIJKLMNOPQRSTUVWXYZ
abcdefghijklmnopqrstuvwxyz[([1234567890)]]
@#$%`´€¢ŸŒÉÁÓÚÅÑÍÇØ––=+\|/–·¸'""''°º«»‹›ß™¿¡!?

Combine styles to create overlay effects.

SPLICE
SPLICE
SPLICE

SPLICE PIXEL GENES
SPLICE PIXEL GENES
SPLICE PIXEL GENES

atomicmedia.net   443

HARRY SPECIALIZED IN MAKING VERY QUAINT WAX TOYS

AABbCcDDEEFFGGHHIIJJKkLLMMNNOoPPQQRRSsTTUUVvWwXxYYZz$1234567890!

A TRAIN, CAR, BOAT, DOLL, AND DOG

Pack my liquor box with five dozen vintage Atari ST joysticks, please.

abcdefghijklmnopqrstuvwxyzABCDEFGHIJKL   A Full Character Set
MNOPQRSTUVWXYZ@#$%^&*œéáóÚÑåÉÁÓÜÂÎçø   1234567890!?]]}

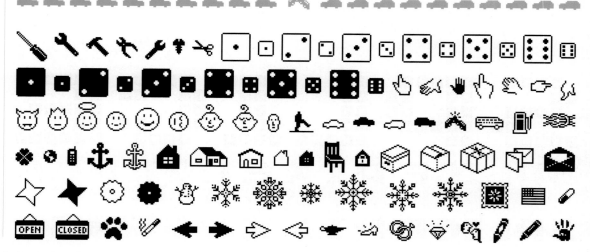

Regular

Watch all five questions asked by experts amaze the judge

AaBbCcDdEeFfGgHhIiJjKkLlMmNnOoPpQqRrSsTtUuVvWwXxYyZz{([$1234567890!?])}
Yes, this font has diacritics and punct, and even your precious British currency: @#%^&*æñéáóüåçÉÁÓÜÅÎ£

Italic

How quickly five daft jumping zebras vex the lions

AaBbCcDdEeFfGgHhIiJjKkLlMmNnOoPpQqRrSsTtUuVvWwXxYyZz{([$1234567890!?])}
*Italic also has diacritics and punct, and your precious British currency: @#%^&*ñéáóüåçÉÁÓÜÅÎ£*

Bold

Sphinx of black quartz, judge my five vows

AaBbCcDdEeFfGgHhIiJjKkLlMmNnOoPpQqRrSsTtUuVvWwXxYyZz{([$1234567890!?])}
Bold also has all the good stuff, plus your fine British currency: @#%^&*ñéáóüåçÉÁÓÜÅÎ£

--- Set big fields of type with **Kare Five Dots** ---

Sure, Kare Five Dots can handle your copious body copy. Everything you need to churn out paragraphs of prose is included. "Quote" from a *Magazine*. **Bold random phrases** to your heart's content. Publish it all on any screen without fuzzy antialiasing. Unlike pixel fonts from other vendors, Kare Five Dots is Flash-compatible. Like all Atomic Media fonts, it is specially designed not to blur or fill. Jaggy is good.

Regular

A mix of big juicy steaks sizzled in a pan as

AaBbCcDdEeFfGgHhIiJjKkLlMmNnOoPpQqRrSsTtUuVvWwXxYyZz{([$1234567890!?])}
Diacritics and punct, and even your lovely British currency: @#%^&*æñéáóüåçÉÁÓÜÅÎ£

Bold

Five workmen left the quarry to grub

AaBbCcDdEeFfGgHhIiJjKkLlMmNnOoPpQqRrSsTtUuVvWwXxYyZz1234567890!?
Diacritics and punct, and your British currency: {([$@#%^&*ñéáóüåçÉÁÓÜÅÎ£

TINY TYPE YOU CAN READ.

How did Susan Kare fit legible letters into a space just 5 pixels high?
ANSWER: More than 20 YEARS of practicing BITHAPPY MAGIC.

Regular

Watch all six questions asked by experts amaze judge

AaBbCcDdEeFfGgHhIiJjKkLlMmNnOoPpQqRrSsTtUuVvWwXxYyZz{([$1234567890!?])}

Yes, this font has diacritics and punct, and even your precious British currency: @#%^&*œñéáóüåçÉÁÓÜÂÎ£

Italic

How quickly six jumping zebras vex the lions

AaBbCcDdEeFfGgHhIiJjKkLlMmNnOoPpQqRrSsTtUuVvWwXxYyZz{([$1234567890!?])}

*Italic also has diacritics and punct, and your fine British currency: @#%^&*ñéáóüåçÉÁÓÜÂÎ£*

Bold

Sphinx of black quartz, judge my six vows

AaBbCcDdEeFfGgHhIiJjKkLlMmNnOoPpQqRrSsTtUuVvWwXxYyZz{([$1234567890!?])}

Bold also has all the good stuff, plus your fine British currency: @#%^&*ñéáóüåçÉÁÓÜÂÎ£

––– Set gobs of type with **Kare Six Dots** –––

Sure, Kare Six Dots can handle your copious body copy. Everything you need to churn out paragraphs of prose is included. "Quote" from a *Magazine*. **Bold random phrases** to your heart's content. Publish it all on any screen without fuzzy antialiasing. Unlike pixel fonts from other vendors, Kare Six Dots is Flash–compatible. Like all Atomic Media fonts, it is specially designed not to blur or fill. Jaggy is good.

Regular

A mix of juicy steaks sizzled in the pan as

AaBbCcDdEeFfGgHhIiJjKkLlMmNnOoPpQqRrSsTtUuVvWwXxYyZz{([$1234567890!?])}

Diacritics and punct, and even your lovely British currency: @#%^&*œñéáóüåçÉÁÓÜÂÎ£

Bold

Five workmen left the quarry to grub

AaBbCcDdEeFfGgHhIiJjKkLlMmNnOoPpQqRrSsTtUuVvWwXxYyZz1234567890

Diacritics, punct, and your British currency: {([!?$@#%^&*ñéáóüåçÉÁÓÜÂÎ£

SIX DOTS: TINY TYPE YOU CAN READ.

How did Susan Kare fit a legible letter into a space just 6 pixels high?

ANSWER: More than 20 YEARS of practicing BITMAPPY MAGIC.

Macroscopic A

WILT THE STILT HAS A POSSE

ABCDEFGHIJKLMNOPQRSTUVWXYZ

{[([1234567890])]}@#$%¢£¥Æ©

ÊÀØÜÑÎÇ⌀Øẞ!? <>«» ™©®

Macroscopic B

WILT THE STILT HAS A POSSE

ABCDEFGHIJKLMNOPQRSTUVWXYZ

{[([1234567890])]}@#$%¢£¥Æ©

Macroscopic C

WILT THE STILT HAS A POSSE

ABCDEFGHIJKLMNOPQRSTUVWXYZ

{[([1234567890])]}@#$%¢£¥Æ©

ÊÀØÜÑÎÇ⌀Øẞ!? <>«» ™©®

Macroscopic D

WILT THE STILT HAS A POSSE

ABCDEFGHIJKLMNOPQRSTUVWXYZ

{[([1234567890])]}@#$%¢£¥Æ©

Macroscopic E

WILT THE STILT HAS A POSSE

ABCDEFGHIJKLMNOPQRSTUVWXYZ

{[([1234567890])]}@#$%¢£¥Æ©

Macroscopic

Matthew Bardram
2001

All the Macroscopic styles are
built with the same stem width,
allowing them to be used together at
the same point size to apply emphasis
or create other effects

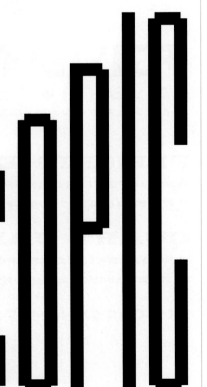

MACROSCOPIC

{ CHICHÉN ITZÁ }

ABCDEFGHIJKLMNOPQRSTUVWXYZ

‹ KUKULKÁN ›

[¢¢¥€$] (0123456789)

チコソシイチキクニマノ柔モ三

チコソシイハキクニマノリモ三ラセタストカナヒテサンツ

タテイスカンナニラセチトシハキクマノリレツサソヒコ三モネル×ヌフアウエオヤユヨワホダ ディズガ二ゼドジバギグツザソヒゴ

Regular

FREIGHT ME PIXELS IN SIXTY DOZEN

ABCDEFGHIJKLMNOPQRSTUVWXYZABCDEFGHIJKLMNOPQRSTU
VWXYZ!1234567890@#$%^˜&*ŒÉÁÓÚÅÑÎÉÁÓÚÅÎÎÇØ ---=+\|/◆·.,"₽₂«»

Bold

QUART JARS & TWELVE SACKS

ABCDEFGHIJKLMNOPQRSTUVWXYZABCDEFGHIJKLMNOPQRSTUV
WXYZ!1234567890@#$%^˜&*ŒÉÁÓÚÅÑÎÉÁÓÚÅÎÎÇØ ---=+\|/◆·.,"₽₂«»

HIS CATS' NAMES ARE "ROCK, SCISSORS, AND PAPER"

MICROFONT

DON'T BE FOOLED BY THE TINY SIZE
{[(1234567890)]}
IT'S GOT DIACRITICS & PUNCT

ABCDEFGHIJKLMNOPQRSTUVWXYZ#$%^&* [ONLY 4 PIXELS HIGH] ŒÉÁÓÚÅÑÎÉÁÓÚÅÎÎÇØ ---=+\|/·.,"ªº«»

MiniFood

Susan Kare
2001

Pixel illustrations for bullets,
dividers, watermarks, or borders.

Atomic Media

BLACK SPHINX QUARTZ & JUDGE MONO

MONOCULE-IS-MONOSPACED ABCDEFGHIJKLMNOPQRSTUVWXYZ! 1234567890

@#$%^&*ŒÉÁÓÚÂÑÎÇØ ---=+\|/•·.,"' ªº«»<>() <>ʳᶜ™÷ FULL-CHAR-SET

· : · . · ⠇ · · ⠄ · ⠐ · ⠆ · · ⠁ · : ⠇ · · ⠐ · ⠐ · ⠆ ⠄ ⠁ · · ⠐ · · ⠆ · : · . · · · . · ⠁ ·

· : · . · ⠇ · · ⠄ · ⠐ · ⠆ · · ⠁ · : ⠇ · · ⠐ · ⠐ · ⠆ ⠄ ⠁ · · ⠐ · · ⠆ · : · . · · · . · ⠁ ·

JACKDAWS LOVE MY PURPLE LYNX MADE OF

DON'T BE FOOLED BY THE TINY SIZE

{ [(1 2 3 4 5 6 7 8 9 0)] }

IT'S GOT DIACRITICS & PUNCT

ABCDEFGHIJKLMNOPQRSTUVWXYZ@#$%^¢*ŒÉÁÓÚÂÑÎÉÁÓÚÂÎÇØ ---=+\|/•·.,"'ªº«»

A pixelated script for the nerd of distinction

AaBbCcDdEeFfGgHhIiJjKkLlMmNnOoPpQqRrSsTtUuVvWwXxYyZz1234567890!

He found love on the net

Regular

Hey guys! I've spent the past several days (that's right,

abcdefghijklmnopqrstuvwxyzABCDEFGHIJKLMNOPQRSTUVWXYZ Don't be fooled by the tiny size

!@#$%^¢*œéáóúãñîÉÁÓÚÂÎçø ---=+\|/•·.,"'ªº«» { [(1 2 3 4 5 6 7 8 9 0)] }

Bold

haven't eaten, slept, done any work...) playing a

abcdefghijklmnopqrstuvwxyzABCDEFGHIJKLMNOPQRSTUVWXYZ A full character set included

!@#$%^¢*œéáóúãñîÉÁÓÚÂÎçø ---=+\|/•·.,"'ªº«» { [(1 2 3 4 5 6 7 8 9 0)] }

Small

pre-release version of Silicon Beach's new game, Dark Castle.

abcdefghijklmnopqrstuvwxyzABCDEFGHIJKLMNOPQRSTUVWXYZ Don't be fooled by the tiny size

!@#$%^¢*œéáóúãñîÉÁÓÚÂÎçø ---=+\|/•·.,"'ªº«» { [(1 2 3 4 5 6 7 8 9 0)] }

Small Bold

This game is AMAZING! [comp.sys.mac 12.08.1986]

abcdefghijklmnopqrstuvwxyzABCDEFGHIJKLMNOPQRSTUVWXYZ A full character set is included

Matthew Bardram
2001

Atomic Media

Regular

Announcing the long-awaited update of

Oregon Trail Deluxe!

Transformed from the MS-DOS version, far beyond the outdated graphics in the Apple][version. The hot new look supports the current industry standard of

256-Color Graphics!

abcdefghijklmnopqrstuvwxyzABCDEFGHIJKLMNOPQRSTUVWXYZ!
1234567890@#$%^&*œéáóüåñíéñóüåîçø ---=+\|/·.,"'ªº«»

SanScript

The game is mouse-driven, making it even more accessible to all youngsters.

Retailing for $59.95

Oregon Trail requires 2 megabytes of RAM, a VGA graphics card, and a hard drive.
abcdefghijklmnopqrstuvwxyzABCDEFGHIJKLMNOPQRSTUVWXYZ!
1234567890@#$%^&*œéáóüåñíéñóüåîçø ---=+\|/·.,"'ªº«»

Matthew Bardram
1999

Regular

TWO HARDY BOXING KANGAROOS JET FROM

ABCDEFGHIJKLMNOPQRSTUVWXYZABCDEFGHIJKLMNOPQRSTUVWXYZ
!1234567890@#$%^+*œÉÁÓÜÅÑÎÇθ ---:+\|/·.,"'ªº«»

Bold

SALT LAKE TO ZAMBIA BY PIXEL PLANE

ABCDEFGHIJKLMNOPQRSTUVWXYZABCDEFGHIJKLMNOPQRSTUVWXYZ
!1234567890@#$%^+*œÉÁÓÜÅÑÎÇθ ---:+\|/·.,"'ªº«»

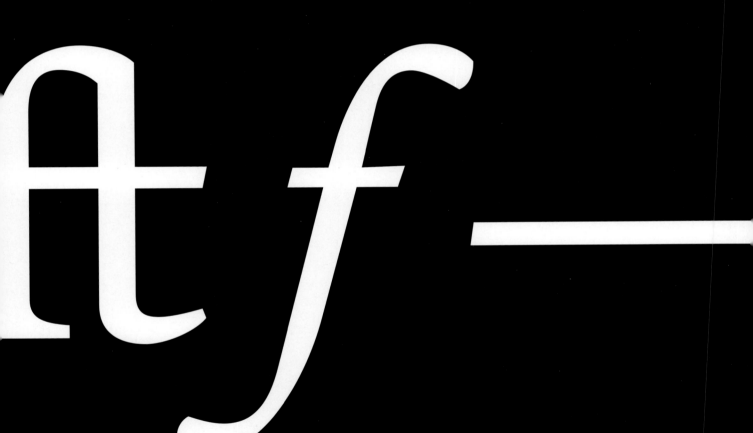

FELICIANO
TYPE
FOUNDRY

Feliciano Type Foundry is an independent
type foundry based in Lisbon, providing quality
font software for both platforms, Pc Windows
and Macintosh. The worldwide right to license
the typefaces BsArchae, BsKombat, BsLooper,
BsMandrax, BsMonofaked, BsRetchnov, FTF Merlo,
FTF Morgan Sans, FTF Morgan Sans Condensed,
FTF Morgan Bog, FTF Morgan Poster, FTF Morgan
Tower, FTF Rongel, and FTF Stella, belongs
exclusively to the Feliciano Type Foundry.

T: +351 21 390 61 40
F: +351 21 394 07 04
E: ftfinfo@secretonix.pt

To buy online go to myfonts.com

Bs-Archae

Mário Feliciano
1999

Regular, Bold, Heavy

Bs-Archae Regular

AaBCDEEFGHIiJKLMMNNOPQRΓSTtUVVWXYYZ,&1234567890!?

Bs-Archae Bold

AaBCDEEFGHIiJKLMMNNOPQRΓSTtUVVWXYYZ,&12345678

Bs-Archae Heavy

AaBCDEEFGHIiJKLMMNNOPQRΓSTtUVVWXYYZ,&12345

STAR

SUPERJET AIRCRAFTS

WIN

ENDLESS

DIFFERENT TIME ZONES

MICKEY SPILLANE

JACK

GRAVITY IS LESS ON THE

BRAIN

MR

SIR

GARFIELD

ARTHUR STERLING

THE

INVENTOR

Feliciano

Bs-Kombat

Mário Feliciano
1998

Normal, Alternate

Bs-Kombat & Kombat Alternate

ABCDEFGHIJKLMNOPQRSTUVWXYZ abcdefghijklmnopqrstuvwxyz áâàãäå ç

1234567890&!?.,: — æmnrty ÁÂÀÃÄ ç % $€ ... ª º ¶

FRESH

AIR

SEQUENCE

GR165

spacecraft

SUDDENLY

BASS

Electronique

DRIVERS

Science instruments

Bs-Looper

Mário Feliciano
2000

Regular Stencil, Black Stencil

Bs-Looper Black Stencil

ABCDEFGHIJKLMNOPQRSTU
VWXYZÆŒ&1234567890!?.;

BS3

SPECTROMETER

HANDUBES

SOUTH OF THE BORDER

ROCKIE

Bs-Looper Regular Stencil

ABCDEFGHIJKLMNOPQRSTU
VWXYZÆŒ&1234567890!?.;

ftfinfo@secretonix.pt

Mário Feliciano
2000

Regular, Italic, Bold, Heavy

Bs-Mandrax Bold, Regular e Italic 7.5pt

There are approximately two billion children (persons under 18) in the world. However, since Santa does not visit children of Muslim, Hindu, Jewish or Buddhist religions, this reduces the workload for Christmas night to 15% of the total, or 378 million (according to the population reference bureau). At an average rate of 3.5 children per household, that comes to 108 million homes, presuming that there is at least one good child in each. Santa has about 31 hours of Christmas to work with, thanks to the different time zones and the rotation of the earth, assuming he travels east to west. This works out to 967.7 visits per second. This is to say that, for each Christian household with a good child, Santa has around 1/1000th of a second to park the sleigh, hop out, jump down the chimney, fill the stockings, distribute the remaining presents under the tree, eat whatever snacks have been left for him, get back up the chimney, jump into the sleigh, and get on to the next house. Assuming that each one of these 108 million stops is evenly distributed around the earth (which, of course, *we know to be false, but will accept for the purposes of our calculations), we are now talking about 0.78 miles per household; a total trip of 75.5 million miles, not counting bathroom stops or breaks. This means Santa's sleigh is moving at 650 miles per second (3000 times the speed of sound). For purposes of comparison, the fastest man-made vehicle, the Ulysses space probe, moves at a poky 27.4 miles per second, and a conventional*

Bs-Mandrax Regular 6pt

The payload of the sleigh adds another interesting element. Assuming that each child gets nothing more than a medium-sized Lego set (two pounds), the sleigh is carrying over 500 thousand tons, not counting Santa himself. On land, a conventional reindeer can pull no more than 300 pounds. Even granting that the flying reindeer could pull 10 times that amount, the job can't be done with eight or even nine of them; Santa would need 360,000 of them. This increases the

Bs-Mandrax Italic 6pt

The payload of the sleigh adds another interesting element. Assuming that each child gets nothing more than a medium-sized Lego set (two pounds), the sleigh is carrying over 500 thousand tons, not counting Santa himself. On land, a conventional reindeer can pull no more than 300 pounds. Even granting that the flying reindeer could pull 10 times that amount, the job can't be done with eight or even nine of them; Santa would need 360,000 of them. This increases the

There are approximately two billion children in the world

Thermoelectric converter

Ultraviolet

The instrument looks for specific colors

Bs-Mandrax Regular complete character set

abcdefghijklmnopqrstuvwxyzABCDEFGHIJKLMNOPQRSTUVWXYZ_12345678 90,.%‰!?&æœøßÆŒØ.:,; fifl° # ªº «»"‹›"''(—) †‡*¡¿–¥€f¢$©\|// [@] ™ [•] áâàäãå çéêèëíîìïñóôòöõúûùüÿÁÂÀÄÃÅÇÉÊÈËÍÎÌÏÑÓÔÒÖÕÚÛÙÜŸ+−×÷<=>´`¨˜˘

FTF Merlo

Mário Feliciano
1997-2003

Roman (osf, lining, caps, figures, pi font), Italic (osf, lining, caps, figures, pi font)

Hujus difficillimæ absolutionis rarissimam laudem eximiè consecutus est Joachim Ibarra qui longe eminuit in splendidissima illa, et vere in omnibus regiâ, optimæ Salustii versionis Editione [...], quæ pariter stupendibus viris Hispanicarum, Latinarum, Hebraicarum, Phoenicia rumque literarum, necnon et artis *Typographiæ* peritissimis, prodiit Matriti, anno 1772, in fol. Et quid ab illa ingenios issimâ et acuratissi mâ gente. Quæ pretiosissimas Bibliothecas, et doctissimos earum catalogos habet, quid ad hispanicis musis omni disciplinarum et art-

E tudo isso porque, numa velha cidade alemã, alguem criara o processo facil de divulgar as ideias. depois foi a corrida vertiginosa da humanidade para as grandes invenções que tornaram pequeno o mundo e autorizam todas as esperanças. na base das conquistas maravilhosas do progresso, por detrás dos inventos que transformaram o mundo estão as pequenas e frágeis letras de Gutenberg.

Hahj*&a*

NATIONBUS DISPERGERET

STUPENDIBUS

Adinventionibus Dest

FTF Merlo Roman complete charcter set

abcdefghijklmnopqrstuvwxyzABCDEFGHIJKLMNOPQRS TUVWXYZ_1234567890,%‰!?&æœøßÆŒØ.:,;ABCDEFGHIJ KLMNOPQRSTUVWXYZ&ÆŒøfbfhffffiffkflftffiffflſtſtðłþÐŁÞÐŁÞ° #ªº«»"‹›"'(—)⁰¹²³⁴⁵⁶⁷⁸⁹⁄₀₁₂₃₄₅₆₇₈₉⁽⁶⁾½¼¾†‡*¡¿–¥€ƒ¢$©ɪ|// [@]™{·}āáâàäãåçčēéêèğíïîìñōóôòöõšūúûùüýÿž _1234567890ĀÁÂÀÄÃÅÇČĒÉÊÈĚĞĪÍÎÌÏÑÒÓÔÒÖÕŠŪÚ ÛÙÜÝŸŽÁÂÀÄÃÅÇÉÊÈĚÍÍÎÌÏÑÓÔÒÖÕÚÛÙÜŸ+−×÷<=>≠≤±≥´`¨˜

Hujus difficillimæ absolutionis rarissimam laudem eximiè consecutus est Joachim Ibarra qui longe eminuit in splendidissima illa, et vere in omnibus regiâ, optimæ Salustii versionis Editione [...], quæ pariter stupendibus viris Hispanicarum, Latinarum, Hebraicarum, Phoenicia rumque literarum, necnon et artis Typographiæ peritissimis, prodiit Matriti, anno 1772, in fol. Et quid ab illa ingenios issimâ et acuratissi mâ gente. Quæ pretiosissimas Bibliothecas, et doctissimos earum catalogos habet, quid ad hispanicis musis omni disciplinarum.

Chancillería

CRUZ

Sucedido en la ciudad de Lorca

Joaquim Ibarra 1772

FTF Merlo Italic complete charcter set

*abcdefghijklmnopqrstuvwxyzABCDEFGHIJKLMNOPQRSTUV WXYZ1234567890, % ‰!?ɢæœøßÆŒØ.:,;ᴀʙᴄᴅᴇꜰɢʜɪᴊᴋʟᴍɴᴏᴘ ǫʀꜱᴛᴜᴠᴡxʏᴢ&ÆŒØ&fbffiffifjfkflftfffflꜱꜱꜱꝺłþ ÐŁÞ ᴅʟᴘ°#ᵃᵒ«»“‹›”‘›
(—)⁰¹²³⁴⁵⁶⁷⁸⁹‰/₀₁₂₃₄₅₆₇₈₉ ⁽⁶⁾½¼¾†‡*¡¿−¥€f¢$©ɪ|//[@]&{·}
āáâàãåçčēéêèëġīíîìïñōóôòõŏšūúûùüýÿž1234567890ĀÁÂÀÄÃÅ ÇČĒÉÊÈËĞĪÍÎÌÏÑŌÓÔÒÖÕŠŪÚÛÙÜÝŸŽÁÂÀÄÃÅÇÉÊÈËÍÎÌÏÑÓ ÔÒÖÕÚÛÙÜŸ+−×÷<=>≠≤±≥´^`¨˜*

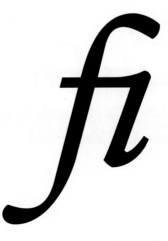

FTF Morgan Big

Mário Feliciano
2001

Big1 Regular, Big1 Oblique,
Big1 Bold, Big1 Bold Oblique,
Big2 Regular, Big2 Oblique,
Big2 Bold, Big2 Bold Oblique,
Big3 Regular, Big3 Oblique,
Big3 Bold, Big3 Bold Oblique

BLOW

PI

OK

BEN

INVESTIGATE

GRAN

SOLAR

WIK

RUN FOR THE DOOR WHILE THEY SEARCH

STRONG

GUARDIANS OF THE UNIVERSE

POPULATION

MASTERMIND OF THE T-MEN

POWER-PACKED PAGES OF ADVENTURE

TWISTED BRAINS

PROFESSOR JEANS RIVER

NOW INTRODUCING THE SPACE CONQUERORS

INVENTION

FLYING SAUCERS

DRIVER

MILLION-DOLLAR

ftfinfo@secretonix.pt

ATOM

GRANGER

FT

COSMIC SCIENTIST

INTRODUCING A NEW BUDGET OF ADVENTURE FANTASY AND FUN

SCREEN-SEARING STORY

DRAW ATTENTION TO THE LAVISH EXPENS

ADVENTURE

FIELD

61058WE

SHOCK ENTERTAINMENT!

218E

SOUNDS

WE1

THE BIG RUN

AMPHIBASTRO

WHERE TEMPTATION

FTF Morgan Poster

Mário Feliciano
2001

Poster Regular, Poster Oblique,
Poster Bold, Poster Bold Oblique,
Poster Black, Poster Black Oblique

Feliciano

Mário Feliciano
2001

Regular (office, lining, caps, expert, pi font, figures), Italic (office, lining, caps, expert, pi font), Bold (office, lining, caps, expert, pi font, figures), Bold Italic (office, lining, caps, expert, pi font)

1) Science instrument performance was nominal for all activities during this period. One frame of GS-4 data was recorded this week. The EDR backlog is 16 days.

Hafnz *afi*

2) There was one real-time schedule change made on 12/23 [DOY 358] when 4.9 hours of DSS-43 support substituted for DSS-45 released to NEAR. The total actual support for the period was 62.6 hours, of which 9.7 hours were large aperture coverage.

At some distance from the Sun, the supersonic solar wind will be held back from further expansion by the interstellar wind. The first feature to be encountered by a spacecraft as a result of this interstellar wind/solar wind interaction will be the termination shock, where the solar wind slows from supersonic to subsonic speed, and large changes in plasma flow direction and magnetic field orientation occur. Passage through the termination shock ends the termination shock phase and begins the heliosheath exploration phase. While the exact location of the termination shock is not known, it is very possible that Voyager 1 will complete the termination shock phase of the mission between the years 2001 and 2003 *when the spacecraft will be between 80 and 90 AU from the Sun. Most of the current estimates place the termination shock at around 85 ± 5 AU. After passage through the termination shock, the spacecraft will be operating in the heliosheath environment, which is still dominated by the Sun's magnetic field and particles contained in the solar wind.*

0123456789 High command transmissions

ABCDEFGHIJKLMNOPQRSTUVWXYZ123456

Three RTG units, electrically parallel-connected, are the central power sources for the mission module. Each RTG is made up of an isotopic heat source, a thermoelectric converter, a gas pressure venting system, temperature transducers, connectors, a heat rejecting CYLINDRICAL container, and bracketry. The RTGs are mounted in tandem (end-to-end) on a deployable boom as part **of the MM. The heat source radioisotopic fuel is Plutonium-238**

There are seven operating instruments on board each Voyager spacecraft, although the Plasma instrument on Voyager 1 is not returning useful data. Five of these instruments directly support the five science investigation teams.

These five instruments are:
MAG *Magnetic field investigation*
LECP *Low energy charged particle investigation*
PLS *Plasma investigation*
CRS *Cosmic ray investigation*
PWS *Plasma wave investigation*

Place verification operations 0123456789

Planet Earth

ftfinfo@secretonix.pt

Greetings to the Universe

The Voyager spacecraft will be the third and fourth human artifacts to escape entirely from the solar system. Pioneers 10 and 11, which preceded Voyager in outstripping the gravitational attraction of the Sun, both carried small metal plaques identifying their time and place of origin for the benefit of any other spacefarers that might find them in the distant future. With this example before them, NASA placed a more ambitious message aboard Voyager 1 and 2–a kind of time capsule, intended to communicate a story of our world to extraterrestrials. The Voyager message is carried by a phonograph record–a 12-inch goldplated copper disk containing sounds and images selected to portray the diversity of life and culture on Earth. The contents of the record were selected for NASA by a committee chaired by Carl Sagan of Cornell University. Dr. Sagan and his associates assembled 115 images and a variety of natural sounds, such as those made by surf, wind, and thunder; birds, whales, and other animals. To this, they added musical selections from different cultures and eras, spoken greetings from Earth-people in fifty-five languages, and printed messages from President Carter and U.N. Secretary-General Waldheim. Each record is encased in a protective aluminum jacket, together with a cartridge and a needle. Instructions, in symbolic language, explain the origin of the spacecraft, and indicate how the record is to be played. The 115 images are encoded

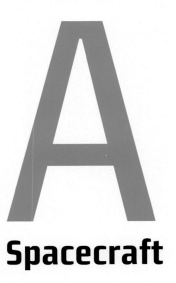

A Spacecraft

FTF Morgan Sans Cond

Mário Feliciano
2001

Regular (office, lining, caps, expert, pi font, figures), Italic (office, lining, caps, expert, pi font), Bold (office, lining, caps, expert, pi font, figures), Bold Italic (office, lining, caps, expert, pi-font)

Feliciano

ABILITY TO STORE *HGA* POINTING INFORMATION ON-BOARD

BACKUP MISSION LOAD DESCRIPTION

Flight system performance

RANGE, VELOCITY AND ROUND TRIP LIGHT TIME AS OF 12/29/00

Distance from the Sun (Km)	11,930,000,000	9,402,000,000
Distance from the Sun (Mi)	7,413,000,000	5,842,000,000
Distance from the Earth (Km)	12,039,000,000	9,533,000,000
Distance from the Earth (Mi)	7,481,000,000	5,923,000,000
Total Distance Traveled Since Launch (Km)	13,742,000,000	12,913,000,000
Total Distance Traveled Since Launch (Mi)	8,539,000,000	8,024,000,000
Velocity Relative to Sun (Km/sec)	17.259	15.768
Velocity Relative to Sun (Mi/hr)	38,606	35,271
Velocity Relative to Earth (Km/sec)	31.140	36.697
Velocity Relative to Earth (Mi/hr)	69,657	82,089
Round Trip Light Time (Hours:Minutes:Seconds)	22:18:34	17:39:58

The Voyager Interstellar Mission (VIM) has the potential for obtaining useful interplanetary—and possibly interstellar—fields, particles, and waves (FPW) science data until around the year 2020, when the spacecraft's ability to generate adequate electrical power for continued science instrument operation will come to an end. In order to capitalize on this lengthy data acquisition potential, it is imperative that the spacecraft have a continuing sequence of instructions for acquiring the desired science data, and that the spacecraft High Gain Antenna (HGA) remain boresighted on the Earth for continuous data transmission. Because of the long mission duration, and the likelihood of periodic spacecraft anomalies, it is also advantageous to continue the use of the onboard fault protection capability for automated responses to specific subsystem anomalies, and to provide an onboard sequence to continue spacecraft operation in the specific event of the future loss of command reception capability. All of these factors are considered in the VIM sequencing strategy. The

KGB

SQUADRON

ftfinfo@secretonix.pt

ROAMER

ACTION

Feliciano

FTF Rongel

Mário Feliciano
1999

Roman (osf, osf table, lining,
lining table, expert, pi font, figures),
Italic (osf, osf table, lining,
lining table, expert, pi font, figures)

Na óptica de Simmel, nesta teoria é excluído de todo o sentido relativo à essência e ao valor da arte aquilo que não é totalmente interno àesfera estética. Há um enclausurar manifesto, uma tentativa fascizante de preservar a pureza estética

Adinventionibus Dest

hujus difficillimæ absolutionis rarissimam laudem eximiè consecutus est Joachim Ibarra qui longe eminuit in splendidissima illa, et vere in omnibus regiâ, optimæ Salustii versionis Editione [...], quæ pariter stupendibus viris Hispanicarum, Latinarum, Hebraicarum, Phoeniciarumque literarum, necnon et artis Typographiæ peritissimis, prodiit Matriti, anno 1772, in fol. Et quid ab illa ingenios issimâ et acuratissimâ gente. Quæ pretiosissimas Bibliothecas, et doctissimos earum catalogos habet, quid ad hispanicis musis omni disciplinarum et artium genere sperandum sit, hoc illustrissimo exemplo abundè comprobavit.

NATIONBUS DISPERGERET

A B C D E F G H I J K L M N O P Q R S T U V W X Y Z &

Na óptica de Simmel, nesta teoria é excluído de todo
o sentido relativo à essência e ao valor da arte aquilo que não é
totalmente interno à esfera estética. Há um enclausurar manifesto,
uma tentativa fascizante de preservar a pureza estética

ftfinfo@secretonix.pt

En este manuscrito tenemos
un exemplo sumamente persuasivo
de quán necesaria es la critica para
hacer juicio de los libros

Eiffißen

A B C D E F G H I J K L M N O P Q R S T U V W X Y Z &

Bibliotheca

FTF Stella

Mário Feliciano
2000

Regular (osf, lining, osf table, lining
table, expert, figures, pi font), Italic
(osf, lining, osf table, lining table,
expert, pi font), Bold (osf, lining,
osf table, lining table, expert,
figures, pi font), Bold Italic (osf,
lining, osf table, lining table, expert,
pi font)

There are approximately two billion children (persons under 18) in the world. However, since Santa does not visit children of Muslim, Hindu, Jewish or Buddhist religions, this reduces the workload for Christmas night to 15% of the total, or 378 million (according to the population reference bureau). At AN AVERAGE RATE OF 3.5 CHILDREN

There are approximately two billion children (persons under 18) in the world. However, since Santa does not visit children of Muslim, Hindu, Jewish or Buddhist religions, this reduces the workload for Christmas night to 15% of the total, or 378 million (according to the population reference bureau). At an average rate of 3.5 CHILDREN PER HOUSEHOLD, THAT

ABC
Santa Claus
Engineer's Perspective

The payload of the sleigh adds another interesting element. Assuming that each child gets nothing more than a medium-sized *Lego* set (two pounds), the sleigh is carrying over 500 thousand tons, not counting Santa himself. On land, a conventional REINDEER CAN PULL NO MORE THAN 300 POUNDS

THE PAYLOAD OF THE SLEIGH *adds another interesting element. Assuming that each child gets nothing more than a medium-sized* Lego *set (two pounds), the sleigh is carrying over 500 thousand tons, not counting Santa himself. On land, a conventional reindeer can pull no more than 300 pounds. Even granting that the flying reindeer could pull 10 times that amount, the job can't be done with eight or even nine of them; Santa would need 360,000 of them. This increases the payload, not counting the weight of the sleigh, another 54,000 tons, or roughly seven times the weight of the* Queen Elizabeth *(the ship, not the monarch).*

There are approximately two billion children (persons under 18) in the world. However, since Santa does not visit children of Muslim, Hindu, Jewish or Buddhist religions, this reduces the workload for Christmas night to 15% of the total, or 378 million (according to the population reference bureau). **At AN AVERAGE RATE OF 3.5 CHILDREN**

There are approximately two billion children (persons under 18) in the world. However, since Santa does not visit children of Muslim, Hindu, Jewish or Buddhist religions, this reduces the workload for Christmas night to 15% of the total, or 378 million (according to the population reference bureau). At an average rate of 3.5 CHILDREN PER HOUSEHOLD, THAT

THE PAYLOAD OF THE SLEIGH adds another interesting element. Assuming that each child gets nothing more than a medium-sized *Lego* set (two pounds), the sleigh is carrying over 500 thousand tons, not counting Santa himself. On land, a conventional reindeer can pull no more than 300 pounds. Even granting that the flying reindeer could pull 10 times that amount, the job can't be done with eight or even nine of them; Santa would need 360,000 of them. This increases the payload, not counting the weight of the sleigh, another 54,000 tons, or roughly seven times the weight of the *Queen Elizabeth* (the ship, not the

Abe*fghist*
H*a*bcdefg*hijk*lmnop

HUISHOUDELIJK

THE SPACECRAFT WILL BE BETWEEN

FORTIES

Como é seu habito, tantas vezes, Graham Greene escolheu

RESEARCH CONTROLS

Stan

SHIPBUILDER

Engineering equipment

Jornalista incomparável, um dos escritores mais

Plaques kilométriques

Em Londres os Serviços Secretos acreditam em tudo e Wormold é considerado

ABC

SEQUENCING

Æ

Atmosphere

&

Civil engineering developers

DRAWING

The incredible

METEOR

 Galápagos Design Group

Since its inception in 1994, Galápagos Design Group continues to provide cost effective custom font technology solutions and creative type services for corporate identity and branding in numerous business sectors. Galápagos also continues to add new flavor to its unique type library.

Galápagos clients include many major font foundries, as well as original equipment manufacturers, independent software vendors, and design firms, such as:

Agilent Technologies, Apple, BP, DigitalVision, Eli Lilly, Hewlett Packard, Lockheed Martin, Microsoft, Qwest, Saatchi & Saatchi, and Wachovia Financial.

Galápagos Design — Font Technology and Design Solutions.

Contact: Larry Oppenberg or Mike Allen
Website: www. galapagosdesign.com
Telephone: 978 952 6200
Fax: 978 952 6260
email: info@galapagosdesign.com

Robusto

George Ryan
2002

Burly and athletic, vigorous and strong, Robusto will add puissance to your project. The powerful build of each character portrays health and vitality, while the suave curvy tails add a seductive allure. Inspired by the lettering of Oz Cooper, George Ryan delivers another highly functional display type.

"Life will not be full and complete with me until I see the right type named 'Robusto'. I have awakened in the stilly night snickering at that name. I see a fat boy in a circus, a playful St. Bernard pup, an elephant, a Mack truck, or what have you... It should be a comic type".

**Thoughts on Robusto — Oswald Cooper
from The Book of Oz Cooper**

Galápagos

Bartholemé Open

Dennis Pasternak
2002

Bartholemé Open
Bartholemé SC Open

An award-winning classical
design, Bartholemé Open
features a large x-height, tightly
curved counters, and crisp serifs
with tight bracketing.

SENATUS·POPULUSQUE·ROMANUS
IMP·CAESARI·DIVI·NERVAE·F·NERVAE
TRAIANO·AVG·GERM·DACICO·PONTIF
·MAXIMO·TRIB·POT·
XVII·IMP·VI·COS·VI·P·P·ADDECLARAN
DUM·QUANTAE·ALTITUDINIS·MONS·ET
LOCUS·TANTIS·OPERIBUS·SIT·E·GESTUS

The base inscription on the Trajan Column
commemorating Trajan's victories over
King Decebalus in the Dacian wars of
the Danube · Carpathian territory.

978-952-6200

AÆBCDEFGHIJKLMNOØŒPQRSTUVWXYZ&aæb
cdeffiflghijklmnoøœpqrsßtuvwxyz $12345€67890
(.,:;?¿!¡...‹›«» """'',,) @*§†‡¶ ÅÇÉÏÔÑÙ åçéïôñù

Bartholemé Regular

Dennis Pasternak
2002

Bartholemé Regular
Bartholemé Medium
Bartholemé Bold
Bartholemé Extrabold

A letter is a designed area. It is a pattern made within a space. Its outlines have the effect of motion. It begins and ends. The things are true about the shapes of letters that are true about all designs that have pattern and motion. The pattern of a letter may be graceful or it may be awkward, and the fact of its

A letter is a designed area. It is a pattern made within a space. Its outlines have the effect of motion. It begins and ends. The things are true about the shapes of letters that are true about all designs that have pattern and motion. The pattern of a letter may be graceful or it may be awkward, and the fact of its

A letter is a designed area. It is a pattern made within a space. Its outlines have the effect of motion. It begins and ends. The things are true about the shapes of letters that are true about all designs that have pattern and motion. The pattern of a letter may be graceful or it may be awkward, and

A letter is a designed area. It is a pattern made within a space. Its outlines have the effect of motion. It begins and ends. The things are true about the shapes of letters that are true about all designs that have pattern and motion. The pattern of a letter may be graceful or it may be awk

The four-weight semicondensed Bartholemé family came into existence as a family expansion based on the designer's earlier concept, Bartholemé Open. This hybrid family was inspired by–and loosely based on–a number of mid-twentieth century type concepts having Old Face or Modern influences. Those inspirational type designs were primarily designed for various proprietary photolettering technologies of the times. Design qualities include a large x-height, tightly curved counters and crisp serifs with tight bracketing. The Bartholemé family was designed for display use in titling and short passages of text.

AÆBCDEFGHIJKLMNOØŒPQRSTUVWXYZ&aæb
cdeffiflghijklmnoøœpqrsßtuvwxyz $12345€67890
(.,:;?¿!¡...‹›«» """'',,) @§†‡¶ ÅÇÉÏÔÑÙ åçéïôñù*

Bartholemé Italic

Dennis Pasternak
2002

Bartholemé Italic
Bartholemé Medium Italic
Bartholemé Bold Italic
Bartholemé Extrabold Italic

Galápagos

A letter is a designed area. It is a pattern made within a space. Its outlines have the effect of motion. It begins and ends. The things are true about the shapes of letters that are true about all designs that have pattern and motion. The pattern of a letter may be graceful or it may be awkward, and the fact of its

A letter is a designed area. It is a pattern made within a space. Its outlines have the effect of motion. It begins and ends. The things are true about the shapes of letters that are true about all designs that have pattern and motion. The pattern of a letter may be graceful or it may be awkward, and the fact of its

A letter is a designed area. It is a pattern made within a space. Its outlines have the effect of motion. It begins and ends. The things are true about the shapes of letters that are true about all designs that have pattern and motion. The pattern of a letter may be graceful or it may be awkward, and

A letter is a designed area. It is a pattern made within a space. Its outlines have the effect of motion. It begins and ends. The things are true about the shapes of letters that are true about all designs that have pattern and motion. The pattern of a letter may be graceful or it may be awk

George Ryan
2002

McLemore Light
McLemore Light Italic
McLemore
McLemore Italic
McLemore Bold
McLemore Bold Italic
McLemore Black
McLemore Black Italic

¶ At a very young age, some children have a particular fascination with the colorful letters carved in the faces of wooden blocks. ¶ As they are *growing to adolescence, they are saturated with with letters of all types — animated letters, vibrant brush lettering, colorful signs and huge billboards.* ¶ Some older children start experimenting with drawing the letters they have in their active memory or in their own environment. *Some of these letters are primitive and others are very interesting.* ¶ **Some teens may attend an art school and others may work a job where working with letters is important.** *They are taught how letters are fit with one another to form fluid words.* ¶ **For some people, letter drawings become type, more refined while starting to understand the minutiæ** *of spacing, curves and proportions of a well-design*

978-952-6200

AÆBCDEFGHIJKLMNOØŒPQRSTU VWXYZ&aæbcdeffifflghijklmnoøœpqr sßtuvwxyz $12345€67890 (.,:;?¿!¡…‹›«»

McLemore Regular

George Ryan
2002

McLemore Light
McLemore Regular
McLemore Bold
McLemore Black

The essence of this superior face is the slightly concave nature of the stems, arms, and serifs of each character. This creates a highly legible typeface with a graceful, natural presence on the page, and at larger point sizes, it's magical!

A letter is a designed area. It is a pattern made within a space. Its outlines have the effect of motion. It begins and ends. The things are true about the shapes of letters that are true about all designs that have pattern and motion. The

A letter is a designed area. It is a pattern made within a space. Its outlines have the effect of motion. It begins and ends. The things are true about the shapes of letters that are true about all designs that have pattern and motion. The

A letter is a designed area. It is a pattern made within a space. Its outlines have the effect of motion. It begins and ends. The things are true about the shapes of letters that are true about all designs that have pattern and motion. The

A letter is a designed area. It is a pattern made within a space. Its outlines have the effect of motion. It begins and ends. The things are true about the shapes of letters that are true about all designs that have pattern and motion. The

AÆBCDEFGHIJKLMNOØŒPQRSTUV WXYZ&aæbcdeffifflghijklmnoøœpqrsßtuv wxyz $12345€67890 (.,:;?¿!¡…‹›«»""'',,) @

McLemore Italic

George Ryan
2002

McLemore Light Italic
McLemore Italic
McLemore Bold Italic
McLemore Black Italic

A letter is a designed area. It is a pattern made with in a space. Its outlines have the effect of motion. It be gins and ends. The things are true about the shapes of letters that are true about all designs that have pat tern and motion. The pattern of a letter may be crude

A letter is a designed area. It is a pattern made with in a space. Its outlines have the effect of motion. It begins and ends. The things are true about the shapes of letters that are true about all designs that have pattern and motion. The pattern of a letter may be

A letter is a designed area. It is a pattern made with in a space. Its outlines have the effect of motion. It begins and ends. The things are true about the shapes of letters that are true about all designs that have pattern and motion. The pattern of a le

A letter is a designed area. It is a pattern made within a space. Its outlines have the effect of motion. It begins and ends. The things are true about the shapes of letters that are true about all designs that have pattern and motion. The

Galápagos

New Age

Alex Kaczun
2002

New Age Regular
New Age Italic

Chapter Eleven

¶ So I travelled, stopping ever and again, in gr eat strides of a thousand years or more, drawn on by the mystery of the earth's fate, watching with a strange fascination the sun grow larger and duller in the western sky, and the life of th e old earth ebb away. At last, more than thirty million years hence, the huge red-hot dome of the sun had come to obscure nearly a tenth pa rt of the darkling heavens. Then I stopped once more, for the crawling multitude of crabs had disappeared, and the red beach, save for its liv id green liverworts and lichens, seemed lifeless. And now it was flecked in white. A bitter cold assailed me.

excerpt from The Time Machine—*H.G.Wells*

978-952-6200

AÆBCDEFGHIJKLMNOØŒPQRSTUVW XYZ&aæbcdeffiflghijklmnoøœpqrsßtuvw xyz $12345€67890 (.,:;?¿!¡...‹›«»""''"‚„) @

A letter is a designed area. It is a pattern made
within a space. Its outlines have the effect of mo
tion. It begins and ends. The things are true about
about the shapes of letters that are true about all

**A letter is a designed area. It is a pattern
made within a space. Its outlines have the ef
fect of motion. It begins and ends. The things
are true about the shapes of letters that are**

New Age Regular

Alex Kaczun
2002

New Age Regular
New Age Bold

New Age: The dawn of a new age
in typography. A sophisticated
design with an air of class and
distinction, New Age blends the
readability of a serif typeface with
the graphic impact of a sans serif.
Numerous cursive elements add
harmony, linking this typeface with
the past. New Age – the best of
both worlds.

AÆBCDEFGHIJKLMNOØŒPQRSTUVW XYZ&aæbcdeffiflghijklmnoøœpqrsßtuvwxy z $12345€67890 (.,:;?¿!¡...‹›«»""''"‚„) @*∫†

A letter is a designed area. It is a pattern made with
in a space. Its outlines have the effect of motion. It
begins and ends. The things are true about the shapes
of letters that are true about all designs that have

**A letter is a designed area. It is a pattern made
within a space. Its outlines have the effect of
motion. It begins and ends. The things are true
about the shapes of letters that are true about**

New Age Italic

Alex Kaczun
2002

New Age Italic
New Age Bold Italic

AÆBCDEFGHIJKLMNOØŒPQRSTUVWXYZ &aæbcdeffiflghijklmnoøœpqrsßtuvwxyz $12 345€67890 (.,:;?¿!¡...‹›«»""''"‚„) @*∫†‡¶ ÅÇ

A letter is a designed area. It is a pattern made with
in a space. Its outlines have the effect of motion. It
begins and ends. The things are true about the shapes
of letters that are true about all designs that have pat

**A letter is a designed area. It is a pattern made
with in a space. Its outlines have the effect of
motion. It begins and ends. The things are true
about the shapes of letters that are true about**

New Age Condensed

Alex Kaczun
2002

New Age Condensed
New Age Bold Condensed

Galápagos

Culpepper Regular

George Ryan
2002

Culpepper Light
Culpepper Regular
Culpepper Extrabold

A Grecian urn inscribed by the artisan. A spiritual Pagan glyph carved in stone. A Celtic bracelet found in an excavation. All these images are brought to mind when Culpepper works its magic across the page. Developed by George Ryan, Culpepper is inspired by the work of Rudolph Koch. This new face is perfect for any artistic design, and will add a sense of antiquity to your work.

AÆBCDEFGHIJKLMNOØŒPQRSTUVWX
YZ&aæbcdeffiflghijklmnoøœpqrsßtuvwxy
z $12345€67890(.,:;?¿!i…‹›«»""''„,) @*†‡§

A letter is a designed area. It is a pattern made within a space. Its outlines have the effect of motion. It begins and ends. The things are true about the shapes of letters that are true about all designs that have pattern and motion. The motion of a letter may be graceful or awkward, and the fact of its grace or awkwardness is apparent at once. Judgement upon these

A letter is a designed area. It is a pattern made within a space. Its outlines have the effect of motion. It begins and ends. The things are true about the shapes of letters that are true a bout all designs that have pattern and motion. The motion of a letter maybe graceful or awkward, and the fact of its grace or awkwardness is apparent at once.

A letter is a designed area. It is a pattern made within a space. Its outlines have the effect of motion. It begins and ends. The things are true about the shapes of letters that are true about all designs that have pattern and motion. The motion of a letter maybe graceful or awkward, and the fact of its grace or awk

Culpepper Regular SC

George Ryan
2002

Culpepper Light SC
Culpepper SC
Culpepper Extrabold SC

AÆBCDEFGHIJKLMNOØŒPQRSTUVW
XYZ&AÆBCDEFFIFLGHIJKLMNOØŒPQRSSST
UVWXYZ $12345€67890(.,:;?¿!i…‹›«»""''„,)

A LETTER IS A DESIGNED AREA. IT IS A PATTERN MADE WITHIN A SPACE. ITS OUTLINES HAVE THE EFFECT OF MOTION. IT BEGINS AND ENDS. THE THINGS ARE TRUE ABOUT THE SHAPES OF LETTERS THAT ARE TRUE ABOUT ALL DESIGNS THAT HAVE PATTERN AND MOTION. THE MOTION OF A LETTER MAY BE GRACEFUL OR AWK WARD, AND THE FACT OF ITS GRACE

A LETTER IS A DESIGNED AREA. IT IS A PATTERN MADE WITHIN A SPACE. ITS OUTLINES HAVE THE EFFECT OF MOTION. IT BEGINS AND ENDS. THE THINGS ARE TRUE ABOUT THE SHAPES OF LETTERS THAT ARE TRUE A BOUT ALL DESIGNS THAT HAVE PATTERN AND MOTION. THE MOTION OF A LETTER MAYBE GRACEFUL OR AWK WARD, AND THE FACT OF ITS GRACE

A LETTER IS A DESIGNED AREA. IT IS A PATTERN MADE WITHIN A SPACE. ITS OUTLINES HAVE THE EFFECT OF MOTION. IT BEGINS AND ENDS. THE THINGS ARE TRUE ABOUT THE SHAPES OF LETTERS THAT ARE TRUE ABOUT ALL DESIGNS THAT HAVE PAT PATTERN AND MOTION. THE MO TION OF A LETTER MAYBE GRACE FUL OR AWKWARD, AND THE FACT

ABCDEFGHIJKLMNOPQRSTUVWXYZ&abcdefgh ijklmnopqrstuvwxyz $12345€67890 (.,:;?¿!¡...<>«»

A sleek flat panel color display

that has a smaller footprint to add more workspace and a high tech look to your home office.

Extreme Sans

Alex Kaczun
2002

A no-frills sans serif of the future, Extreme Sans features clean and simple lines, with no abrupt terminals. Character edges are rounded like high tech routed parts of precise machinery. The overall look speaks of technology and innovation, and holds extreme possibilities for typographic expression today and tomorrow.

ABCDEFGHIJKLMNOPQRSTUVWXYZ&abcdefgh ijklmnopqrstuvwxyz $12345€67890 (.,:;?¿!¡...<>«»

More gigabytes of storage space

let you create all types of multimedia projects without the worry of running out of disk space.

Extreme Sans Oblique

Alex Kaczun
2002

ABCDEFGHIJKLMNOPQRSTUVWXYZ&abcdefg hijklmnopqrstuvwxyz $12345€67890 (.,:;?¿!¡...<>

Clean & simple lines, no abrupt

terminals. Character edges are rounded like high tech routed parts of precise machinery.

Extreme Sans Heavy

Alex Kaczun
2002

Galápagos

ABCDEFGHIJKLMNOPQRSTUVWXYZ&abcdefg hijklmnopqrstuvwxyz $12345€67890 (.,:;?¿!¡...<>

The lightning-quick DSL speed

you have been waiting for. You can now download those huge sound and picture files in a f

Extreme Sans Heavy Obl

Alex Kaczun
2002

Ersatz

Dave Farey, Richard Dawson
2002

Tired of the functional mono-line sans serif fonts? Ersatz has a style with vibrant roots in the Mediterranean climate of modern Spain. It's refreshing and lively. Basic constructions are simple and attractive, with it's soft curves and kickbacks!

AÆBCDEFGHIJKLMNOØŒPQRSTUVWXYZ&aæb
cdeffiflghijklmnoøœpqrsßtuvwxyz $12345€678
90 [.,:;?¿!i...‹›«»""'",,) @*†‡§¶ ÅÇÉÏÔÑÙ åçéïôñ

Saucy Spanish flamencos
Vibrant Roots in the Mediterranean
Lively sans serif with soft curves & kickbacks
Unique biform letters mixing upper with lowercase elements

Ersatz Bold

Dave Farey, Richard Dawson
2002

AÆBCDEFGHIJKLMNOØŒPQRSTUVWXYZ&a
æbcdeffiflghijklmnoøœpqrsßtuvwxyz $12345
€67890 [.,:;?¿!i...‹›«»""'",,) @*†‡§¶ ÅÇÉÏÔÑÙ

Designers who crave color
and sunlight create refreshing fonts
Listen carefully, you can hear the sharp gui
tars and soft tambourine sounds of exciting flamenco music

AÆBCDEFGHIJKLMNOØŒPQRSTUVWXYZ
&aæbcdeffiflghijklmnoøœpqrsßtuvwxyz
$12345€67890(.,:;?¿!i…‹›«»"""'',„)@†‡§¶

Lower tax rates for home
owners that will affect future
town budgets for the next eight years.
This led to a fiery debate between the town council

Prop Ten

George Ryan
2002

A face with a twist! A slant on a classic style, this design features squared-off apexes, bevelled t's and dwarfed tails. This face offers designers the uniformity of a monospaced typeface with the legibility of a proportional one. Prop Ten delivers unequivocal clarity.

AÆBCDEFGHIJKLMNOØŒPQRSTUVWXYZ
&aæbcdeffiflghijklmnoøœpqrsßtuvwx
yz $12345€67890(.,:;?¿!i…‹›«»"""'',„)@

A stronger grassroots po
litical organization is making
a substantial difference in this year's
national election. It has changed the opinion of m

Prop Ten Bold

George Ryan
2002

Galápagos

Jorge

George Ryan
2002

Can you say "Character"? A new cartoon face, Jorge (Hor-hay), brings words to life. Quirky and comical, Jorge will lighten the mood of your design with its wacky personality. Although the font was created in uppercase only, Jorge's four style variations add diversity and verve to the mix.

ABCDEFGHIJKLMNOPQRSTUVWXYZ& $12345€67890
{[(.,;;?¿!¡...<>«»""''"',,,)]} @*§†‡¶ ©®™ ÅÇÉÏÑÔÙÆŒSS
WELCOME TO 4 STYLES OF ZANY FONTS
INSPIRED BY THE FARCICAL SATURDAY MORNING CARTOONS

Jorge Outline

George Ryan
2002

ABCDEFGHIJKLMNOPQRSTUVWXYZ & $12345€67890
{[(.,;;?¿!¡...<>«»""''"',,,)]} @*§†‡¶ ©®™ ÅÇÉÏÑÔÙÆŒSS
OF THE FIFTIES. DO YOU REMEMBER
THE EXPRESSIONS OF THE COYOTE GETTING HIS LATEST ACME GIZMO?

Jorge Drop Shadow

George Ryan
2002

ABCDEFGHIJKLMNOPQRSTUVWXYZ& $12345€67
890 {[(.,;;?¿!¡...<>«»""''"',,,)]} @*§†‡¶ ©®™ ÅÇÉÏÑÔÙ
WILEY NEVER DID GET TO CATCH HIS
NEMESIS, THE ELUSIVE ROADRUNNER, BUT ALWAYS SEEMED

Jorge Outline DS

George Ryan
2002

ABCDEFGHIJKLMNOPQRSTUVWXYZ& $12345€6
7890 {[(.,;;?¿!¡...<>«»""''"',,,)]} @*§†‡¶ ©®™ ÅÇÉÏÑÔ
TO GET TOASTED, BLASTED TO BITS,
OR TAKE A NEVERENDING FREEFALL INTO A DEEP CANYON.

ABCDEFGHIJKLMNOPQRSTUVW XYZ&abcdefghijklmnopqrstuvx

A three element

font inspired by classic theatre

Bing Inline

Dennis Pasternak
2002

Bing takes its inspiration from a combination of the classic cinema marquee and contemporary fabricated signage. The Bing family's versatility is what makes this typeface so stellar. Bing Script allows you to create a simple handwritten look on the page, while Bing Black can be used as a poster face to increase the visibility and punch of your message. Bing Inline combines the two faces to energize the prose in your project.

ABCDEFGHIJKLMNOPQRSTUV WXYZ&abcdefghijklmnopqrst

marquees and fa

bricated contemporary signage

Bing Black

Dennis Pasternak
2002

Galápagos

ABCDEFGHIJKLMNOPQRSTUVWXYZ &abcdefghijklmnopqrstuvwxyz $123

A script having roots

in irregular handblown tubular glass used in traditional neon signs of the

Bing Script

Dennis Pasternak
2002

Bisco Condensed

Dennis Pasternak
2002

Sleek and streetwise, Bisco is an expressive display face with irregular contours, giving weight and bounce. This design achieves high readability at all point sizes.

AÆBCDEFGHIJKLMNOØŒPQRSTUVWXYZ&AÆ
BCDEFFIFLGHIJKLMNOØŒPQRSSSTUVWXYZ $12345€6
7890 (.,:;?¿!¡…‹›«»""''‚„) @*†‡§¶ ÅÇÉÏÑÔÙ åç

GRAFITTI ARTISTS PROTEST!

LACK OF AVAILABLE SPACE ON REMAINING DOWNTOWN

BUILDINGS AND PUBLIC FIXTURES. A SPOKESPERSON FOR THE

GROUP STATED THE CITY COUNCIL'S IRRESPONSIBILITY IN PROVIDING ADEQUATE
SPACE FOR FUTURE ENHANCEMENTS. THE PROTESTERS FEEL THEIR CREATIVITY IS BE

Swordtail

Alex Kaczun
2002

Handwriting with passion and flair, Swordtail is a freehand script with a swashbuckling style reminiscent of old Spain. There is an undeniable energy in the strokes, a rhythm and beat of a passionate hand.

AÆBCDEFGHIJKLMNOØŒPQRSTUV
WXYZ&aæbcdeffifighijklmnoøœpqrsßt
uvwxyz $12345€67890 (.,?¿!¡…<>""''‚„) @

Buccaneers or Raiders

Eighteenth century pirates seizing gold and
silver in their swashbuckling style on the high seas
of the Caribbean. Ambushing and outrunning ships

AÆBCDEFGHIJKLMNOØŒPQRST
UVWXYZ&aæbcdeffifflghijklmnoøœp
qrsßtuvwxyz $12345€67890 (.,:;?¿!¡…‹›

Off Broadway comedies made

a strong comeback this past year as reported

in entertainment's source of news, Variety magazine. It

has been reported the upturn in ticket sales is due to appearances by top
name stars, improved stage design, scripts, one-liners and overall appeal

Geis

George Ryan
2002

Curvaceous yet sleek, these well-developed characters create a nostalgic face with a contemporary feel. Bevelled ascenders, and descenders combined with the gradient of thick-to-thin transitions give this typeface balance and rhythm, while the weight adds depth and grace.

Aa Bb Cc Dd Ee Ff Gg Hh Ii Jj Kk Ll
Mm Nn Oo Pp Qq Rr Ss Tt Uu Vv Ww Xx
Yy Zz & $12345€67890 (.,:;?¿!¡…‹›«» """,,,) @

Sophisticated and stylish quill

inspired letterforms add a touch of class, at all point

sizes, in a formal or informal textual page setting. This script adds delicacy to the

the smaller point sizes required for invitations, or in specialized one-line titling usage.

Tiamaria

George Ryan
2002

Soft, sensual lines add subtle touches of the feminine in the form of a delicate script. The graceful Tiamaria adds a touch of class to the page.

Galápagos

Holland Fonts

Holland Fonts. Typefaces by Max Kisman.

...In the early 1980s, Max Kisman became the designer of a small, independent music magazine, *Vinyl*. This Amsterdam-based publication was set up very much as a response to the innovative British magazine, *The Face*. Responding to Neville Brody's radical designs for that magazine, Kisman began to experiment by creating new headline typefaces for each issue... (Emily King. New Faces: type design in the first decade of device-independent digital typesetting. 1987-1997. http://www.typotheque.com/articles/EK_PhD_chapter5.html)

Holland Fonts was founded in 2002.
95 Bolsa Avenue, Mill Valley, California, CA 94941, U.S.A.

www.hollandfonts.com / info@hollandfonts.com

BOEM
PAUKESLAG
PLAT
daar ligt alles

O_____o

weer razen violen cello bassen koperen triangel

trommels PAUKEN

razen rennen razen rennen razen RENNEN

drama in volle slag hoeren slangen werpen zich op eerlijke

mannen het gezin wankelt de fabriek wankelt

de eer wankelt ligt er

alle begrippen VALLEN

HALT!

MaxMix One

Max Kisman
1991

MaxMix One is a compilation of characters from various fonts for the FontFont library and other custom alphabets designed between 1985 and 1991.

"Boem Paukeslag" is a poem by Paul van Ostaijen from the bundle *De Bezette Stad* (The Occupied City), Berlin, 1920.

The remix of the poem using MaxMix One was originally published as a poster by *TYP/Typografisch Papier* in the Netherlands in 1991.

Typefaces by Max Kisman, available at FontFont.com, are: FF Scratch, FF Network, FF Cutout, FF Fudoni, FF Rosetta, FF Jacque and FF Vortex, published by FontShop International, Germany.

Holland Fonts

Bebedot Black

Max Kisman
1998

Bebedot developed from doodles and scribbles in notebooks; irregular forms might very well contain a style for an alphabet.

ABCDEFGHIJKLMNOPQRSTUVWXYZabcdefghijklmnop qrstuvwxyz0123456789$¢€£¥ƒ-.,:;...''""„,¡¿?!&ÁÇÉÎÑÔ

Significant
MODERN

TYPE

Bebedot Blonde

Max Kisman
1998

Bebedot Blonde was first used in an intro spread in *Wired* magazine, designed by Max Kisman (#6.04, April 1998): *"To keep up you need the right answers. To get ahead you need the right questions."*
The name of this typeface was inspired by a women's clothing campaign on San Francisco bus stands. The dot is for the com that never came.

ABCDEFGHIJKLMNOPQRSTUVWXYZabcdefghijklmnop qrstuvwxyz0123456789$¢€£¥ƒ-.,:;...''""„,¡¿?!&ÁÇÉÎÑÔ

Lower case
CAPITAL

LINE

Circuit Closed

Max Kisman
1997

A decorative tech typeface designed for use in station identities and animations for television.

ABCDEFGHIJKLMNOPQRSTUVWXYZabcdefghijklmnopq rstuvwxyz0123456789$¢€£¥ƒ-.,:;...''""„,¡¿?!&ÅÇÉÎÑÔ

Alternatives
SHORT CUT

ICONS

Circuit Open

Max Kisman
1997

The slight reference to the Westinghouse logo (designed by Paul Rand) was inspired by a dinner table created from a huge sign featuring that logo.

ABCDEFGHIJKLMNOPQRSTUVWXYZabcdefghijklmnopq rstuvwxyz0123456789$¢€£¥ƒ-.,:;...''""„,¡¿?!&ÅÇÉÎÑÙ

Motherboard
EXPANSION

CARD

Bfrika

Max Kisman
2001

Bfrika, an "Africa-inspired"
typeface, was first used in *i-juici*
magazine, the Typographic
Issue (#17, 2002, Durban, South
Africa): "National Typographica."
Its geometrical decorative
design represents bold
simplicity, directness and
rhythm. The name evolves from a
text written for the spread in the
magazine. The B replaces the A.
Bfrika. Africa be free.

Holland Fonts

Max Kisman
2001

Originally designed in 1984 for a compilation CD of world music called *Mundenge* (the word for "youth dance" in Zairean dialect Kipende), this typeface took inspiration, not only from the music itself, but also from the hand-painted lettering of barbershop signs.

Modern music from Zaire is often played on instruments made out of utility objects like the *ongong:* traditionally a calabash and an elephant tooth as blow-pipe, now often a can with a plastic or metal blow-pipe; the *kalinda:* a skin-covered 50-liter barrel with strings of rope; or *banjo:* a buffalo or boa skin-covered can with nylon strings.

Percussion instruments may vary from bottles, compact cassette boxes, and cooking pots to friction disks of cars and custom-made metal scrapers. Other popular instruments are self-made guitars, the *likembe* - a thumb piano and the *bass-likembe* with 4 metal lamellas, amplified by a washing tub, or a scraper made of two sardine cans with a spring in between and a car battery-powered megaphone.

ABCDEFGHIJKLMNOPQRSTUVWXYZABCDEFGHIJKLMNO
PQRSTUVWXYZ0123456789$¢€£¥ƒ-.,:;…""''"",„¡¿?!&ÅÇ

MUNDENGE
BROUSSE-ROCK
FROM ZAIRE
'YOUTH DANCE'
ONGONG
KALINDA
BASS-LIKEMBE

ABCDEFGHIJKLMNOPQRSTUVWXYZabcdefghijklmno
pqrstuvwxyz0123456789$¢€£¥ƒ-.,:;…''""„"¡¿?!&ÅÇÉÎÑÖ

LOOK Nevertheless
IT'S TIME

Quickstep Regular

Max Kisman
2001

Quickstep was designed in 1994 for the 25th anniversary of SSP Printing Co. in Amsterdam, the Netherlands, a well-known print shop for the local design community.

ABCDEFGHIJKLMNOPQRSTUVWXYZabcdefghijklmno
pqrstuvwxyz0123456789$¢€£¥ƒ-.,:;…''""„"¡¿?!&ÅÇÉÎÑ

EYES Communicator
SENSITIVE

Quickstep Bold

Max Kisman
1994

Quickstep Bold was used for an intro spread, designed by Max Kisman, of a Brian Eno quote in *Wired* magazine (#3.05, May 1995): *"The problem with computers is that they don't have enough Africa in them. What's pissing me off is that they use so little of my body."*

Quickstep's erratic manual appearance was the perfect complement to the paper cutout-style illustration.

ABCDEFGHIJKLMNOPQRSTUVWXYZabcdefghijklmnopq
rstuvwxyz0123456789$¢€£¥ƒ-.,:;…''""„"¡¿?!&ÅÇÉÎÑÖØ

BURN Mediterranean
FIREPLACE

Quickstep Sans Regular

Max Kisman
2002

ABCDEFGHIJKLMNOPQRSTUVWXYZabcdefghijklmnopq
rstuvwxyz0123456789$¢€£¥ƒ-.,:;…''""„"¡¿?!&ÅÇÉÎÑÖ

SHOW Scandinavian
EXHIBITION

Quickstep Sans Regular

Max Kisman
2002

Holland Fonts

Chip 01

Max Kisman
1996

Chip 01 was designed for use on a "high-tech" transparent telephone card for the Royal Dutch Telecommunications Company. The typeface gave the card its own identity with a technological reference.

ABCDEFGHIJKLMNOPQRSTUVWXYZabcde
fghijklmnopqrstuvwxyz0123456789

Mobile phoney

Chip 02

Max Kisman
2002

Chip 02 is an adapted version of its predecessor, Chip 01, and offers increased legibility.

ABCDEFGHIJKLMNOPQRSTUVWXYZabcde
fghijklmnopqrstuvwxyz0123456789

Long distance

Interlace Single

Max Kisman
1998

Interlace Single was inspired by video technology and designed for use on television station identities; it never quite made it.

ABCDEFGHIJKLMNOPQRSTUVWXYZabcdef
ghijklmnopqrstuvwxyz0123456789$¢€

Video projector

Interlace Double

Max Kisman
1998

ABCDEFGHIJKLMNOPQRSTUVWXYZabcdef
ghijklmnopqrstuvwxyz0123456789$¢€

Frequency rate

Tribe Mono

Max Kisman
2001

A "soft-tech" typeface design for *www.fontshop.com/tribe*, a short-lived online magazine about typography and graphic design.

ABCDEFGHIJKLMNOPQRSTUVWXYZabcde
fghijklmnopqrstuvwxyz0123456789?

Time zone clash

info@hollandfonts.com

ABCDEFGHIJKLMNOPQRSTUVWXYZabcdefghijklmnopqrstuv
wxyz0123456789$-.,:;'""'¡¿?!&ÅÇÉÎÑÒØÜåçéòøüÆæŒœ"'*/\

Sequence signal dip

Submarine Extra Light

Max Kisman
2003

Submarine originates from a typeface design developed for the website identity and logo of a small Dutch media production company bearing the same name.

ABCDEFGHIJKLMNOPQRSTUVWXYZabcdefghijklmnopqrstuv
wxyz0123456789$-.,:;'""'¡¿?!&ÅÇÉÎÑÒØÜåçéòøüÆæŒœ"'*/\

Periscope goes west

Submarine Light

Max Kisman
2003

ABCDEFGHIJKLMNOPQRSTUVWXYZabcdefghijklmnopqrstuv
wxyz0123456789$-.,:;'""'¡¿?!&ÅÇÉÎÑÒØÜåçéòøüÆæŒœ"'*/\

Sonar torpedo blasts

Submarine Regular

Max Kisman
2003

ABCDEFGHIJKLMNOPQRSTUVWXYZabcdefghijklmnopqrstuv
wxyz0123456789$-.,:;'""'¡¿?!&ÅÇÉÎÑÒØÜåçéòøüÆæŒœ"'*/\

Flying go submarine

Submarine Bold

Max Kisman
2003

ABCDEFGHIJKLMNOPQRSTUVWXYZabcdefghijklmnopqrstuvw
xyz0123456789$-.,:;'""'¡¿?!&ÅÇÉÎÑÒØÜåçéòøüÆæŒœ"'*/\

Depth deepest ocean

Submarine Extra Bold

Max Kisman
2003

Holland Fonts

ABCDEFGHIJKLMNOPQRSTUVWXYZabcdefghijklmnopqrstuvwxyz0123456789$¢€£¥ƒ-.,:
;...''""·.,¡¿?!8ÅÇÉÎÑÒØÜåçéòøüÆæŒœ"'*`´/\|(){}[]¶§ß#@©®™ªº·•+<=>%‰±µ

The port of San Francisco
THE GOLDEN GATE BRIDGE
Sunset at Tennessee Valley beach

Pacific Standard Bold

Max Kisman
2001

Inspired by the unpretentious
type and lettering often seen
in ports, Pacific Standard Bold
was originally created as a
poster typeface for the Dutch
*30th International Film Festival
Rotterdam* poster in 2001.

ABCDEFGHIJKLMNOPQRSTUVWXYZabcdefghijklmnopqrstuvwxyz0123456789$¢£¥
ƒ-.,:;...''""·.,¡¿?!8ÅÇÉÎÑÒØÜåçéòøüÆæŒœ"'*`´/\|(){}[]¶§ß#@©®™ªº·•+<=>%‰±µ

Mt. Tamalpais and
HIGHWAY 1 NORTH
Sacramento River Runs

info@hollandfonts.com

Pacific Standard Serif Light

Max Kisman
2002

ABCDEFGHIJKLMNOPQRSTUVWXYZabcdefghijklmnopqrstuvwxyz0123456789$¢£¥ f-.,:;…''""",,¡¿?!8ÅÇÉÎÑØØÜåçéòøüÆæŒœ"'* ˜ ˜/\|(){}[]¶§ß#@©®™ªº•+<=>‰±µ

Hot dogs and short links

BREAKFAST SPECIALIST

Honk your horn 4 homegrown corn

Pacific Standard Serif Bold

Max Kisman
2002

ABCDEFGHIJKLMNOPQRSTUVWXYZabcdefghijklmnopqrstuvwxyz0123456789$¢£¥ f-.,:;…''""",,¡¿?!8ÅÇÉÎÑØØÜåçéòøüÆæŒœ"'* ˜ ˜/\|(){}[]¶§ß#@©®™ªº•+<=>‰±µ

Crossroads ahead

COAST 2 COAST

Roadtrips and adventures

Holland Fonts

ABCDEFGHIJKLMNOPQRSTUVWXYZabcdefghijklmnopqrstuvwxyz0123456789$¢£¥ƒ-.,:
;...''"".,,¡¿?!8ÅÇÉÎÑØØÜàçéòøüÆæŒœ"'*˜`/\|(){}[]¶§ß#@©®™ªº•+<=>%‰±µ

Jazzy swingers in Monterey

NORTH BEACH RESTAURANT

Whale migration Mendecino Coast

ABCDEFGHIJKLMNOPQRSTUVWXYZabcdefghijklmnopqrstuvwxyz0123456789$¢£¥
ƒ-.,:;...""",,¡¿?!8ÅÇÉÎÑØØÜàçéòøüÆæŒœ""*˜`/\|(){}[]¶§ß#@©®™ªº•+<=>%‰±

17-Mile Drive Big Sur

TWENTY9 PALMS, CA

The Joshua Tree Monument

info@hollandfonts.com

ABCDEFGHIJKLMNOPQRSTUVWXYZabcdefghijklmnopqrstuvwxyz0123456789$¢£¥ƒ−.: :…`'""„,.¡¿?!8ÅÇÉÑØ0ÜàçéòøüÆæŒœ"'*`˜/\|(){}[]¶§ß#@©®™ªº•<=>‰±μ

Black birds over Bodega Bay
AND CALIFORNIA INCOGNITO
Summer Sunday BBQ at Rancho Nicasio

ABCDEFGHIJKLMNOPQRSTUVWXYZabcdefghijklmnopqrstuvwxyz0123456789$¢£ Y ƒ−.,:…`'""„,.¡¿?!8ÅÇÉÑØ0ÜàçéòøüÆæŒœ"'*`˜/\|(){}[]¶§ß#@©®™ªº•<=>‰±μ

Point Reyes Station
SHUCKED OYSTERS
Redwoods and deer crossing

ABCDEFGHIJKLMNOPQRSTUVWXYZabcdefghijklmnopqrstuvwxyz0123456789$¢£¥ƒ–..:
:;…'''""„…¡¿?!8ÅÇÉÎÑØØÜåçéòøüÆæŒœ"'*`~/\|()[]{}¶§ß#@©®™ªº•+<=>%‰±µ

The day breaks in the east
THE DISTANT HORIZON CLIPS
Portland, Oregon, and Seattle, Washington

ABCDEFGHIJKLMNOPQRSTUVWXYZabcdefghijklmnopqrstuvwxyz0123456789$¢£¥
ƒ–..:;…'''""„…¡¿?!8ÅÇÉÎÑØØÜåçéòøüÆæŒœ"'*`~/\|()[]{}¶§ß#@©®™ªº•+<=>%‰±µ

Cruisin' the interstate
SNOW–COVERED TOP
Above the long and windy road

info@hollandfonts.com

Xbats

Max Kisman
2002

Make your instant Christmas and winter holiday greeting cards with this *Xbats* picture font. Twenty-six regular (capitals, A-Z) and 26 inverted (lowercase, a-z) images use the upcoming winter holiday season as a theme. Seven instant holiday messages (numerals, 1-5 and inverted on 6-0 for English; ¡, !, ¿ and ? for Spanish) will make your greeting complete in any combination.

Holland Fonts

Max Kisman
1988

The vernacular of southwestern cattle brand marks turned into a typeface.

ABCDEFGHIJKLMNOPQRSTUVWXYZɔbcdefghiʃklmnopqrst
uvwxyz0123456789$¢€£¥ƒ-..:... ''""„ ¡¿?!&ÅÇÊÎÑÒÖÜŞçéòôüÆœ

This Lonesome
COWBOY IS
For away from home

Max Kisman
1988

Originally cut out from red litho film as a headline typeface for *Vinyl* music magazine, the geometric structure was very applicable to early type design experiments on the computer. *Emigre* magazine: "...the reduced template of angles which generates Max Kisman's 1988 Zwartvet, akin to the minimal vocabulary of geometric elements employed in Albers's 1925 stencil letters;..." (Ellen Lupton and J. Abbott Miller, Signs of Novelty, Emigre 15, 1990).

ABCDEFGHIJKLMNOPQRSTUVWXYZabcdefghijklmnopqr
stuvwxyz0123456789$¢€£¥ƒ-.,:;...''""„ ¡¿?!&ÅÇÊÎÑÒÖÜ

Vinyl magazine
ART & MUSIC
Meta Beta Manifesta

info@hollandfonts.com

ABCDEFGHIIKLMNOPQRSTUVWXYZabcdefghijklmnopqrstuvwxyz0123456789$(¢£¥ƒ-.,
:,...''""„,¡¿?!&ªⒸÇÈÎÑÒⒼÜàⒻÉÒⓇÜ€ⒶⒼ""'`´/|()[]¶§ß#®©™²°♦+<=>‰‱µ

The landscape is floating by

ONE HAND ON THE WHEEL

A world of memories vaporizes at night

Traveller Regular

Max Kisman
1990

This geometric typeface was featured in Rick Poynor's *Typography Now 1* (Booth-Clibborn Editions, London UK, 1991).

Later, discussing this type of angular style, the critic Rick Poynor noted that, *"fate has overtaken the angular post-constructivist type design of Neville Brody, Zuzana Licko and Max Kisman."* Poynor described a process by which typefaces, once *"fresh, unexpected, precisely attuned to the moment,"* get used increasingly more often in less and less appropriate contexts, and end up looking *"irredeemably passé."* ("American Gothic", Rick Poynor in *Eye* magazine, June 1992).

ABCDEFGHIJKLMNOPQRSTUVWXYZabcdefghijklmnopqrstuvwxyz0123456789$(¢£
¥ƒ-.,:,...''""„,¡¿?!&ªⒸÇÈÎÑÒⒼÜàⒻÉÒⓇÜ€ⒶⒼ""'`´/|()[]¶§ß#®©™²°♦+<=>‰‱µ

Moments of quiet

STATUES FOR HOPE

Monuments for comfort

Traveller Bold

Max Kisman
1990

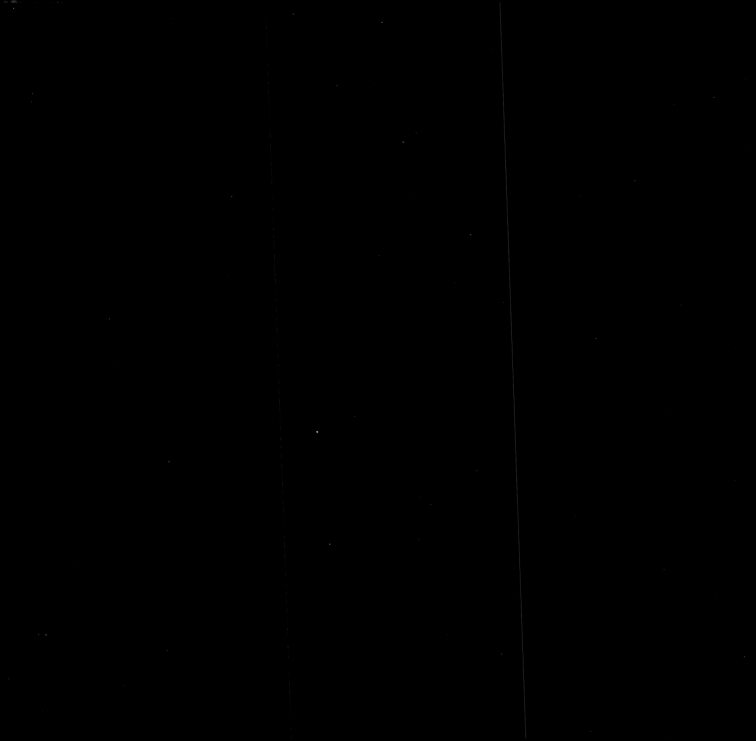

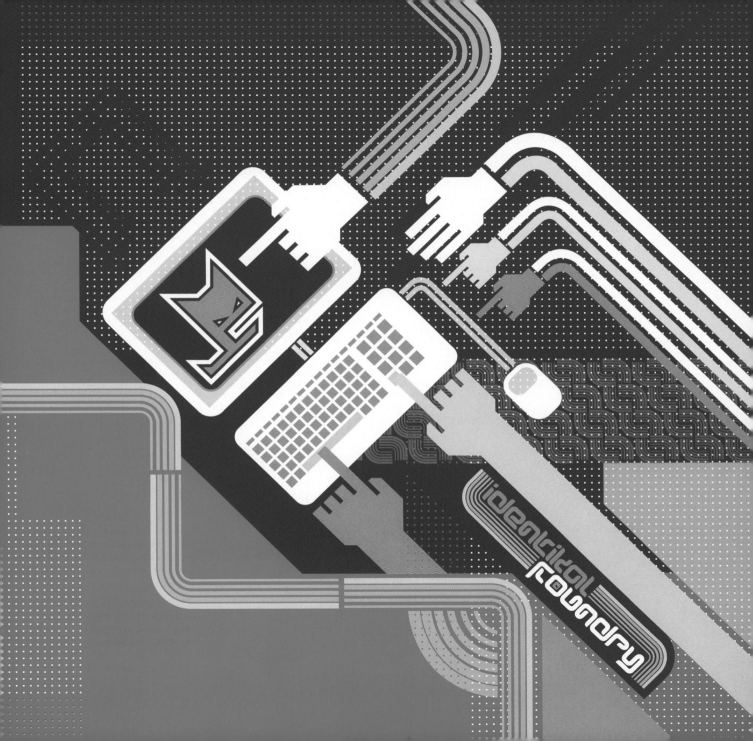

AtomicType

Mailing Address:
Mill House
11 Nightingale Road
Horsham
RH12 2NW
ENGLAND

Sales Enquiries:
Tel: +44 (0) 1403 249 245
Fax: +44 (0) 1403 249 246
Email: paul@atomictype.co.uk
Web: atomictype.co.uk

Background:
AtomicType have represented exclusive font sales for the Identikal Foundry since 1998. There are over 50 separate font families available to purchase from the Identikal Foundry range, along with a whole host of collectable printed catalogs and information.

Identikal Foundry

Contact Details:
Nick Hayes
Creative Director
The Identikal Corporation
Studio 5
The Oasis Buildings
Holloway Road
LONDON N7 6JN
ENGLAND

Tel: +44 (0) 20 7263 2129
Fax: +44 (0) 20 7272 1521
Mobile: +44 (0) 7957 497 569
Email: info@identikal.com
Web: www.identikal.com

Identikal Background:
The Identikal Corporation was founded by identical twins Adam & Nick Hayes whilst studying Graphic Communication at University in the mid-nineties. Since then, it has become recognised for combining an eclectic mixture of sound and vision, capable of producing unique work for any creative problem, from Graphic Design to Moving Image, Multimedia to Sound and Type Design.

Identikal have worked with clients all over the world, from Getty Images in America and Guinness in Eire, to the Drop Club in Hong Kong, whilst managing to keep a very impressive portfolio of work due to their striking and innovative style. They have developed a reputation that attracts some of the world's most desirable clients, such as Sony Computer Entertainment, Universal Music, Virgin, Ministry of Sound, EMAP publishing and many more.

Identikal are the team behind the cult success of the Identikal Foundry. They have created some of the hottest modern fonts of this new century, including worldwide collections of around 250 families. Publications including, *Maxim, Timeout, Dazed and Confused, Create, Mixmag, DJ Magazine, Wired* and many others have used Identikal typefaces throughout their pages. The fonts are also popular amongst various music acts such as, *Truesteppers, Shea Seger, Blue, Beverley Knight, Incognito, Shakira, Elisabeth Troy, MC Luck & DJ Neat,* to name but a few. Ad campaigns such as *PS2 The Third Place,* the launch of the *Nintendo Gameboy Advance,* and *Virgin Money* have also used fonts from the Identikal Foundry Collections. This has given Identikal a name in typography which many believe to be the strength and character behind the team.

If you would like to see more work from Identikal, you can check out the portfolio area on their site: **www.identikal.com.** Alternatively, contact them through email: **info@identikal.com.**

21st Century Typography

21st

Nick Hayes
1998

With its wide range of weights and numerous styles, the 21st typeface family was designed to represent the new century.

Identikal

21st Regular 15pt

AaBbCcDdEeFfGgHhIiJjKkLlMmNnOoPp
QqRrSsTtUuVvWwXxYyZz0123456789
<[{(/!?@£$¢¥%&B::\)}]>

21st Black 9pt

21st century typography for the modern noughties digital designer. Seven weights with seven italics for a diversity of use in style and taste.

21st Bold 9pt

21st century typography for the modern noughties digital designer. Seven weights with seven italics for a diversity of use in style and taste.

21st Regular 9pt

21st century typography for the modern noughties digital designer. Seven weights with seven italics for a diversity of use in style and taste.

21st Fine 9pt

21st century typography for the modern noughties digital designer. Seven weights with seven italics for a diversity of use in style and taste.

21st Superfine 9pt

21st century typography for the modern noughties digital designer. Seven weights with seven italics for a diversity of use in style and taste.

21st Round Black 9pt

21st century typography for the modern noughties digital designer. Seven weights with seven italics for a diversity of use in style and taste.

21st Outline 9pt

21st century typography for the modern noughties digital designer. Seven weights with seven italics for a diversity of use in style and taste.

21st Black Italic 22pt

***21st** Italics*
21st Black Italic

21st Fine & Superfine Italic 22pt

21st Fine Italic
21st Superfine Italic

21st Bold & Regular Italic 22pt

21st Bold Italic
21st Regular Italic

21st Round Black & Outline Italic 22pt

21st Round Black
21st Outline Italic

21st Black 22pt

21st Type Family
21st Black

21st Fine & Superfine 22pt

21st Fine
21st Superfine

21st Bold & Regular 22pt

21st Bold
21st Regular

21st Round Black & Outline 22pt

21st Round Black
21st Outline

45 Degrees

Nick Hayes
1999

45 degrees has 6 variants within its family.

45 Degrees Light 15pt

AaBbCcDdEeFfGgHhIiJjKkLlMmNnOoPp
QqRrSsTtUuVvWwXxYyZz0123456789
≤<[{(/!?@£$¢€¥%&ßfifl:;*"œœ†ø\]}]>≥

45 Degrees Italics 17pt

45 degrees
Regular Italic
45 degrees
Light Italic
45 degrees
Ultra Light Italic

45 Degrees Regular 9pt

45 degrees is a typeface built up of horizontal and vertical lines with 45 degree angles. Its condensed look works well for headlines and logo arrangements for print.

45 Degrees Ultra Light 9pt

45 degrees is a typeface built up of horizontal and vertical lines with 45 degree angles. Its condensed look works well for headlines and logo arrangements for print.

Angol

Nick Hayes
2000

Angol has 6 variants within its family, including 2 styles: Round and Sharp.

Angol Assortment 44pt

AngolRoundSharp

Angol Sharp Black 14pt

The Angol typeface is a set of fonts designed for use in logotype and digital illustration projects.

Angol Round Black 19pt

AaBbCcDdEeFfGgHhIiJjKkLlMmNnOoPp
QqRrSsTtUuVvWwXxYyZz0123456789
≤<[{(/!?@£$¢€¥%&ßfifl:;*"œœ†ø\)}]>≥

Angol Sharp Bold 14pt

The Angol typeface is a set of fonts designed for use in logotype and digital illustration projects.

Angol Round Bold 14pt

The Angol typeface is a set of fonts designed for use in logotype and digital illustration projects.

Angol Round Regular 14pt

The Angol typeface is a set of fonts designed for use in logotype and digital illustration projects.

Angol Sharp Regular 14pt

The Angol typeface is a set of fonts designed for use in logotype and digital illustration projects.

Attac

Nick Hayes
1999

Attac is a typeface family with 8 different variants.

Attac Regular 16pt

AaBbCcDdEeFfGgHhIiJjKkLlMmNnOoPp
QqRrSsTtUuVvWwXxYyZz0123456789
≤<[{(/!?@£$¢€¥%&ßfifl:;*"œæ\)}]>≥

Attac Black 9pt

Attac is a typeface built up of eight different angles to form a family of fonts that look modern and stylish, yet keeping a classical legible flow to body copy and headlines.

Attac Bold 9pt

Attac is a typeface built up of eight different angles to form a family of fonts that look modern and stylish, yet keeping a classical legible flow to body copy and headlines.

Attac Semi-Bold 9pt

Attac is a typeface built up of eight different angles to form a family of fonts that look modern and stylish, yet keeping a classical legible flow to body copy and headlines.

Attac Black Italic 9pt

Attac is a typeface built up of eight different angles to form a family of fonts that look modern and stylish, yet keeping a classical legible flow to body copy and headlines.

Attac Bold Italic 9pt

Attac is a typeface built up of eight different angles to form a family of fonts that look modern and stylish, yet keeping a classical legible flow to body copy and headlines.

Attac Semi-Bold Italic 9pt

Attac is a typeface built up of eight different angles to form a family of fonts that look modern and stylish, yet keeping a classical legible flow to body copy and headlines.

Attac Regular Italic 9pt

Attac is a typeface built up of eight different angles to form a family of fonts that look modern and stylish, yet keeping a classical legible flow to body copy and headlines.

Click

Adam Hayes
2001

The Click typeface family is made up of 6 fonts.

Click Bold 30pt

AaBbCcDdEeFfGgHhIiJjKkLlMm
NnOoPpQqRrSsTtUuVvWwXxY
yZz1234567890<([{o⌀$£&!?}])>

Click Regular 28pt

AaBbCcDdEeFfGgHhIiJjKkLlMmN
nOoPpQqRrSsTtUuVvWwXxYyZz

Click Light 28pt

AaBbCcDdEeFfGgHhIiJjKkLlMmN
nOoPpQqRrSsTtUuVvWwXxYyZz

Click Bold Italic 18pt
ClickBoldItalic

Click Regular Italic 18pt
ClickRegItalic

Click Light Italic 18pt
ClickLightItalic

Curvature

Adam Hayes
1999

The Curvature family consists of 10 typefaces.

Curvature Black 25pt

AaBbCcDdEeFfGgHhIiJjKkLlMmNnOoPpQqRrSs
TtUuVvWwXxYyZz 1234567890 <[{%$£&}]>

Curvature Black Italic 16pt

AaBbCcDdEeFfGgHhIiJjKkLlMmNnOoPpQqRrSsTtUuVvWwXxYyZz

Curvature Bold 16pt
Identikal Curvature Bold TYPE

Curvature Bold Italic 16pt
IDENTIKAL Curvature Bold Italic

Curvature Regular 16pt
Identikal Curvature Regular TYPE

Curvature Regular Italic 16pt
IDENTIKAL Curvature Regular Italic

Curvature Fine 25pt

AaBbCcDdEeFfGgHhIiJjKkLlMmNnOoPpQqRrSs
TtUuVvWwXxYyZz 1234567890 <[{%$£&}]>

Curvature Fine Italic 16pt

AaBbCcDdEeFfGgHhIiJjKkLlMmNnOoPpQqRrSsTtUuVvWwXxYyZz

Curvature Rounded 16pt
Identikal Curvature Rounded

Curvature Rounded 16pt
Curvature Rounded Italic TYPE

Adam Hayes
2000

The Dieppe family consists of 6 typefaces.

Dieppe Bold 20pt

AaBbCcDdEeFfGgHhIiJjKkLlMmNnOoPpQqRrSs TtUuVvWwXxYyZz 1234567890 <[{(@$&£)}]>

Dieppe Bold Oblique 12pt

AaBbCcDdEeFfGgHhIiJjKkLlMmNnOoPpQqRrSsTtUuVvWwXxYyZz1234567890

Dieppe Regular 20pt

AaBbCcDdEeFfGgHhIiJjKkLlMmNnOoPpQqRrSs TtUuVvWwXxYyZz 1234567890 <[{(@$&£)}]>

Dieppe Regular Oblique 12pt

AaBbCcDdEeFfGgHhIiJjKkLlMmNnOoPpQqRrSsTtUuVvWwXxYyZz1234567890

Dieppe Light 20pt

AaBbCcDdEeFfGgHhIiJjKkLlMmNnOoPpQqRrSs TtUuVvWwXxYyZz 1234567890 <[{(@$&£)}]>

Dieppe Light Oblique 12pt

AaBbCcDdEeFfGgHhIiJjKkLlMmNnOoPpQqRrSsTtUuVvWwXxYyZz1234567890

Adam Hayes
1999

The Distilla family consists of 6 typefaces. Distilla was formerly known as Formatt.

Distilla Bold 20pt

AaBbCcDdEeFfGgHhIiJjKkLlMmNnOoPpQqRrSs TtUuVvWwXxYyZz 1234567890 <[{(@$&£)}]>

Distilla Bold Italic 12pt

AaBbCcDdEeFfGgHhIiJjKkLlMmNnOoPpQqRrSsTtUuVvWwXxYyZz123456

Distilla Regular 20pt

AaBbCcDdEeFfGgHhIiJjKkLlMmNnOoPpQqRrSs TtUuVvWwXxYyZz 1234567890 <[{(@$&£)}]>

Distilla Regular Italic 12pt

AaBbCcDdEeFfGgHhIiJjKkLlMmNnOoPpQqRrSsTtUuVvWwXxYyZz123456

Distilla Light 20pt

AaBbCcDdEeFfGgHhIiJjKkLlMmNnOoPpQqRrSs TtUuVvWwXxYyZz 1234567890 <[{(@$&£)}]>

Distilla Light Italic 12pt

AaBbCcDdEeFfGgHhIiJjKkLlMmNnOoPpQqRrSsTtUuVvWwXxYyZz123456

+44 (0) 1403 249 245

ID 01

Nick Hayes
2001

This typeface family has 2 different styles available, and is included on the font disc with this book.

ID 01 Left 27pt

AaBbCcDdEeFfGgHhIiJjKkLlMmNnOoPp
QqRrSsTtUuVvWwXxYyZz0123456789

ID 01 Left 56pt

ID01Left

ID 01Right 56pt

ID01Right

Kanal

Nick Hayes
1997

Kanal has 8 variants within its font family.

Kanal Regular 15pt

AaBbCcDdEeFfGgHhIiJjKkLlMmNnOoPp
QqRrSsTtUuVvWwXxYyZz0123456789
<([{/?!ᴱˢ&-_+=ß;:"|\}])>   Kanal Regular

Kanal Ultra Light 9pt

The Kanal typeface is a monospaced font with condensed features suited to the publishing industry. Headlines as well as intro text flow finely over a longer line length.

Kanal Light 9pt

The Kanal typeface is a monospaced font with condensed features suited to the publishing industry. Headlines as well as intro text flow finely over a longer line length.

Kanal Normal 9pt

The Kanal typeface is a monospaced font with condensed features suited to the publishing industry. Headlines as well as intro text flow finely over a longer line length.

Kanal Ultra Light Italic 9pt

The Kanal typeface is a monospaced font with condensed features suited to the publishing industry. Headlines as well as intro text flow finely over a longer line length.

Kanal Light 9pt

The Kanal typeface is a monospaced font with condensed features suited to the publishing industry. Headlines as well as intro text flow finely over a longer line length.

Kanal Normal Italic 9pt

The Kanal typeface is a monospaced font with condensed features suited to the publishing industry. Headlines as well as intro text flow finely over a longer line length.

Kanal Light 9pt

The Kanal typeface is a monospaced font with condensed features suited to the publishing industry. Headlines as well as intro text flow finely over a longer line length.

Kneeon

Nick Hayes
2001

Kneeon has 8 variants within its font family. Its design has been based on the structure of neon typographic shapes.

Kneeon Regular 17pt

AaBbCcDdEeFfGgHhIiJjKkLlMmNnOoPp
QqRrSsTtUuVvWwXxYyZz0123456789
[([{!?☐£$¢₤¥&&ßfifl;:*"œæéøℓ}])]

Kneeon Regular 17pt

Kneeon typeface
CITY OF LIGHTS
Identikal Corp→

Kneeon Bold 17pt

Kneeon typeface
CITY OF LIGHTS
Identikal Corp→

Kneeon Square 17pt

Kneeon typeface
CITY OF LIGHTS
Identikal Corp→

Kneeon Light 17pt

Kneeon typeface
CITY OF LIGHTS
Identikal Corp→

Kneeon Bold Italic 17pt

Kneeon typeface
CITY OF LIGHTS
Identikal Corp→

Kneeon Square Italic 17pt

Kneeon typeface
CITY OF LIGHTS
Identikal Corp→

Kneeon Light Italic 17pt

Kneeon typeface
CITY OF LIGHTS
Identikal Corp→

Monark Black 20pt

AaBbCcDdEeFfGgHhIiJjKkLlMmNnOoPpQq
RrSsTtUuVvWwXxYyZz1234567890{(@$)}

Monark Black Italic 12pt

AaBbCcDdEeFfGgHhIiJjKkLlMmNnOoPpQqRrSsTtUuVvWwXxYyZz1234

Monark Bold 12pt

AaBbCcDdEeFfGgHhIiJjKkLlMmNnOoPpQqRrSsTtUuVvWwXxYyZz1234

Monark Bold Italic 12pt

AaBbCcDdEeFfGgHhIiJjKkLlMmNnOoPpQqRrSsTtUuVvWwXxYyZz1234

Monark Regular 12pt

AaBbCcDdEeFfGgHhIiJjKkLlMmNnOoPpQqRrSsTtUuVvWwXxYyZz1234

Monark Regular Italic 12pt

AaBbCcDdEeFfGgHhIiJjKkLlMmNnOoPpQqRrSsTtUuVvWwXxYyZz1234

Monark Light 20pt

AaBbCcDdEeFfGgHhIiJjKkLlMmNnOoPpQq
RrSsTtUuVvWwXxYyZz1234567890{(@$)}

Monark Light Italic 12pt

AaBbCcDdEeFfGgHhIiJjKkLlMmNnOoPpQqRrSsTtUuVvWwXxYyZz1234

Orbita Regular 26pt

AaBbCcDdEeFfGgHhIiJjKkLlMmNnOoPp
QqRrSsTtUuVvWwXxYyZz0123456789

Orbita Heavy 14pt

AaBbCcDdEeFfGgHhIiJj
KkLlMmNnOoPpQqRrSs
TtUuVvWwXxYyZz0123

Orbita Light 14pt

AaBbCcDdEeFfGgHhIiJj
KkLlMmNnOoPpQqRrSs
TtUuVvWwXxYyZz0123

Orbita Oblique Versions 20pt

HeavyOblique
RegularOblique
LightOblique

Phat Bold 20pt

AaBbCcDdEeFfGgHhIiJjKkLlMmNnOoPp
QqRrSsTtUuVvWwXxYyZz1234567890

Phat Bold Italic 12pt

PhatFont BoldItalic

Phat Regular Italic 12pt

PhatFont RegularItalic

Phat Regular 12pt

AaBbCcDdEeFf
GgHhIiJjKkLlMm
NnOoPpQqRrSs

Phat Light Italic 12pt

*AaBbCcDdEeFf
GgHhIiJjKkLlMm
NnOoPpQqRrSs*

Phat Light 12pt

AaBbCcDdEeFf
GgHhIiJjKkLlMm
NnOoPpQqRrSs

+44 (0) 1403 249 245

Phuture ODC

Phuture ODC Ultra 30pt

AaBbCcOdEeFfGgHhIiJjKKLl
MmNnOoPpQqRrSsTtUuVvWW
wXxYyZz1234567890‹‹(‹%?›»

Phuture ODC

Adam Hayes
1998

The "Original" Phuture typeface was drawn up on the back of a sketchpad in 1993. It was then drawn electronically in 1995. More styles were added, as well as the ODC series.

Phuture ODC Ultra Italic 12pt

AaBbCcOdEeFfGgHhIi
JjKKLlMmNnOoPpQqR
rSsTtUuVvWwXxYyZz

Phuture ODC Black 12pt

AaBbCcOdEeFfGgHhIiJ
jKKLlMmNnOoPpQqRrS
sTtUuVvWwXxYyZz

Phuture ODC Black Italic 12pt

AaBbCcOdEeFfGgHhIiJ
jKKLlMmNnOoPpQqRrS
sTtUuVvWwXxYyZz

Phuture Squared Closed Bold 28pt

AaBbCcOdEeFfGgHhIiJjKKLlMmN
nOoPpQqRrSsTtUuVvWwXxYyZz

Phuture Squared Closed

Adam Hayes
1995

Phuture Squared Closed contains 6 fonts within its family. The Phuture typeface family is a collection of 28 fonts.

Phuture Squared Closed Plain 12pt

AaBbCcOdEeFfGgHhIiJj
KKLlMmNnOoPpQqRrSs

Phuture Squared Closed Italic 12pt

AaBbCcOdEeFfGgHhIiJj
KKLlMmNnOoPpQqRrSs

Phuture Squared Closed Fine 12pt

AaBbCcOdEeFfGgHhIiJj
KKLlMmNnOoPpQqRrSs

Phuture Squared Closed Outline 12pt

PHUTURE SQUARED CLOSED OUTLINE

Phuture Squared Closed A-Italic 12pt

PHUTURE SQUARED CLOSED A-ITALIC

Phuture Squared Open Bold 12pt

PHUTURE SQUARED OPEN BOLD

Phuture Squared Open Plain 12pt

PHUTURE SQUARED OPEN PLAIN

Phuture Squared Open Fine 12pt

PHUTURE SQUARED OPEN FINE

Phuture Squared Open A-Italic 12pt

PHUTURE SQUARED OPEN A-ITALIC

Phuture Squared Open Outline 12pt

PHUTURE SQUARED OPEN OUTLINE

Phuture Squared Open Italic 12pt

PHUTURE SQUARED OPEN ITALIC

Phuture Squared Open

Adam Hayes
1995

Phuture Squared Open contains 6 fonts within its family.

Phuture Rounded Open Bold 28pt

AaBbCcOdEeFfGgXhIiJjKKLlMm
NnOoPpQqRrSsTtUuWwXxYyZz

Phuture Rounded Open

Adam Hayes
1995

Phuture Rounded Open contains 6 fonts within its family. The Phuture font family is seen as one of our most original and inspiring typefaces.

Phuture Rounded Open Plain 12pt

AaBbCcOdEeFfGgXhIiJj
KKLlMmNnOoPpQqRrSs

Phuture Rounded Open Italic 12pt

AaBbCcOdEeFfGgHhIiJj
KKLlMmNnOoPpQqRrSs

Phuture Rounded Open Fine 12pt

AaBbCcOdEeFfGgXhIiJj
KKLlMmNnOoPpQqRrSs

Phuture Rounded Open Outline 12pt

PHUTURE ROUNDED OPEN OUTLINE

Phuture Rounded Open A-Italic 12pt

PHUTURE ROUND CLOSED A-ITALIC

Phuture Rounded Closed Bold 12pt

PHUTURE ROUNDED CLOSED BOLD

Phuture Rounded Closed Plain 12pt

PHUTURE ROUNDED CLOSED PLAIN

Phuture Rounded Closed Fine 12pt

PHUTURE ROUNDED CLOSED FINE

Phuture Rounded Closed A-Italic 12pt

PHUTURE ROUNDED CLOSED A-ITALIC

Phuture Rounded Closed Outline 12pt

PHUTURE ROUNDED CLOSED OUTLINE

Phuture Rounded Closed Italic 12pt

PHUTURE ROUNDED CLOSED ITALIC

Phuture Rounded Closed

Adam Hayes
1995

Phuture Rounded Closed contains 6 fonts within its family.

Plotta Bold 20pt

AaBbCcDdEeFfGgHhIiJjKkLlMmNnOoPpQqRr
SsTtUuVvWwXxYyZz1234567890 <(((@\$£)))>

Plotta Bold Italic 12pt

AaBbCcDdEeFfGgHhIi JjKkLlMmNnOoPpQqRrSsTtUuVvWwXxYyZz

Plotta Bold 20pt

AaBbCcDdEeFfGgHhIiJjKkLlMmNnOoPpQqRr
SsTtUuVvWwXxYyZz1234567890 <(((@\$£)))>

Plotta Regular Italic 12pt

AaBbCcDdEeFfGgHhIi JjKkLlMmNnOoPpQqRrSsTtUuVvWwXxYyZz

Plotta Light 20pt

AaBbCcDdEeFfGgHhIiJjKkLlMmNnOoPpQqRr
SsTtUuVvWwXxYyZz1234567890 <(((@\$£)))>

Plotta Light Italic 12pt

AaBbCcDdEeFfGgHhIi JjKkLlMmNnOoPpQqRrSsTtUuVvWwXxYyZz

Adam Hayes
1999

Podium was originally drawn up
for a V.I.P. club called Drop, based
in Hong Kong. We had so many
enquiries about it that we decided
to make it into a font family.
The Podium family consists of
6 typefaces.

Podium Bold 20pt

**AaBbCcDdEeFfGgHhIiJjKkLlMmNnOoPpQq
RrSsTtUuVvWwXxYyZz1234567890((&\$))**

Podium Bold Italic 12pt

AaBbCcDdEeFfGgHhIiJjKkLlMmNnOoPpQqRrSsTtUuVvWwXxYyZz

Podium Regular 20pt

AaBbCcDdEeFfGgHhIiJjKkLlMmNnOoPpQq
RrSsTtUuVvWwXxYyZz1234567890((&\$))

Podium Regular Italic 12pt

AaBbCcDdEeFfGgHhIiJjKkLlMmNnOoPpQqRrSsTtUuVvWwXxYyZz

Podium Light 20pt

AaBbCcDdEeFfGgHhIiJjKkLlMmNnOoPpQq
RrSsTtUuVvWwXxYyZz1234567890((&\$))

Podium Light Italic 12pt

AaBbCcDdEeFfGgHhIiJjKkLlMmNnOoPpQqRrSsTtUuVvWwXxYyZz

Reaction Heavy 20pt

AaBbCcDdEeFfGgHhIiJjHkLlMmNnOoPpQqRr SsTtUuVvWwXxYyZz1234567890 «{{(a$£)}}»

Reaction Heavy Italic 12pt

AaBbCcDdEeFfGgHhIiJjHKLlMmNnOoPpQqRrSsTtUuVvWwXxYyZz

Reaction Ultra 12pt

AaBbCcDdEeFfGgHhIiJjHKLlMmNnOoPpQqRrSsTtUuVvWwXxYyZz

Reaction Ultra Italic 12pt

AaBbCcDdEeFfGgHhIiJjHKLlMmNnOoPpQqRrSsTtUuVvWwXxYyZz

Reaction Bold Italic 12pt

AaBbCcDdEeFfGgHhIiJjHKLlMmNnOoPpQqRrSsTtUuVvWwXxYyZz

Reaction Bold Italic 12pt

AaBbCcDdEeFfGgHhIiJjHKLlMmNnOoPpQqRrSsTtUuVvWwXxYyZz

Reaction Regular Italic 12pt

AaBbCcDdEeFfGgHhIiJjHKLlMmNnOoPpQqRrSsTtUuVvWwXxYyZz

Reaction Regular Italic 12pt

AaBbCcDdEeFfGgHhIiJjHKLlMmNnOoPpQqRrSsTtUuVvWwXxYyZz

Reaction Fine Italic 12pt

AaBbCcDdEeFfGgHhIiJjHKLlMmNnOoPpQqRrSsTtUuVvWwXxYyZz

Reaction Fine Italic 12pt

AaBbCcDdEeFfGgHhIiJjHKLlMmNnOoPpQqRrSsTtUuVvWwXxYyZz

Reaction

Adam Hayes
2000

The Reaction typeface family is made up of 10 fonts.

Rebirth Ultra 18pt

AaBbCcDdEeFfGgHhIiJjKkLlMmNnOoPp QqRrSsTtUuVvWwXxYyZz1234567890

Rebirth Ultra Italic 12pt

AaBbCcDdEeFfGgHhIiJjKkLlMmNnOoPpQqRrSsTtUuVvWw

Rebirth Black 12pt

AaBbCcDdEeFfGgHhIiJjKkLlMmNnOoPpQqRrSsTtUuVvWw

Rebirth Black Italic 12pt

AaBbCcDdEeFfGgHhIiJjKkLlMmNnOoPpQqRrSsTtUuVvWw

Rebirth Regular 12pt

AaBbCcDdEeFfGgHhIiJjKkLlMmNnOoPpQqRrSsTtUuVvWw

Rebirth Regular Italic 12pt

AaBbCcDdEeFfGgHhIiJjKkLlMmNnOoPpQqRrSsTtUuVvWw

Rebirth Fine 18pt

AaBbCcDdEeFfGgHhIiJjKkLlMmNnOoPp QqRrSsTtUuVvWwXxYyZz1234567890

Rebirth Fine Italic 12pt

AaBbCcDdEeFfGgHhIiJjKkLlMmNnOoPpQqRrSsTtUuVvWw

Rebirth

Adam Hayes
1999

The Rebirth family consists of 8 typefaces.

Nick Hayes
2002

The Revalo family consists of a Modern version, which is rounded, and a Classic version, which has flat edges. This collection of fonts has been specifically designed for the publishing industry and corporate identity design teams.

Various Revalo Modern Weights at 54pt

Revalo™**Modern** Font Family

Revalo Modern Regular 24pt

AaBbCcDdEeFfGgHhIiJjKkLlMmNnOoPp
QqRrSsTtUuVvWwXxYyZz0123456789
‹‹[{(/!?@£$¢€¥%&ßfifl:;*"œæ†ø\)}]››

Revalo Modern Black 10pt

The Revalo Modern Classic font family has been crafted with the Modern Digital Designer in mind. The classic version has a sharp formal look to its characteristics, whereas the Modern version oozes style and definition.

Revalo Modern Bold 10pt

The Revalo Modern Classic font family has been crafted with the Modern Digital Designer in mind. The classic version has a sharp formal look to its characteristics, whereas the Modern version oozes style and definition.

Revalo Modern Light 10pt

The Revalo Modern Classic font family has been crafted with the Modern Digital Designer in mind. The classic version has a sharp formal look to its characteristics, whereas the Modern version oozes style and definition.

Revalo Modern Thin 10pt

The Revalo Modern Classic font family has been crafted with the Modern Digital Designer in mind. The classic version has a sharp formal look to its characteristics, whereas the Modern version oozes style and definition.

Revalo Modern Italics 22pt

Modern Black Italic
Modern Bold Italic

Modern Bold Italic
Modern Black Italic

Modern Regular Italic
Revalo™Modern Family

Various Revalo Classic Weights at 54pt

Revalo™**Classic** Font Family

Revalo Classic Regular 24pt

AaBbCcDdEeFfGgHhIiJjKkLlMmNnOoPp
QqRrSsTtUuVvWwXxYyZz0123456789
‹‹[{(/!?@£$¢€¥%&ßfifl:;*"œæ†ø\)}]››

Revalo Classic Black 10pt

The Revalo Modern Classic font family has been crafted with the Modern Digital Designer in mind. The classic version has a sharp formal look to its characteristics, whereas the Modern version oozes style and definition.

Revalo Classic Bold 10pt

The Revalo Modern Classic font family has been crafted with the Modern Digital Designer in mind. The classic version has a sharp formal look to its characteristics, whereas the Modern version oozes style and definition.

Revalo Classic Light 10pt

The Revalo Modern Classic font family has been crafted with the Modern Digital Designer in mind. The classic version has a sharp formal look to its characteristics, whereas the Modern version oozes style and definition.

Revalo Classic Thin 10pt

The Revalo Modern Classic font family has been crafted with the Modern Digital Designer in mind. The classic version has a sharp formal look to its characteristics, whereas the Modern version oozes style and definition.

Revalo Classic Italics 22pt

Classic Black Italic
Classic Light Italic

Classic Bold Italic
Classic Thin Italic

Classic Regular Italic
Revalo™Classic Family

+44 (0) 1403 249 245

Robustik Bold 20pt

AaBbCcDdEeFfGgHhIiJjKkLlMmNnOoPp
QqRrSsTtUuVvWwXxYyZz1234567890

Robustik Bold Oblique 12pt

AaBbCcDdEeFfGgHhIiJjKkLlMmNnOoPpQqRrSsTtUuVvWwXxYyZz

Robustik Regular 20pt

AaBbCcDdEeFfGgHhIiJjKkLlMmNnOoPp
QqRrSsTtUuVvWwXxYyZz1234567890

Robustik Regular Oblique 12pt

AaBbCcDdEeFfGgHhIiJjKkLlMmNnOoPpQqRrSsTtUuVvWwXxYyZz

Robustik Light 20pt

AaBbCcDdEeFfGgHhIiJjKkLlMmNnOoPp
QqRrSsTtUuVvWwXxYyZz1234567890

Robustik Bold Light 12pt

AaBbCcDdEeFfGgHhIiJjKkLlMmNnOoPpQqRrSsTtUuVvWwXxYyZz

Seize Regular 25pt

AaBbCcDdEeFfGgHhIiJjKkLlMmNnOoPpQqRrSs
TtUuVvWwXxYyZz1234567890<[{(@$&£)}]>

Seize Regular 18pt

AaBbCcDdEeFfGgHhIiJjKkLlMmNnOoPpQqRrSsTtUuVvWwXxYyZz

Seize Light & Seize Light italic

AaBbCcDdEeFfGgHhIi
JjKkLlMmNnOoPpQqRr
SsTtUuVvWwXxYyZz
Identikal Seize Light Italic

Seize Bold & Seize Bold Italic 25pt

AaBbCcDdEeFfGgHhIi
JjKkLlMmNnOoPpQqRr
SsTtUuVvWwXxYyZz
Identikal Seize Light Italic

Seize Regular 25pt

AaBbCcDdEeFfGgHhIiJjKkLlMmNnOoPpQqRrSs
TtUuVvWwXxYyZz1234567890<[{(@$&£)}]>

Seize Regular 18pt

AaBbCcDdEeFfGgHhIiJjKkLlMmNnOoPpQqRrSsTtUuVvWwXxYyZz

Sharp was originally drawn up as a logotype for Salt Records, back in 1998. A year later, we decided to turn it into a typeface family. It has now become one of our most used fonts, and is great for illustration and logo work.

RaBbCcDdEeFfGgHhIi
JjKkLlMmNnOoPpQqR
RrSsTtUuVvWwXxYyZz
1234567890 <[[[@$&]]>

Sharp Ultra Italic 20pt
Identikal present: Sharp Ultra Italic

Sharp Bold

Adam Hayes
1999

RaBbCcDdEeFfGgHhIiJjKkLlMmN
nOoPpQqRrSsTtUuVvWwXxYyZz

Sharp Bold Italic 18pt
Identikal present: Sharp Bold Italic

Sharp Regular

Adam Hayes
1999

RaBbCcDdEeFfGgHhIiJjKkLlMmN
nOoPpQqRrSsTtUuVvWwXxYyZz

Sharp Regular Italic 18pt
Identikal present: Sharp Regular Italic

Sharp Light

Adam Hayes
1999

RaBbCcDdEeFfGgHhIiJjKkLlMmN
nOoPpQqRrSsTtUuVvWwXxYyZz

Sharp Light Italic 18pt
Identikal present: Sharp Light Italic

Sharp Bold 20pt
<[[[@?!$&]]]>

Sharp Regular 20pt
<[[[@?!$&]]]>

Sharp Light 20pt
<[[[@?!$&]]]>

Stak Bold 26pt

AaBbCcCDdEeFFGgHHnIiJjKKLLmm
NnOOPPpDqGrrSsTtCuUvVvWxXyY22
0123456789<((□!ø£$%&.*I€?†¥B])}>

Stak Bold Italic 26pt

AaBbCcCDdEeFFGgHHnIiJjKKLLmm
NnOOPPpDqGrrSsTtCuUvVvWxXyY22
0123456789<((□!ø£$%&.*I€?†¥B])}>

Stak Light 16pt

AaBbCcCDdEeFFG
gHHnIiJjKKLLmm
NnOOPPpDqGrrSsT
tCuUvVvWxXyY22

Stak Light Italic 16pt

AaBbCcCDdEeFFG
gHHnIiJjKKLLmm
NnOOPPpDqGrrSsT
tCuUvVvWxXyY22

Stak Regular16pt

AaBbCcCDdEeFFG
gHHnIiJjKKLLmm
NnOOPPpDqGrrSsT
tCuUvVvWxXyY22

Stak Regular 26pt

IDENTIKAL Stak ITaLIC ReguLar

Stak

Nick Hayes
2001

Stak consists of 6 typefaces.

Trak Black 26pt

**AaBbCcDdEeFfGgHhliJjKkLlMmNnOoPpQ
qRrSsTtUuVvWwXxYyZz1234567890**

Trak Black 14pt

AaBbCcDdEeFfGgHhliJjKkLlMmNnOoPpQqRrSsTtUuVvWwXxYyZz1234567

Trak Fine 26pt

AaBbCcDdEeFfGgHhliJjKkLlMmNnOoPpQ
qRrSsTtUuVvWwXxYyZz1234567890

Trak Fine Italic 14pt

AaBbCcDdEeFfGgHhliJjKkLlMmNnOoPpQqRrSsTtUuVvWwXxYyZz1234567

Trak Semi Bold 14pt

**AaBbCcDdEeFfGgHhliJj
KkLlMmNnOoPpQqRrSs
TtUuVvWwXxYyZz123**

Trak Semi Bold Italic 14pt

**AaBbCcDdEeFfGgHhliJj
KkLlMmNnOoPpQqRrSs
TtUuVvWwXxYyZz123**

Trak Regular 14pt

AaBbCcDdEeFfGgHhliJj
KkLlMmNnOoPpQqRrSs
TtUuVvWwXxYyZz123

Trak Regular Italic 14pt

AaBbCcDdEeFfGgHhliJj
KkLlMmNnOoPpQqRrSs
TtUuVvWwXxYyZz123

Trak Bold 14pt

**AaBbCcDdEeFfGgHhliJj
KkLlMmNnOoPpQqRrSs
TtUuVvWwXxYyZz123**

Trak Bold Italic 14pt

**AaBbCcDdEeFfGgHhliJj
KkLlMmNnOoPpQqRrSs
TtUuVvWwXxYyZz123**

Trak

Adam Hayes
1999

Trak consists of 10 typefaces.

Tremble

Adam Hayes
1999

The Tremble family consists of 8 typefaces.

Tremble Ultra 20pt

AaBbCcDdEeFfGgHhIiJjKkLlMmNnOoPpQqRrSsTt
UuVvWwXxYyZz 1234567890 ‹[{((@/^¿&£?!"·:|\$))}]›

Tremble Ultra Italic 12pt

AaBbCcDdEeFfGgHhIiJjKkLlMmNnOoPpQqRrSsTtUuVvWwXxYyZz1234567

Tremble Bold 13pt

AaBbCcDdEeFfGgHhIiJj
KkLlMmNnOoPpQqRrSs
TtUuVvWwXxYyZz1234

Tremble Bold Italic 13pt

AaBbCcDdEeFfGgHhIiJj
KkLlMmNnOoPpQqRrSs
TtUuVvWwXxYyZz1234

Tremble Regular 13pt

AaBbCcDdEeFfGgHhIiJj
KkLlMmNnOoPpQqRrSs
TtUuVvWwXxYyZz1234

Tremble Regular Italic 13pt

AaBbCcDdEeFfGgHhIiJj
KkLlMmNnOoPpQqRrSs
TtUuVvWwXxYyZz1234

Tremble Light 13pt

AaBbCcDdEeFfGgHhIiJj
KkLlMmNnOoPpQqRrSs
TtUuVvWwXxYyZz1234

Tremble Light Italic 13pt

AaBbCcDdEeFfGgHhIiJj
KkLlMmNnOoPpQqRrSs
TtUuVvWwXxYyZz1234

UNDA Series

Nick Hayes
1998

UNDA Series consists of 15 typefaces. The original concept of UNDA was to offer a variety of effects within one set of fonts.

UNDA Series Square 35pt

AaBbCcDdEeFfGgHhIiJjKkLlMmN
nOoPpQqRrSsTtUuVvWwXxYyZz

UNDA Series Circle 35pt

AaBbCcDdEeFfGgHhIiJjKkLlMmN
nOoPpQqRrSsTtUuVvWwXxYyZz

UNDA Series Triangle 35pt

AaBbCcDdEeFfGgHhIiJjKkLlMmN
nOoPpQqRrSsTtUuVvWwXxYyZz

UNDA Series Vertical 35pt

AaBbCcDdEeFfGgHhIiJjKkLlMmN
nOoPpQqRrSsTtUuVvWwXxYyZz

UNDA Series Horizontal 35pt

AaBbCcDdEeFfGgHhIiJjKkLlMmN
nOoPpQqRrSsTtUuVvWwXxYyZz

UNDA Angle 30pt

AaBbCcDdEeFfGgHhIiJjKkLlMmNnOoPpQ
qRrSsTtUuVvWwXxYyZz0123456789

Nick Hayes
1998

UNDA Series consists of 15 typefaces. The original concept of UNDA was to offer a variety of effects within one set of fonts.

UNDA Angle Italic 18pt

AaBbCcDdEeFfGgHh
IiJjKkLlMmNnOoPpQq
RrSsTtUuVvWwXxYy

UNDA Angle Fine 18pt

AaBbCcDdEeFfGgHh
IiJjKkLlMmNnOoPpQq
RrSsTtUuVvWwXxYy

UNDA Angle Fine Italic 18pt

AaBbCcDdEeFfGgHh
IiJjKkLlMmNnOoPpQq
RrSsTtUuVvWwXxYy

UNDA Bitmap 18pt

AaBbCcDdEeFfGgHh
IiJjKkLlMmNnOoPpQq
RrSsTtUuVvWwXxYy

UNDA Bitmap Italic 18pt

AaBbCcDdEeFfGgHh
IiJjKkLlMmNnOoPpQq
RrSsTtUuVvWwXxYy

UNDA Bitmap Fine 18pt

AaBbCcDdEeFfGgHh
IiJjKkLlMmNnOoPpQq
RrSsTtUuVvWwXxYy

UNDA Bitmap Fine Italic 18pt

AaBbCcDdEeFfGgHh
IiJjKkLlMmNnOoPpQq
RrSsTtUuVvWwXxYy

UNDA Outline 18pt

AaBbCcDdEeFfGgHh
IiJjKkLlMmNnOoPpQq
RrSsTtUuVvWwXxYy

UNDA Outline Italic 18pt

AaBbCcDdEeFfGgHh
IiJjKkLlMmNnOoPpQq
RrSsTtUuVvWwXxYy

Wired

Adam Hayes
1999

Wired is a family of 8 typefaces.

Wired Black 20pt

AaBbCcDdEeFfGgHhIiJjKkLlMmNnOoPpQqRrSs
TtUuVvWwXxYyZz1234567890 ‹([{%£&?!$}])›

Wired Black Italic 11pt

AaBbCcDdEeFfGgHhIiJjKkLlMmNnOoPpQqRrSsTtUuVvWwXxYyZz

Wired Regular 11pt

AaBbCcDdEeFfGgHhIiJjKkLlMm

Wired Regular Italic 11pt

AaBbCcDdEeFfGgHhIiJjKkLlMm

Wired Light Italic 11pt

AaBbCcDdEeFfGgHhIiJjKkLlMm

Wired Light Italic 11pt

AaBbCcDdEeFfGgHhIiJjKkLlMm

Wired Serif 11pt

AaBbCcDdEeFfGgHhIiJjKkLlMm

Wired Serif Italic 11pt

AaBbCcDdEeFfGgHhIiJjKkLlMm

Zero

Nick Hayes
2000

Zero consists of 6 typefaces.

Zero Open Regular 22pt

AaBbCcDdEeFfGgHhIiJjKkLlMmNnOoPp
qRrSsTtUuVvWwXxYyZz1234567890

Zero Open Bold 19pt

Zero Open Bold

Zero Open Regular 19pt

Zero Open

Zero Open Fine 19pt

Zero Open Fine

Zero Closed Bold 19pt

Zero Closed Bold

Zero Closed Regular 19pt

Zero Closed

Zero Closed Fine 19pt

Zero Closed Fine

ingoFonts

Fonts ℗ and © by Ingo Zimmermann
since 1994

Ingo Zimmermann ____ *1967 son of a graphic designer ____ graffiti, then studied graphic design, typography, and calligraphy, as well as photography ____ exhibitions ____ work for numerous magazines, preferring own typefaces ____

ingoFonts
Fonts ® and © by Ingo Zimmermann
since 1994

www.ingo-zimmermann.de

At ingoFonts all fonts can be downloaded.
Gratis. Free.
Here's the catch: The files offered here to
download contain only a reduced font.
That means, the font only consists of uppercase
and lowercase from A to Z, or rather, a to z.
The complete font, including numbers, umlauts,
punctuation, and especially ligatures, is only
available with your order and your cash.

Kreitmayrstraße 3O/3Oa
86165 Augsburg (Germany)
info@ingo-zimmermann.de

Anatole France

Ingo Zimmermann
1997

Bold, decorative poster type in the style of Art Deco.

An old portfolio of script patterns from the 1920s or 1930s includes among its pages a handwritten poster script, very typical for the 1920s. To begin with, there is the emphasized decorative character, which stands out due to stressing the stems. Next, the attempt to portray the character forms with the help of a few – but always recurring – basic elements is driven to the limits. Theoretically speaking, that which should have led to a contrived, geo-metrically determined type, obtains a likeable and pleasant look through the ductus of the manually guided brush.

A few fonts already exist which have been drawn in accordance with the exact same principles. But these are just drawn – only drawn. Anatole France retains the hand script character, in spite of its stringent composition.

ingoFonts

ABCDEFGHIJKLMN

OPQRSTUVWXYZ

abcdefffiflghijklmn

opqrstßuvvrvwxyz

0123456789

&/!?---- .,;;„""´

Charpentier Renaissance

Ingo Zimmermann
1996

Very readable Antiqua typeface in three styles: Renaissance, Baroque and Classicism.

Charpentier is the Antiqua form of the sans serif "Graz2006" (the very first ingoFont). The uppercase of Charpentier is developed from Roman monumental lettering; the lowercase is modeled on the Carolingian minuscule.

Charpentier Renaissance

ABCDEFGHIJKLMNOPQRSTUVWXYZ
abbecchckdeffffififlftghijklllmmmnnuoppæqrrasſſ ſchſiſſ ſtß
ttitzuunrvwxyz 0123456789 & / ! ? - – — . , : ; „ " » « ( )

Charpentier Baroque

Ingo Zimmermann
1996

Charpentier Baroque

ABCDEFGHIJKLMNOPQRSTUVWXYZ
abcdeffiflghijklmnopqrsſßtuvwxyz
0123456789 & / ! ? - – — . , : ; „ " » « ( )

Charpentier Classicistique

Ingo Zimmermann
1996

Charpentier Classicistique

ABCDEFGHIJKLMNOPQRSTUVWXYZ
abcdeffiflghijklmnopqrsſßtuvwxyz
0123456789 & / ! ? - – — . , : ; „ " » « ( )

Charpentier Classicistique Italique

ABCDEFGHIJKLMNOPQRSTUVWXYZ
abcdeffiflghijklmnopqrsſßtuvwxyz
0123456789 & / ! ? - – — . , : ; „ " » « ( )

DeFonte Léger

ABCDEFGHIJKLMNOPQRSTUVWXYZ
abcdeffiflghijklmnopqrsßtuvwxyz
0123456789 / ! ? - – — . , : ; „ " » « ( )

DeFonte Normale

ABCDEFGHIJKLMNOPQRSTUVWXYZ
abcdeffiflghijklmnopqrsßtuvwxyz
0123456789 / ! ? - – — . , : ; „ " » « ( )

DeFonte DemiGras

ABCDEFGHIJKLMNOPQRSTUVWXYZ
abcdeffiflghijklmnopqrsßtuvwxyz
0123456789 / ! ? - – — . , : ; „ " » « ( )

DeFonte Gros

ABCDEFGHIJKLMNOPQRSTUVWXYZ
abcdeffiflghijklmnopqrsßtuvwxyz
0123456789 / ! ? - – — . , : ; „ " » « ( )

DeFonte

Ingo Zimmermann
1995

Variation of "Helvetica"
according to the "blur" principle.

The underlying typeface is
based on Helvetica, the only true
"run-of-the-mill" typeface of the
twentieth century. The distorted
principle used simulates the
photographic effect of halation
and/or overexposure.
The light typestyle, DeFonte
Léger, nearly breaks on the thin
points, whereas on those points
where the lines meet or cross,
dark spots remain. The characters are "nibbled at" from the
inner and outer brightness.
On the normal and semi-bold
typestyles, DeFonte Normale
and DeFonte Demi Gras,
the effect is limited almost
exclusively to the end strokes
and corners, which appear to
be strongly rounded off. The
bold version DeFonte Gros is
especially attractive. As a result
of "overexposure," counters
(internal spaces) are closed in,
while characters become blurred
and turn into spots; new
characteristic forms are created
which are astoundingly legible.

ingoFonts

Ingo Zimmermann
1995

Deconstructivist variation on the Clarendon style.

Déformé was born out the distortion of the time-honored Clarendon letterforms, in which the stems and thin strokes have been reversed. Thus, a typeface was created which will remind some readers of a Western typeface, and others of the ordinary typeface of a typewriter. Actually, it is still a robust Clarendon, which has survived its disfigurement quite well. Déformé, like its "mother," is easily legible, in spite of the inherent emphasis which one is not used to seeing.

Déformé

ABCDEFGHIJKLMNOPQRSTUVWXYZ
abcdeffiflghijklmnopqrsßtuvwxyz
0123456789 &/!?--— .,:;„"»«()

DeKunst

Ingo Zimmermann
1995

Deconstructivistic initials; each character in two variations.

Typefaces are defined by vectors – contours descriptive of the inner and outer form of the letter – and their filled-in sections. DeKunst was created by distorting and overlapping vectorized lines and shapes. Nearly similar forms and reflections lend an ornamental effect to some of the characters. Geometrical gimmicks sometimes remind one of Kurt Schwitters' compositions. Incidental amorphous forms call to mind the paintings and sculptures of Hans Arp or Alexander Calder.

info@ingo-zimmermann.de

DePixel IIIegible

ABCDEFGHIJKLHNOPQRSTUVWXYZ

abcdckde ΓΓΠΓcghIJklmnooarsΓßcuvwxyz

0123456789 ∕∕ | ? - - —

· , : ; „ ˆˇ ˜ ˝ » « ( )

Die ILLEGIBLE DEPIXEL encscand aus der Übercreibung des Pixeleffekcs. Wie andere Screenfoncs auch
isc sie aus einzelnen Pixeln aufgebauc. Nur becrägc die Versalhöhe lediglich 5 Pixel, die n-Höhe gar nur 4
Pixel. Dazu zeigc sie den aus dem Web bekannten Effekc einer zu kleinen Schrifcdarscellung, der Texce nahezu unleserlich erscheinen lässc.

DePixel

Ingo Zimmermann
1999

Simulation of a pixel typeface
made up of not enough pixels.

Illegible DePixel was developed
from the exaggeration of the
pixel effect on Apple's renowned
Geneva. As with all screen fonts,
it simulates the composition
of individual pixels. Only here,
the cap height amounts to only
5 pixels, and the x-height a mere
4 pixels. Furthermore, this
typeface shows the well-known
effect found on the Web of
a font design which is too small,
and makes texts appear almost
illegible.

ingoFonts

Deutsche Schrift Callwey

ABCDEFGHIJKLMNOPQRSTUVWXYZ

abcdeffifflghijklmnopqrstßtuvwxyz – – . , : ; „ "

Diese Schrift erscheint auf einem Blatt einer Schreibustermappe des Callwey-Verlags aus den zwanziger-
er oder dreißiger Jahren. Sie ist dort als „Deutsche Schrift" bezeichnet. Eine sogenannte Deutsche Schrift ist eine im
neunzehnten Jahrhundert entstandene Schreibschrift. Nach ihrem Erfinder kennt man sie auch unter dem
Namen „Sütterlinschrift".

Deutsche Schrift Callwey

Ingo Zimmermann
1998

So-called Deutsche Schreibschrift (German handwriting),
according to a sample from
ca. 1920/30.

"Deutsche Schrift" is a script
type which appeared in the 19th
century, and is also called
"Sütterlinschrift", after its
creator. An example of the
typeface appears in a portfolio
of script samples from the
Callwey-Verlag from the '20s
or '30s. In that example, the
script is called Deutsche Schrift.

Ingo Zimmermann
1998

Sans serif headline font; characters are also available in alternative forms.

The characters of Die Überschrift range between the narrow boundaries of cap height and baseline. No ascender or descender breaks through this range. The legibility is ensured particularly by the classic Roman proportions and the greatest possible distinctions in the letterforms. The uppercase letters of Die Überschrift were originally designed as a headline font for the magazine *motion*. Their versatility and flexibility, even with deformity and distortion, made them a favorite for *motion* layouts. Die Überschrift runs very tight. In order to open up a wider spectrum of utilization for this letter type, minuscules were also conceived with time, adding to the original, exclusively uppercase, typeface.

>> Josef
>> Josefov

DIE ÜBERSCHRIFT ELEGANT

AΛBBCCDDEFGGHIIJKLMMNOPQRRSTUVWWXYZ
O123456789 /!?-–—.,:;„" "»«()

DIE ÜBERSCHRIFT Normal

AΛBBCCDDEFGGHIIJKLMMNOPQRRSTUVWWXYZ
abcchckdeffflflgghijklmnopqrsßtuvwxyz
O123456789 /!?-–—.,:;„" "»«()

DIE ÜBERSCHRIFT Gequetscht

AΛBBCCDDEFGGHIIJKLMMNOPQRRSTUVWWXYZ
abcchckdeffflflghijklmnopqrsßtuvwxyz
O123456789 /!?-–—.,:;„" "»«()

DIE ÜBERSCHRIFT Halbfett

AΛBBCCDDEFGGHIIJKLMMNOPQRRSTUVWWXYZ
abcdeffflflghijklmnopqrsßtuvwxyz
O123456789 /!?-–—.,:;„" "»«()

info@ingo-zimmermann.de

Faber Eins/Zwei Normal

ABCDEFGHIJKLMNOPQRSTUVWXYZ
aabcdeɛfffiflfiflgghijkllmnopqrrsʃʃßttuuvwxyz 0123456789 /!?--—.,:;„""«»()

Faber Eins/Zwei Schmal Normal

ABCDEFGHIJKLMNOPQRSTUVWXYZ
aabcdeɛfffiflgghijkllmnopqrrsʃʃßttuuvwxyz 0123456789 /!?--—.,:;„""«»()

Faber Eins/Zwei Breit Normal

ABCDEFGHIJKLMNOPQRSTUVWXYZ
abcdeɛfffiflgghijkllmnopqrrsʃʃßttuuvwxyz 0123456789 /!?--—.,:;„""«»()

Faber Eins Normal Kursiv

ABCDEFGHIJKLMNOPQRSTUVWXYZ
abcdeffiflghijklmnopqrsʃßtuuvwxyz 0123456789 / !?--—.,:;„"«»()

Faber Eins/Zwei Kräftig

ABCDEFGHIJKLMNOPQRSTUVWXYZ
aabcdeɛfffiflffiflgghijkllmnopqrrsʃʃßttuuvwxyz 0123456789 /!?--—.,:;„""«»()

Faber Eins/Zwei Halbfett

ABCDEFGHIJKLMNOPQRSTUVWXYZ
aabcdeɛfffiflgghijkllmnopqrrsʃʃßttuuvwxyz 0123456789 /!?--—.,:;„""«»()

Faber Eins/Zwei Fett

ABCDEFGHIJKLMNOPQRSTUVWXYZ
aabcdeɛfffiflgghijkllmnopqrrsʃʃßttuuvwxyz 0123456789 /!?--—.,:;„""«»()

Faber Eins/Zwei

Ingo Zimmermann
1996

Easily legible sans serif types; many letters are also available in alternative styles.

Faber Eins (one) is actually two fonts. Its capital letters are directly derived from the Roman Capitalis Monumentalis. The minuscules combine modern perception with traditional forms. There are two types of some of the minuscules: a standard design in a Gill Sans style, and a more abstract variant in conformity with medieval uncials of the letters a, e, f, g, l, r, t, and u. Faber Eins and Faber Zwei (two) differ only in the standard assignment of the characters on the keyboard: in the case of Faber Eins, the "standard" forms represent the standard assignment, while Faber Zwei represents the uncials.

Display characters are Faber Eins/Zwei Halbfett (bold) and Fett (black). The circular interiors in some of its letter-forms lend a special character to Faber Eins Fett.

›› Faber Drei

ingoFonts

Ingo Zimmermann
1998

Roman variant of Faber Eins.

Faber Drei (Faber Three) is the Roman typeface which was born out of the sans serif design Faber Eins (Faber One). The proportions are nearly identical to those of Faber Eins, which means two things: The capitals are based on the classical example of the Roman Monumental Lettering, and the lowercase characters originated in the written Carolingian Minuscule. In comparison, Faber Drei has heavy - although very short - serifs. The character of contrasting strokes is not very pronounced; therefore, this font is closely related to the first Roman typefaces from the 15th century. The Kursiv also has very reserved serifs, which are quite appealing to modern reading habits.

<< Faber Eins/Zwei

Faber Drei Normal

ABCDEFGHIJKLMNOPQRRSTUVWXYZ
abcchckdeffffiflftghijklmmmnopqrsßtttuvwxyz
0123456789 /!?&-–—.,:;„"""»«()

Die »Faber Drei« hat ihren Ursprung in der serifenlosen »Faber Eins«, deren Antiquaversion sie ist. Die Proportionen sind nahezu mit denen der »Faber Eins« identisch. Die Versalien orientieren sich am klassischen Vorbild der Römischen Capitalis Monumentalis, die Minuskeln haben ihren Ursprung in der geschriebenen Karolingischen Minuskel. Die »Faber Drei« hat vergleichsweise kräftige, wenn auch sehr kurze Serifen. Der Wechselzug-Charakter ist nicht sehr stark ausgeprägt. Damit steht sie in der Nähe der allerersten Antiquas aus dem

Faber Drei Kursiv

ABCDEFGHIJKLMNOPQRRSTUVWXYZ
abcchckdeffffiflftghijklmmmnopqrsſßtttuvwxyz
0123456789 /!?&-–—.,:;„"""»«()

15. Jahrhundert. Ihren charakteristischen Ausdruck erhält sie durch die offenen Formen von CDGOQ und bcdeopq. Aber auch die Spitzen von AMNVWZ sind typisch für die »Faber Drei«. Die relativ langen Ober- und Unterlängen verhelfen der Schrift zu sehr prägnanten Wortbildern. Die »Faber Drei« ist eine sehr gut lesbare Mengensatzschrift, die auch in sehr grosser Anwendung reizvolle Details bietet. Die Verwendung der Ligaturen ergibt ein geschlosseneres Satzbild, kann aber auch zu einer willkommenen Störung der Sehgewohnheit führen. Ganz in Tradition der

Faber Drei Kräftig

ABCDEFGHIJKLMNOPQRSTUVWXYZ
abcchckdeffffiflftghijklmnopqrsßtuvwxyz
0123456789 /!?&-–—.,:;„"""»«()

ersten Kursivschriften steht die »Faber Drei Kursiv«. Ihre Formen ergeben ein geschlossenes fließendes Satzbild. Dabei behält sie die charakteristischen offenen Einzelformen der geraden »Faber Drei«. Auch die Kursiv hat sehr zurückhaltende Serifen, was den modernen Lesegewohnheiten sehr entgegenkommt. Für die negative Anwendungen steht die »Faber Drei Kräftig« zur Verfügung. Ihre kräftigeren Striche verschaffen ihr ein sichereres Auftreten. Als Auszeichnungsschrift zur »Faber Drei Normal« ist sie jedoch zu schwach. Die »Faber Drei« ist eine

Faber Fraktur Normal

ABCDEFGHIJKLMNOPQRSTUVWXYZ

abcchckddeffffiflstoghijkkelllllmmmnopqrslisstktzuvowxyz 0123456789 /!?=--.,:;„""»«()

Faber Fraktur Kurrent

ABCDEFGHIJKLMNOPQRSTUVWXYZ

abcchckdefghijkllllllmmmnopqrsßktzuvowxyz 0123456789 /!?=--.,:;„""»«()

Faber Fraktur Halbfett

ABCDEFGHIJKLMNOPQRSTUVWXYZ

abcchckdeffffiflstghijkelllllmmmnopqrslisstktzuvowxyz 0123456789 /!?=--.,:;„""»«()

Faber Gotik Text

ABCDEFGHIJKLMNOPQRSTUVWXYZ

abcchckdeffffiflftghijklmnopqrsßktzuvowxyz 0123456789 /!?---.,:;„""»«○

Faber Gotik Gothic

ABCDEFGHIJKLMNOPQRSTUVWXYZ

abcchckdeffffiflftghijklmnopqrsßttzuvowxyz 0123456789 /!?---.,:;„""»«○

FABER GOTIK CAPITALS

ABCDEFGHIJKLMNOPQRSTUVWXYZ

ABCDEFGHIJKLMNOPQRSTUVWXYZ 0123456789 /!?---.,:;„""»«○

Faber Fraktur

Ingo Zimmermann
1994

An easy-to-read modern Fraktur without flourish.

Faber Fraktur omits the frills which often make typefaces difficult to read. This font also features the repetition of a few similar basic type forms. At the same time, the typical contrasting strokes of a historical handwritten Fraktur are retained. All characters are reduced to their basic skeletons. The fanciness and manifold breaks (or fractures) typical of blackletter typefaces are reduced considerably, to a few instances. Faber Fraktur does not appear nearly so foreign and archaic as the old broken fonts. Alternative forms are available for the characters d, g, k, s, x, and l. Typical for a blackletter typeface: the long s, which is replaced only at the end of a word or syllable by the round s.

Faber Gotik

Ingo Zimmermann
2002

Contrived Gothic, according to modern form principles, in three variations.

Faber Gotik is reminiscent of Gutenberg, who created the first movable block letters 555 years ago. The characters are composed of squares, which are lined up straight or in a more or less slanted manner. The principle of breaking applied here is analogous to the historical model. Even the form of the characters is based on the model from the Middle Ages.

In Faber Gotik Text, the historical form is most loyally retained, whereas Faber Gotik Gothic is almost a contrived modern typeface. Somewhat unusual, Faber Gotik Capitals is a Gothic caps font.

ingoFonts

Fixogum

Ingo Zimmermann
1998

A capital letter typeface written freely with a tube of *Fixogum*.

Who can forget the green tube which was always present on any graphic artist's table? *Fixogum* is an adhesive which is removable and leaves no traces of its use, since the dried glue can be rubbed away with your fingers. All layouts were glued with *Fixogum* until the Apple Macintosh was introduced. In the hand of the calligrapher, this green tube resulted - in a roundabout way - in the creation of the typeface Fixogum. Fixogum is composed of capitals only; however, they are joined in such a peculiar way that a typeface which is more or less fluent is produced. The forms are archaic, and represent a basic script. Fixogum results in a pleasantly structured typeface. The rows appear to be closed. As a whole, Fixogum is somewhat reminiscent of graffiti handwriting, which might have something to do with the writer's past...

info@ingo-zimmermann.de

Josef Leicht

AΛBBCDEFGGHIIJKLMMNOPQRRSTUVWWXYZ
abcchckddeffffifflgghijkllmnopqrsßßtuvwxyz
0123456789 /!?--—.,:;„""“"»«()

Josef Normal

AΛBBCDEFGGHIIJKLMMNOPQRRSTUVWWXYZ
abcchckddeffffifflgghijkllmnopqrsßßtuvwxyz
0123456789 /!?--—.,:;„""“"»«()

Josef Kursiv

AΛBBCDEFGGHIIJKLMMNOPQRRSTUVWWXYZ
abcchckddeffffifflgghijkllmnopqrsßßtuvwxyz
0123456789 /!?--—.,:;„""“"»«()

Josef Halbfett

AΛBBCDEFGGHIIJKLMMNOPQRRSTUVWWXYZ
abcddefffifflghijkllmnopqrsßßtuvwxyz
0123456789 /!?--—.,:;„""“"»«()

Josef Fett

AΛBBCDEFGGHIIJKLMMNOPQRRSTUVWWXYZ
abcddefffifflghijkllmnopqrsßßtuvwxyz
0123456789 /!?--—.,:;„""“"»«()

Josef

Ingo Zimmermann
2000

A sans serif body type developed from "Die Überschrift."
In memory of Josef Zimmermann, 1912–2000.

Josef evolved out of Die Überschrift. Josef uses the capitals from Die Überschrift, while the finer points of the minuscules have been revised, so that the result is an excellent readable body type. Josef extenders go far beyond those of Die Überschrift, as the ascenders and descenders are noticeably longer than the H-height. Classical and modern type forms are united in Josef. Going against the typographical trend, a and g are modern, but the alternative classical form is also available as an optional keyboard layout. Other characters also have two variations. Rigid, rational forms have been drawn for d, f, j, and l, as well as playful versions. Together with the familiar variations of the capitals in Die Überschrift, a number of combinations are possible.

<< Die Überschrift
>> Josefov

ingoFonts

Josefov

Ingo Zimmermann
2003

Slab serif variation of the sans serif, Josef.

Strictly speaking, Josefov is not a Roman typeface, in spite of its serifs. The sans serif Josef, the underlying typeface, was decorated wirh heavy, rectangular serifs. The serifs merge into the stems rounded, but the stems and hairlines themselves also run together in a rounded form. On the round characters, the serifs are attached horizontally, against all tradition, whereas the double-sided serifs reflect examples of the ascenders of some early printers of the 15th century.

<< Die Überschrift
<< Josef

Josefov Leicht

ABCDEFGHIJKLMNOPQRSTUVWXYZ
abcchckdeffiflghijklmnopqrsßtuvwxyz
0123456789 /!?-—.,:;„"""»«()

Josefov Normal

ABCDEFGHIJKLMNOPQRSTUVWXYZ
abcchckdeffiflghijklmnopqrsßtuvwxyz
0123456789 /!?-—.,:;„"""»«()

Josefov Halbfett

ABCDEFGHIJKLMNOPQRSTUVWXYZ
abcchckdeffiflghijklmnopqrsßtuvwxyz
0123456789 /!?-—.,:;„"""»«()

Klex

Ingo Zimmermann
1996

A calligraphic alphabet in bold/light brushstrokes.

Actually, a typeface like this one should be written with a wide brush; this one was written with a thick, pointed brush. Thus were created the round or misshapen ends of the stems, and the sometimes excessively pointed ends of the hairlines. For each character of Klex, the large brush was dipped in the ink anew. Using this method, the forms turned out very soft, in spite of their geometrical rigidity. The individual characters are heavy, simple, and monumental, so that they are also suitable as initials.

Maier's Nr. 8 Mager

ABCDEFGHIJKLMNOPQRSTUVWXYZ
abcchckdDefffffiflghijklmnopqrsßttttzuvwxyz
0123456789 /!?=--.,:j „ „ " " »«()

Maier's Nr. 8 Halbfett

ABCDEFGHIJKLMNOPQRSTUVWXYZ
abcchckdDefff fiflghijklmnopqrsßttttzuvwxyz
0123456789 /!?=--.,:j „ " " »«()

Maier's Nr. 8

Ingo Zimmermann
2002

A sketched "script for tech-
nicians" from ca. 1900.
Very geometrical, rigid forms
characterized by typical signs
of Jugendstil/Art Nouveau.

A magazine from ca. 1900
carries the title *Schriften-
sammlung für Techniker:
Verkleinerte Schriften der
wichtigsten Alphabete*
(Collection of scripts for
technical specialists: reduced
scripts of the most important
alphabets), by Karl O. Maier.
It served as the model for
technical professions in which,
at that time, the captions of
drawings were still done by
hand. The high degree of ab-
straction in Maier's Nr. 8
presents a strange effect to
those who know the age of the
original. In comparison, many
of today's so-called ultramodern
types suddenly look quite
old-fashioned.

ingoFonts

Maier's Nr. 21 Mager

ABCDEFGHIJKLMNOPQRSTUVWXYZ
ABCDEFGHIJKLMNOPQRSTUVWXYZ
abcdefff fiflghijklmnopqrsſsttttuvwxyz
0123456789 /!?=--.,:j „ " " »«()

Maier's Nr. 21 Normal

ABCDEFGHIJKLMNOPQRSTUVWXYZ
ABCDEFGHIJKLMNOPQRSTUVWXYZ
abcdefff fiflghijklmnopqrsſsttttuvwxyz
0123456789 /!?=--.,:j „ " " »«()

Maier's Nr. 21

Ingo Zimmermann
2002

A sketched "script for tech-
nicians" from ca. 1900.
Very geometrical, rigid forms
characterized by typical signs
of Jugendstil/Art Nouveau.

Worthy of note are the Art
Nouveau forms of Maier's Nr. 21
that were characteristic around
the turn of the 20th century.
The characters of the original
models have been scanned,
digitized, and greatly magnified.
In the process, special attention
was also given to keep the
"messy" edges, typical of
handwritten scripts, effectively
noticeable in the digitized form.
In this way, this "technical"
typefaces maintains a handmade
flavor.

Schwabacher DR

Ingo Zimmermann
1998

Heavy, broken Script;
Rudolf Koch's first print
from 1909.

On an old page full of script
examples from the 1930s,
this script is described as
"Schwabacher (used by the
Deutsche Reichsbahn)." As a
matter of fact, it is the first print
of the Offenbach script master
Rudolf Koch, who came out with
this script in 1909. At that time,
it was given the name Neudeutsch
(New German). Later, it became
very popular under the name
Koch-Schrift, and was at times
the official script of the Deutsche
Reichsbahn (German National
Railway).

Schwabacher der Deutschen Reichsbahn

ABCDEFGHIJKLMN
OPQRSTUVWXYZ
abcchckdefffffffififlstghijklmno
pqrsßsiſſſtßttittzuvwxyz
0123456789
/!?=~——•,:;„" » « ()

info@ingo-zimmermann.de

Wendelin Normal

ABCDEFGHIJKLMNOPQRSTUVWXYZ abbecchckdftefffiflftghijkl
mmmnruoppeqrrasßttiuvwxyz 0123456789 /!?-–—.,:;„""»«()

Wendelin Normal Kapitälchen

ABCDEFGHIJKLMNOPQRSTUVWXYZ
ABCDEFGHIJKLMNOPQRSTUVWXYZ 0123456789 /!?-–—.,:;„""»«()

Wendelin Normal Kursiv

ABCDEFGHIJKLMNOPQRSTUVWXYZ abbecchckdftefffiflftghijkl
mmmnruoppeqrrasßttiuvwxyz 0123456789 /!?-–—.,:;„""»«()

Wendelin Kräftig

ABCDEFGHIJKLMNOPQRSTUVWXYZ abbecchckdftefffiflftghijkl
mmmnruoppeqrrasßttiuvwxyz 0123456789 /!?-–—.,:;„""»«()

Wendelin Halbfett Kursiv

ABCDEFGHIJKLMNOPQRSTUVWXYZ abbecchckdftefffiflftghijkl
mmmnruoppeqrrasßttiuvwxyz 0123456789 /!?-–—.,:;„""»«()

Wendelin Fett

ABCDEFGHIJKLMNOPQRSTUVWXYZ abcdeffifighijkl
mnopqrsßtuvwxyz 0123456789 /!?-–—.,:;„""»«()

Wendelin Fett Kursiv

ABCDEFGHIJKLMNOPQRSTUVWXYZ abcdeffifighijkl
mmmnopqrsßtuvwxyz 0123456789 /!?-–—.,:;„""»«()

Wendelin Breitfett

ABCDEFGHIJKLMNOPQRSTUVWXYZ abcdeffifighijkl
mnopqrsßtuvwxyz 0123456789 /!?-–—.,:;„""»«()

Wendelin

Ingo Zimmermann
1996

Easy to read modern sans serif.

Originally, Wendelin was created
as a body type for the magazine
motion. With time, this type
continued to be elaborated on
and further developed. Wendelin
Normal brings Franklin Gothic
very much to mind. All other
versions, especially Kursiv, are
new creations, in some cases
with quite unusual details.

ingoFonts

DELUXE TYPE FOR THE POST-ATOMIC AGE...

Jukebox, created by Jason Walcott in 2003, began as an independent type foundry in 2000 under the name "JAW Fonts". Jason became interested in type and typography while studying Illustration and Graphic Design at Kean College of New Jersey. After graduating in 1997, he moved to Southern California, where Jukebox is now located. Jason's original designs are often inspired by the whimsical and ingenious designs of hand lettering, found in retro signage, old movie titles, television, and even product labels. Many of these sources serve as the starting point for the development of full typefaces. The Jukebox library also includes a small selection of digital revivals based on older photolettering/metal typefaces. Jason continues to develop new fonts, and Jukebox strives to supply designers and anyone interested in type with fresh and inventive faces.

Jukebox type is available through Veer.com. All Jukebox fonts are available for both Mac and PC, in PostScript and TrueType formats, and contain full accented character sets and kerning pairs.

Jukebox
1116 North Spaulding Ave. Unit D
West Hollywood, CA 90046
Phone: 323·650·2740   email: jasonwalcott@earthlink.net
Web: www.JAWarts.com
to purchase Jukebox type, please visit www.veer.com

Special Thanks to my father, Andrew, my grandparents, Mary and John,
and my mother, Ann, whose continued generosity and support
have made Jukebox possible.   —Jason Walcott
I dedicate this section to my dear, departed grandfather, John W. Walcott "Pappah". 1921-2003

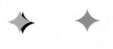

ABCDEFGHIJKLMNOPQRSTUVWXYZ
abcdefghijklmnopqrstuvwxyz 1234567890 ÁáÊêÑñ &€$

Too Much of a Good Thing is Never Enough!

Acroterion JF

Jason Walcott
2002

An elegant high-class script, digitally revived from an older photo/letterpress face.

ABCDEFGHIJKLMNOPQRSTUVWXYZ
abcdefghijklmnopqrstuvwxyz 1234567890 ÁáÊêÑñ ¥€$

Don't underestimate the Power of Laughter.

Adage Script JF

Jason Walcott
2002

A warm "downhome" script font, digitally revived from an older photo/letterpress face.

ABCDEFGHIJKLMNOPQRSTUVWXYZ
abcdefghijklmnopqrstuvwxyz 1234567890 ÁáÊêÑñ &€$

I scaled the Matterhorn and danced the Polka.

Alpengeist JF

Jason Walcott
2001

A blackletter face with an old-world feel. Perfect for a fairy tale, a horror novel, or even personalizing your alpenhorn.

ABCDEFGHIJKLMNOPQRSTUVWXYZ
abcdefghijklmnopqrstuvwxyz 1234567890 ÁáÊêÑñ &€$

Merry Christmas and Happy New Year!

Annabelle JF

Jason Walcott
2002

A flowing script font named after the designer's mother.

Jukebox

Jason Walcott
2001-2002

A family of three typefaces and one dingbat font, designed to be used together or separately. The dingbat font contains an alternate set of numerals. This type family is dedicated to the child in all of us.

Blairesque JF-Curly

ABCDEFGHIJKLMNOPQRSTUVWXYZ AMRT
abcdefghijklmnopqrstuvwxyz yg 1234567890 ÁáÊêÑñ &€$

Blairesque JF-Festive

ABCDEFGHIJKLMNOPQRSTUVWXYZ llff Th
abcdefghijklmnopqrstuvwxyz 1234567890 ÁáÊêÑñ &€$

Blairesque JF-Gothic

ABCDEFGHIJKLMNOPQRSTUVWXYZ
abcdefghijklmnopqrstuvwxyz 1234567890 ÁáÊêÑñ &€$

Blairesque JF-Happy Grams

1234567890

Blairesque Curly

Jason Walcott
2001

When in Rome, eat some Spaghetti!

The Many Faces of Paris

Blairesque Festive

Jason Walcott
2002

I Sailed around the World.

The Big Book of Children's Stories

323-650-2740

International Summit cancelled for Beach Party!

Do you know the way home?

Blairesque Gothic

Jason Walcott
2001

Blairesque Happy Grams

Jason Walcott
2001

Jukebox

ABCDEFGHIJKLMNOPQRSTUVWXYZ

abcdefghijklmnopqrstuvwxyz 1234567890 ÁáÊêÑñ &€$ favm

Antique Car Shows on Television.

ABCDEFGHIJKLMNOPQRSTUVWXYZ

abcdefghijklmnopqrstuvwxyz 1234567890 ÑáÊêÑñ &~€$

A Cruise to Alaska is best in June?

ABCDEFGHIJKLMNOPQRSTUVWXYZ

abcdefghijklmnopqrstuvwxyz 1234567890 ÁáÊêÑñ &€$

He got lost in Wichita, Kansas.

ABCDEFGHIJKLMNOPQRSTUVWXYZ
abcdefghijklmnopqrstuvwxyz 1234567890 ÁáÊêÑñ &€$

The quick Brown Fox jumps over the Lazy Dog. 9 pt.
The quick Brown Fox jumps over the Lazy Dog. 10 pt.
The quick Brown Fox jumps over the Lazy Dog. 12 pt.
The quick Brown Fox jumps over the Lazy Dog. 14 pt.

Cavetto Italic

ABCDEFGHIJKLMNOPQRSTUVWXYZ
abcdefghijklmnopqrstuvwxyz 1234567890 ÁáÊêÑñ &€$

Cavetto Italic Alternate

ABCDEFGHIJKLMNOPQRSTUVWXYZ
d, fghklmnry 1234567890 &
A A K K M R R Th T V W &

Summer Clouds Roll By

Summer Clouds Roll By

Cavetto JF-Italic/Alt.

Jason Walcott
2002

The italic and italic alternate
variants of the Cavetto family.

ABCDEFGHIJKLMNOPQRSTUVWXYZ
abcdefghijklmnopqrstuvwxyz 1234567890 ÁáÊêÑñ &€$

The Year of the Dragon is here!

Charade JF

Jason Walcott
2001

A whimsical font that's full
of fun and charm.

ABCDEFGHIJKLMNOPQ
RSTUVWXYZ
abcdefghijklmnopqrstuvwxyz 1234567890 ÁáÊêÑñ &€$

Join us for an Evening at the Opera House

Debonair JF

Jason Walcott
2000-2001

An elegant script digitally
revived from an older
photo/letterpress face.

Jukebox

Fairy Tale JF

Jason Walcott
2000

An "almost-but-not-quite" blackletter face, inspired by a popular fairy tale.

ABCDEFGHIJKLMNOPQRSTUVWXYZ
abcdefghijklmnopqrstuvwxyz 1234567890 ÁáÊêÑñ & €$

The Prince and Princess lived happily ever after.

Fenway Park JF

Jason Walcott
2001

This athletic-style script font, useful for a variety of applications, has proven to be one of Jukebox's most popular.

ABCDEFGHIJKLMNOPQRSTUVWXYZ
abcdefghijklmnopqrstuvwxyz 1234567890 ÁáÊêÑñ & €$

Take Me Out To The Ballgame!

Friki Tiki JF

Jason Walcott
2001

Inspired by a popular tiki-themed attraction, this font says "Aloha."

ABCDEFGHIJKLMNOPQRSTUVWXYZ THTi
ABCDEFGHIJKLMNOPQRSTUVWXYZ THTaFFFa
1234567890 ÁÁÊÊÑÑ & €$

WHEN YOU GO TO HAWAii, YOU MIGHT GET LEi'D...

Gypsy Switch JF

Jason Walcott
2002

A fun and light typeface, useful for a variety of purposes.

ABCDEFGHIJKLMNOPQRSTUVWXYZ
abcdefghijklmnopqrstuvwxyz 1234567890 ÁáÊêÑñ & €$

I had Fun playing my Xylophones.

ABCDEFGHIJKLMNOPQRSTUVWXYZ
abcdefghijklmnopqrstuvwxyz 1234567890 ÁáÈêÑñ ¿€$

Once Upon a Time in Las Vegas...

Holiday Times JF

Jason Walcott
2000

A festive and fun font, so named because it was inspired by a beloved Christmas source.

ABCDEFGHIJKLMNOPQRSTUVWXYZ
abcdefghijklmnopqrstuvwxyz 1234567890 ÁáÈêÑñ &€$

Congratulations on your Wedding Day!

Jeffriana JF

Jason Walcott
2001

A handwriting-style script font, named after a dear friend of the designer.

Kon Tiki Aloha

ABCDEFGHIJKLMNOPQRSTUVWXYZ
ABCDEFGHIJKLMNOPQRSTUVWXYZ 1234567890 ÁÁÊÊÑÑ &€$

Kon Tiki Aloha Ligatures

TA EB CK ND EN FA FO FE FU FI KO LI AM ON OA OP OR RE SE TH TU TE TI TR LY TY
AT CA TCE DEA FRG ANGA KK KI KE LO MAN TO OE PNA RA TS TOA DE DMEE S
UT VO WA VIR Y ZOUT ER KA LS VE VA KO ANLE LA LUST RUMO OO BA BI BUB

WELCOME TO THE POLYNESIAN TRADERS

WELCOME TO THE POLYNESIAN TRADERS

Kon Tiki JF-Aloha/Ligs.

Jason Walcott
2002

The Kon Tiki font family was inspired by the Polynesian kitch of the 1950s and 1960s. It consists of seven typefaces with full character sets and one alternate ligature font.

Jukebox

Kon Tiki JF-Enchanted

Jason Walcott
2002

ABCDEFGHIJKLMNOPQRSTUVWXYZ
abcdefghijklmnopqrstuvwxyz 1234567890 ÁáÊêÑñ &€$

Take an Exciting Cruise and go Surfing!

Kon Tiki JF-Hula

Jason Walcott
2002

ABCDEFGHIJKLMNOPQRSTUVWXYZ
1234567890 ÁÁÊÊÑÑ &€$

PALM TREES LOOK BEST AT THE BEACH.

Kon Tiki JF-Kona

Jason Walcott
2002

ABCDEFGHIJKLMNOPQRSTUVWXYZ
abcdefghijklmnopqrstuvwxyz
1234567890 ÁáÊêÑñ &€$

Tiki Joe says, "Buy my Pineapples!"

Kon Tiki JF-Lanai

Jason Walcott
2002

ABCDEFGHIJKLMNOPQRSTUVWXYZ
1234567890 ÁÁÊÊÑÑ &€$

WELCOME TO KAUAI ISLAND

ABCDEFGHIJJKLMNOPQRR STUVWXY3
abcdefghijklmnopqrstuvwxyz 1234567890 ÁáÊêÑñ &€$

Dine at the famous Tahitian Lanai!

ABCDEFGHIJKLMNOPQRSTUVWXYZ
abcdefghijklmnopqrstuvwxyz 1234567890 ÁáÊêÑñ &€$

Climb the slopes of Mauna Loa.

ABCDEFGHIJKLMNOPQRSTUVWXYZ U
abcdefghijklmnopqrstuvwxyz asvw
1234567890 ÁáÊêÑñ &€$

Thank You for all your kindness.

Manual Script JF

Jason Walcott
2002

A calligraphic script face
based on a hand-lettered
alphabet in a "how-to" book
about calligraphy.

Jukebox

ABCDEFGHIJKLMNOPQRSTUVWXYZ
abcdefghijklmnopqrstuvwxyz 1234567890 ÁáÊêÑñ &€$
A W Ye-llrs crexor

Call me when you get back to North Carolina...

Mary Helen JF

Jason Walcott
2002

Free-flowing and light,
this font is named
after the designer's
paternal grandmother.

ABCDEFGHIJKL MNOPQRSTUVWXYZ
abcdefghijklmnopqrstuvwxyz 1234567890 ÁáÊê Ññ &€$

You are cordially invited to the Embassy Ball.

ABCDEFGHIJKLMNOPQRSTUVWXYZ
abcdefghijklmnopqrstuvwxyz 1234567890 ÁáÊêÑñ &€$

Delicious candy is a must for Halloween!

ABCDEFGHIJKLMNOPQRSTUVWXYZ
abcdefghijklmnopqrstuvwxyz 1234567890 ÁáÊêÑñ &€$

Never leave home without Clean Underwear.

ABCDEFGHIJKLMNOPQRSTUVWXYZ
abcdefghijklmnopqrstuvwxyz 1234567890 ÁáÊêÑñ &€$

Let's go for a Spin in my Astro Jets!

Randolph JF

Randolph JF-Regular

ABCDEFGHIJKLMNOPQRSTUVWXYZ
abcdefghijklmnopqrstuvwxyz 1234567890 ÁáÊêÑñ &€$

Randolph JF-Italic

ABCDEFGHIJKLMNOPQRSTUVWXYZ
abcdefghijklmnopqrstuvwxyz 1234567890 ÁáÊêÑñ &€$

Randolph JF-Swash

ABCDEFGHIJKLMNPQRSTUVWXY
fhkmnrvw ÁÊÑñ & KRTh riviwi

Randolph JF-Swash Italic

ABCDEFGHIJKLMNPQRSTUVWXY
fhkmnrvw ÁÊÑñ & KRTh riviwi

Regular and Swash

Where are all the Flowers?

Italic and Swash Italic

Where are all the Flowers?

Randolph JF

Jason Walcott
2002

A heavy engravers-style family consisting of a roman, italic, and two swash variants. Named for the designer's hometown in New Jersey.

Jukebox

ABCDEFGHIJKLMNOPQRSTUVWXYZ
abcdefghijklmnopqrstuvwxyz 1234567890 ÁáÊêÑñ &€$

"Quality and Customer Satisfaction" is our Motto!

Retro Repro JF

Jason Walcott
2002

A new version of an old typeface called "Repro Script," originally designed by Jerry Mullen in 1953.

Saharan JF

Jason Walcott
2001

Inspired by some hotel signage, this font is perfect for any Vegas, desert, or Arabian theme. Or use it on vanity plates for your camel.

ABCDEFGHIJKLMNOPQRSTUVWXYZ
1234567890 ÁáÊÊÑÑ &€$

ELVIS HAS ENTERED THE BUILDING.

Scriptorama JF-Hostess

Jason Walcott
2002

The Scriptorama family consists of three script faces that can be used separately or together. They celebrate the hand-lettered signage of days gone by.

The Hostess variant is reminiscent of 1960s style and class.

ABCDEFGHIJKLMNOPQRSTUVWXYZ
abcdefghijklmnopqrstuvwxyz 1234567890 ÁáÊêÑñ &€$

The Art and Style of Hollywood

Scriptorama JF-Markdown

Jason Walcott
2002

The Markdown variant is done in the style of hand-painted window lettering.

ABCDEFGHIJKLMNOPQRSTUVWXYZ
1234567890 ÁáÊÊÑÑ &€$

HUGE SALE ON FACTORY-DIRECT SOFAS!

Scriptorama JF-Tradeshow

Jason Walcott
2002

The Tradeshow variant captures the charm of hand-painted signs from the 1950s.

ABCDEFGHIJKLMNOPQRSTUVWXYZ
abcdefghijklmnopqrstuvwxyz 1234567890 ÁáÊêÑñ &€$

Amish Craft Fair in September

Shirley Script JF

Jason Walcott
2003

A casual script font with a touch of flair. Named after a dear friend of the designer.

ABCDEFGHIJKLMNOPQRSTUVWXYZ

abcdefghijklmnopqrstuvwxyz 1234567890 ÁáÊêÑñ &€$

Friends Are The Family We Choose For Ourselves.

Southland JF

Jason Walcott
2002

A unique typeface with heavy contrast and dynamic flourishes. Based on a hand-lettered alphabet.

ABCDEFGHIJKLMNOPQRSTUVWXYZ

abcdefghijklmnopqrstuvwxyz 1234567890 ÁáÊêÑñ &€$

California Sunshine is Good for Everyone.

Spaulding Sans JF

Jason Walcott
2001

The Spaulding Sans family is a sans serif design with Venetian proportions.

Spaulding Sans Regular

ABCDEFGHIJKLMNOPQRSTUVWXYZ

abcdefghijklmnopqrstuvwxyz 1234567890 ÁáÊêÑñ & € $

Spaulding Sans Italic

ABCDEFGHIJKLMNOPQRSTUVWXYZ

abcdefghijklmnopqrstuvwxyz 1234567890 ÁáÊêÑñ &€$

The quick Brown Fox jumps over the Lazy Dog.   12 pt Regular
The quick Brown Fox jumps over the Lazy Dog.   14 pt Regular

The quick Brown Fox jumps over the Lazy Dog.   12 pt Italic
The quick Brown Fox jumps over the Lazy Dog.   14 pt Italic

Jukebox

Stanzie JF

Jason Walcott
2000

A script face with a hand-lettered feel, digitally revived from an older photo/letterpress face.

ABCDEFGHIJKLMNOPQRSTUVWXYZ
abcdefghijklmnopqrstuvwxyz 1234567890 ÁáÊêÑñ &€$

Please don't feed the Type Designers.

Valentina JF

Jason Walcott
2001

A lighthearted script font with a slightly retro feel. Named after one of the designer's dearest friends.

ABCDEFGHIJKLMNOPQRSTUVWXYZ
abcdefghijklmnopqrstuvwxyz 1234567890 ÁáÊêÑñ &€$

A Trip to Seattle Uncovers Hilarious Family Secret!

Varsity Script JF

Jason Walcott
2001

This font is reminiscent of the hand-embroidered lettering on athletic jerseys.

ABCDEFGHIJKLMNOPQRSTUVWXYZ
abcdefghijklmnopqrstuvwxyz 1234567890 ÁáÊêÑñ &€$

Little League Team wins the big game on Friday!

Viceroy JF

Jason Walcott
2000-2002

An heavier, yet elegant, script font, digitally revived from an older photo/letterpress face.

ABCDEFGHIJKLMNOPQRSTUVWXYZ
abcdefghijklmnopqrstuvwxyz 1234567890 ÁáÊêÑñ & €$ Tôerxz

An Evening of Classical Music at Carnegie Hall

Walcott Gothic Fountain

ABCDEFGHIJKLMNOPQRSTUVWXYZ
ABCDEFGHIJKLMNOPQRSTUVWXYZ 1234567890 ÁÁÊÊÑñ &€$

Walcott Gothic Hollywood

ABCDEFGHIJKLMNOPQRSTUVWXYZ
ABCDEFGHIJKLMNOPQRSTUVWXYZ 1234567890 ÁÁÊÊÑñ &€$

Walcott Gothic Sunset

ABCDEFGHIJKLMNOPQRSTUVWXYZ
ABCDEFGHIJKLMNOPQRSTUVWXYZ 1234567890 ÁÁÊÊÑñ &€$

IT'S AN HONOR JUST TO BE NOMINATED.

IT'S AN HONOR JUST TO BE NOMINATED.

IT'S AN HONOR JUST TO BE NOMINATED.

Walcott Gothic

Jason Walcott
2001

The Walcott Gothic family consist of three styles that celebrate the golden age of Hollywood.

Jukebox

ABCDEFGHIJKLMNOPQRSTUVWXYZ
abcdefghijklmnopqrstuvwxyz
1234567890 ÁáÊêÑñ ¢€$

"I am Wonder the Wonderboy!"

Wonderboy JF

Jason Walcott
2002

Fun and boisterous, this typeface is sure to be noticed.

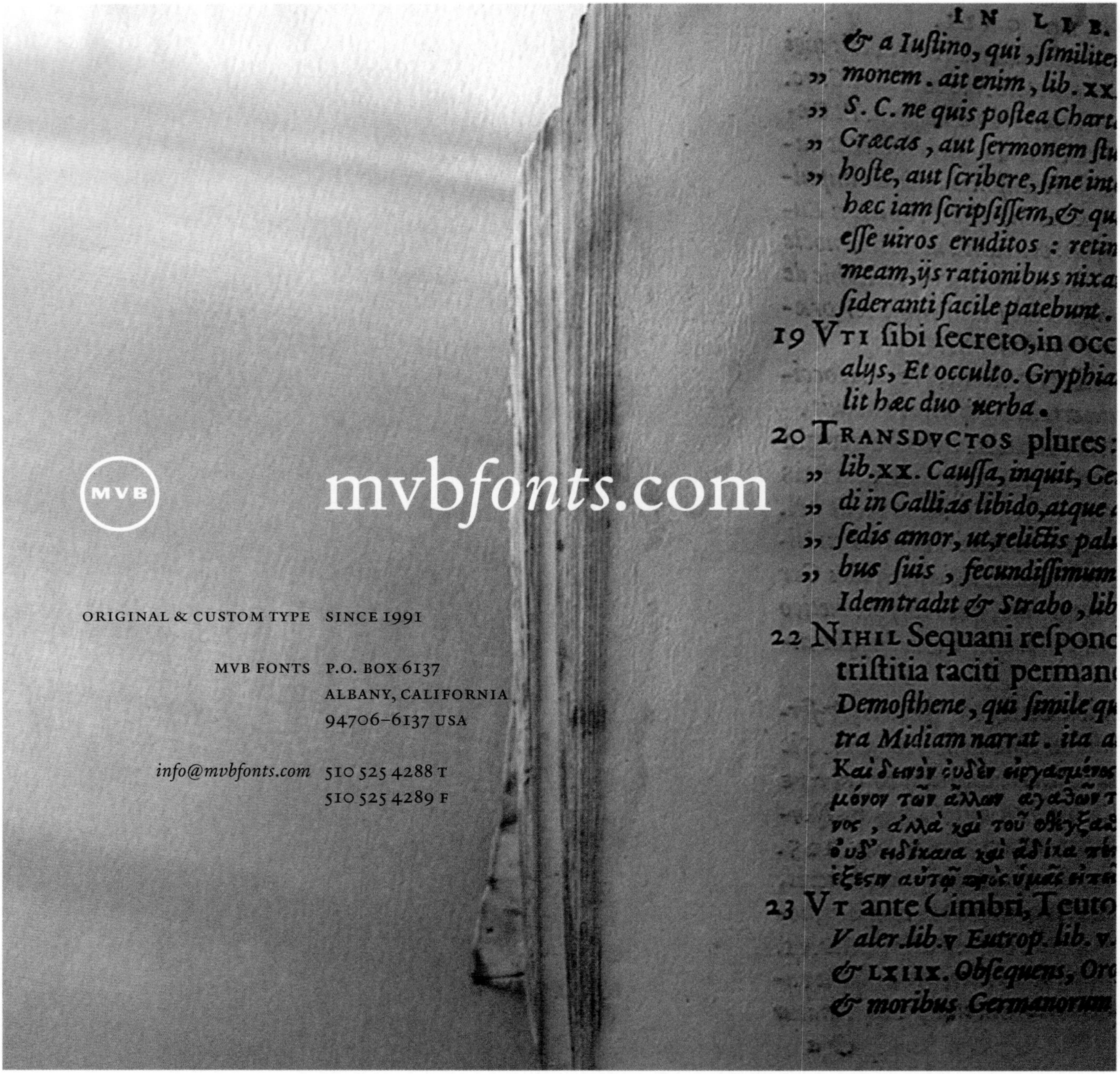

mvbfonts.com

ORIGINAL & CUSTOM TYPE   SINCE 1991

MVB FONTS   P.O. BOX 6137
ALBANY, CALIFORNIA
94706–6137 USA

info@mvbfonts.com   510 525 4288 T
510 525 4289 F

ABCDEFGHIJKLMNOPQRSTUVWXYZ&ÆŒ
abcdefghijklmnopqrstuvwxyz æœfiflß 1234567890 ?!
ABCDEFGHIJKLMNOPQRSTUVWXY&Z

ABCDEFGHIJKLMNOPQRSTUVWXYZ&ÆŒ
abcdefghijklmnopqrstuvwxyz æœfiflß 1234567890 ?!

The quick brown fox jumps over a lazy dog pack my box
with five dozen liquor jugs jaded zombies acted quaintly

The quick brown fox jumps over a lazy dog pack my box with five
dozen liquor jugs jaded zombies acted quaintly but kept driving

MVB Verdigris™

Mark van Bronkhorst
2003

A new text family inspired by
sixteenth-century typefaces
of French punchcutters
Robert Granjon (roman)
and Pierre Haultin (italic).

Release scheduled for
Summer 2003 will include
Roman, Italic, Small Caps,
Bold, Bold Italic, and Extras
for all weights.

We promptly judged antique ivory buckl
es for the next prize. How razorback jum
ping frogs can level six piqued gymnasts
Sixty zippers were quickly picked from th
e woven jute bag. Crazy Fredericka boug
ht many very exquisite opal jewels. Jump
by vow of quick, lazy strength in Oxford
Pack my box with five dozen liquor jugs. J
ackdaws love my big sphinx of quartz. Wa
ltz nymph, for quick jigs vex bud. The qu
ick brown fox jumps over a lazy dog. Pack

We promptly judged antique ivory buckles for t
he next prize. How razorback jumping frogs ca
n level six piqued gymnasts. Sixty zippers were
quickly picked from the woven jute bag. Crazy
Fredericka bought many very exquisite opal je
wels. Jump by vow of quick, lazy strength in Ox
ford. Pack my box with five dozen liquor jugs. J
ackdaws love my big sphinx of quartz. Waltz
nymph, for quick jigs vex bud. The quick brow
n fox jumps over a lazy dog. Pack my box with
five dozen liquor jugs. Jaded zombies acted qua

WE PROMPTLY JUDGED ANTIQUE IVORY
BUCKLES FOR THE NEXT PRIZE. HOW R
AZORBACK JUMPING FROGS CAN LEVEL
SIX PIQUED GYMNASTS. SIXTY ZIPPERS
WERE QUICKLY PICKED FROM THE WOV
EN JUTE BAG. CRAZY FREDERICKA BOUG
HT MANY VERY EXQUISITE OPAL JEWELS
JUMP BY VOW OF QUICK, LAZY STRENGT
H IN OXFORD. PACK MY BOX WITH FIVE
DOZEN LIQUOR JUGS. JACKDAWS LOVE M
Y BIG SPHINX OF QUARTZ. WALTZ, NYMP

Verdigris

starz
@do3*
rgeck
s.com
Quep>

ABCDEFGHIJKLMNOPQRS
TUVWXY&Zabcdefghijk
lmnopqrstuvwxyz@123
4567890 The quick br
own fox jumps over a
lazy dog pack my box

ABCDEFGHIJKLMNOPQRS
TUVWXY&Zabcdefghijk
lmnopqrstuvwxyz@123
4567890 The quick br
own fox jumps over a
lazy dog pack my box

ABCDEFGHIJKLMNOPQRS
TUVWXY&Zabcdefghijk
lmnopqrstuvwxyz@123
4567890 The quick br
own fox jumps over a
lazy dog pack my box

ABCDEFGHIJKLMNOPQRS
TUVWXY&Zabcdefghijk
lmnopqrstuvwxyz@123
4567890 The quick br
own fox jumps over a
lazy dog pack my box

ABCDEFGHIJKLMNOPQRS
TUVWXY&Zabcdefghijk
lmnopqrstuvwxyz@123
4567890 The quick br
own fox jumps over a
lazy dog pack my box

ABCDEFGHIJKLMNOPQRS
TUVWXY&Zabcdefghijk
lmnopqrstuvwxyz@123
4567890 The quick br
own fox jumps over a
lazy dog pack my box

Sarge
Sarge
Sarge
Sarge
Sarge
Sarge

MVB Fantabular™

Akemi Aoki
2002

Regular
Regular Italic
Medium
Medium Italic
Bold
Bold Italic

ABCDEFGHIJKLMNOPQRS
TUVWXY&Zabcdefghijk
lmnopqrstuvwxyz@123
4567890 The quick br
own fox jumps over a
lazy dog pack my box

ABCDEFGHIJKLMNOPQRS
TUVWXY&Zabcdefghijk
lmnopqrstuvwxyz@123
4567890 The quick br
own fox jumps over a
lazy dog pack my box

ABCDEFGHIJKLMNOPQRS
TUVWXY&Zabcdefghijk
lmnopqrstuvwxyz@123
4567890 The quick br
own fox jumps over a
lazy dog pack my box

ABCDEFGHIJKLMNOPQRS
TUVWXY&Zabcdefghijk
lmnopqrstuvwxyz@123
4567890 The quick br
own fox jumps over a
lazy dog pack my box

ABCDEFGHIJKLMNOPQRS
TUVWXY&Zabcdefghijk
lmnopqrstuvwxyz@123
4567890 The quick br
own fox jumps over a
lazy dog pack my box

ABCDEFGHIJKLMNOPQRS
TUVWXY&Zabcdefghijk
lmnopqrstuvwxyz@123
4567890 The quick br
own fox jumps over a
lazy dog pack my box

Sarge
Sarge
Sarge
Sarge
Sarge
Sarge

MVB Fantabular™ Sans

Akemi Aoki
2002

Regular
Regular Italic
Medium
Medium Italic
Bold
Bold Italic

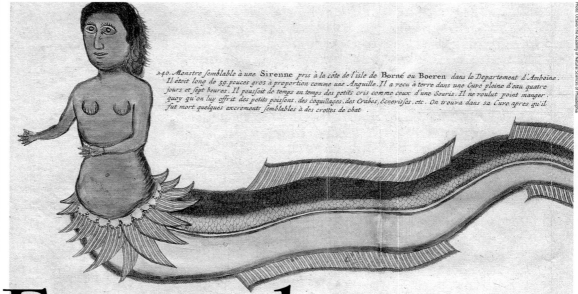

240. Monstre semblable à une Sirenne pris à la côte de l'isle de Borné ou Boeren dans le Departement d'Amboine. Il étoit long de 59 pouces gros à proportion comme une Anguille. Il a recu à terre dans une Cuve pleine d'eau quatre jours et sept heures. Il poussoit de temps en temps des petits cris comme ceux d'une Souris. Il ne voulut point manger quoy qu'on luy offrit des petits poissons, des coquillages, des Crabes, Ecrevisses, etc. On trouva dans sa Cuve, apres qu'il fut mort quelques excrements semblables à des crottes de chat.

Engraved captions

in an old *S and weird* natural history *L* book inspired Alan Greene and Mark van Bronkhorst to develop MVB SIRENNE. Louis Renard's *Poissons, Ecrevisses et Crabes* (1719) claimed that a Sirenne (mermaid) had been captured and observed in a tub of water for four days and seven hours before expiring.

GIVEN AMPLE TIME TO VIEW THE SPECIMEN, Samuel Fallours (the artist whose illustrations were the basis for Renard's book) made the drawing of the mermaid, after which the engraved image (above) was made for publication. The caption with the image reads: *"A Monster resembling a Sirenne caught on the coast of the island of Borné or Boeren [Buru] in the Province of Ambon. It was fifty-nine inches long, and of an eel-like proportion. It lived on shore in a tank of water for four days and seven hours. It uttered occasional cries similar to those of a mouse. It would not eat, although it was offered small fishes, molluscs, crabs, crayfishes, etc. After its death, a few feces similar to those of a cat were found in its tank."* One might wonder: did Fallours have something sexy in his tub, or was the whole story—right down to the catlike droppings—merely a tall tale?

MVB **Sirenne** offers four optical sizes: *'Six'* for small print (used here), *'Text'* (for text like that at left), *'Eighteen'* for text & display, and *'Seventy-Two'* for initials and very large settings.

A 40-page **Specimen Book** of MVB Sirenne tells the complete story of the mermaid and is available from MVB Fonts while supplies last. Email *info@mvbfonts.com* to request a copy.

ABCDEFGHIJKLMNOPQRSTUVWXYZ&ÆŒ1234567890
ABCDEFGHIJKLMNOPQRSTUVWXYZ&ÆŒ
abcdefghijklmnopqrstuvwxyzßfffifflffiffl1234567890
()[]{}?!@#$¢ƒ£€¥%*¼½¾⅛⅜⅝⅞⅓⅔.,abdeilmnorst

ABCDEFGHIJKLMNOPQRSTUVWXYZ&ÆŒ1234567890
abcdefghijklmnopqrstuvwxyzßfffifflffiffl1234567890
()[]{}?!@#$¢ƒ£€ *¼½¾⅛⅜⅝⅞⅓⅔.,abdeilmnorst

MVB Sirenne™ Six

Alan Greene
2002

Roman OSF and TF
Roman Small Caps
Roman Extras
Italic OSF and TF
Italic Extras

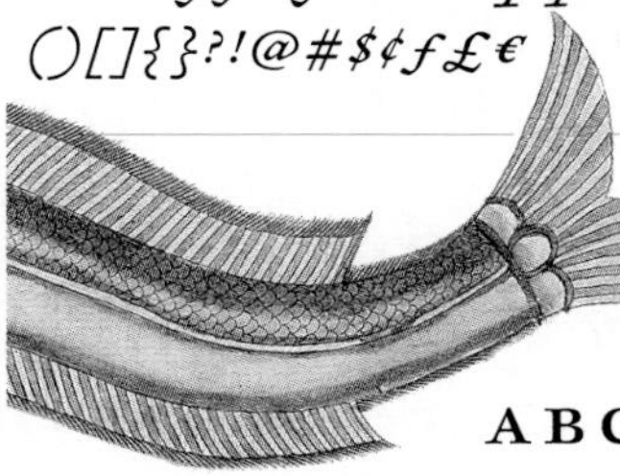

MONSTRE SEMBLABLE À UNE SIRENNE pris à la côte de l'isle de Borné ou Boeren dans le Departement d'Amboine. Il étoit long de 59 pouces gros à proportion comme une Anguille. Il a vecu à terre dans une Cuve pleine d'eau quatre jours et sept heures. Il poussoit de *temps en temps des petits cris comme ceux d'une Souris. Il ne voulut point manger quoy qu'on luy offrit des petits poissons, des coquillages, des Crabes, Ecrevisses, etc. On trouva dans sa Cuve apres qu'il fut mort quelques excrements semblables à des crottes de chat.*

ABCDEFGHIJKLMNOPQRS
TUVWXYZ&ÆŒ1234567890
ABCDEFGHIJKLMNOPQRSTUVWXYZ&ÆŒ
abcdefghijklmnopqrstuvwxyzßfffifflffiffl1234567890
()[]{}?!@#$¢ƒ£€¥%*¼½¾⅛⅜⅝⅞⅓⅔.,abdeilmnorst

AABBCCDDEEFFGGHIJKLMMNNOPP
QRRSSTUVVWXXYZ&ÆŒ1234567890
abcdefghijklmnopqrstuvwxyzßfffifflffiffl1234567890
()[]{}?!@#$¢ƒ£€¥%*¼½¾⅛⅜⅝⅞⅓⅔.,abdeilmnorst

ABCDEFGHIJKLMNOPQRSTUVWXYZ&1234567890
abcdefghijklmnopqrstuvwxyz?!@$¢ƒ£€¥1234567890
ABCDEFGHIJKLMNOPQRSTUVWXYZ&1234567890
abcdefghijklmnopqrstuvwxyz?!@$¢ƒ£€¥1234567890

MVB Sirenne™ Text

Alan Greene
2002

Roman OSF and TF
Roman Small Caps
Roman Extras
Italic OSF and TF
Italic Swash
Italic Extras
Bold OSF and TF
Bold Extras
Bold Italic OSF and TF
Bold Italic Extras

Monstre semblable à une Sirenne pris à la côte de l'isle de Borné ou Boeren d ans le Departement d'Amboine. Il étoit long de 59 pouces gros à proportion comme une Anguille. Il a vecu à terre dans une Cuve pleine d'eau quatre jou rs et sept heures. Il poussoit de temps en temps des petits cris comme ceux d'une Souris. Il ne voulut point man ger quoy qu'on luy offrit des petits poi

Monstre semblable à une Sirenne pris à la côte de l'isle de Borné ou Boeren da ns le Departement d'Amboine. Il étoit l ong de 59 pouces gros à proportion com me une Anguille. Il a vecu à terre dans une Cuve pleine d'eau quatre jours et se pt heures. Il poussoit de temps en temps des petits cris comme ceux d'une Souris. Il ne voulut point manger quoy qu'on luy offrit des petits poissons, des coquil

Monstre semblable à une Sirenne pr is à la côte de l'isle de Borné ou Boe ren dans le Departement d'Amboine. Il étoit long de 59 pouces gros à pro portion comme une Anguille. *Il a ve cu à terre dans une Cuve pleine d'e au quatre jours et sept heures. Il pousso it de temps en temps des petits cris co mme ceux d'une Souris. Il ne voulut p oint manger quoy qu'on luy offrit des*

MVB Fonts

Alan Greene
2002

Eighteen Roman
Eighteen Roman Small Caps
Eighteen Roman Extras
Eighteen Italic
Eighteen Italic Swash
Eighteen Italic Extras

ABCDEFGHIJKLMNOPQRSTUVWXYZ&ÆŒ
ABCDEFGHIJKLMNOPQRSTUVWXYZ&ÆŒ1234567890
abcdefghijklmnopqrstuvwxyz ß ff fi fl ffi ffl
()[]{}?!@#$¢ƒ£€¥%*¼½¾⅛⅜⅝⅞⅓⅔., abdeilmnorst

AABBCCDDEEFFGGHIJKLMMNNOPP
QRRSSTUVVWXXYZ&ÆŒ1234567890
abcdefghijklmnopqrstuvwxyz ß ff fi fl ffi ffl
()[]{}?!@#$¢ƒ£€¥% *¼½¾⅛⅜⅝⅞⅓⅔., abdeilmnorst

MVB Sirenne Eighteen

ONSTRE semblable à une Sirenne pris à la côte de l'isle de Borné ou Boeren dans le Departement d'Amboine. Il étoit long de 59 pouces gros à proportion comme une Anguille. Il a vecu à terre dans une Cuve pleine d'eau quatre jours et sept heures. Il poussoit de temps en temps des petits cris comme ceux d'une Souris. Il ne voulut point manger quoy qu'on luy offrit des petits poissons, des coquillages, des Crabes, Ecrevisses, etc. On trouva dans sa Cuve apres qu'il fut mort quelques excrements semblables à des crottes de chat.

MVB Sirenne Seventy-Two Swash Italic

MVB Sirenne Eighteen

info@mvbfonts.com

SIRENNE

Regulation 215

Maestro Jones

PEASANT GIRL

OBLITERATES

Bartholomew's

Safflower Queen

MVB Sirenne Seventy-Two

MVB Sirenne™ Display

Alan Greene
2002

Seventy-Two Roman
Seventy-Two Roman Small Caps
Seventy-Two Roman Extras
Seventy-Two Italic
Seventy-Two Italic Swash
Seventy-Two Italic Extras

MVB Fonts

info@mvbfonts.com

ABCDEFGHIJKLMNOPQRSTUVWXYZ&ÆŒ
abcdefghijklmnopqrstuvwxyz1234567890?!
Ultra

ABCDEFGHIJKLMNOPQRSTUVWXYZ&ÆŒ
abcdefghijklmnopqrstuvwxyz1234567890?!@
Ultra Italic

ABCDEFGHIJKLMNOPQRSTUVWXYZ&ÆŒ
abcdefghijklmnopqrstuvwxyz1234567890?!@$
Black

ABCDEFGHIJKLMNOPQRSTUVWXYZ&ÆŒ
abcdefghijklmnopqrstuvwxyz1234567890?!@$¢
Black Italic

ABCDEFGHIJKLMNOPQRSTUVWXYZ&ÆŒ
abcdefghijklmnopqrstuvwxyz1234567890?!@$¢
Extra Bold

ABCDEFGHIJKLMNOPQRSTUVWXYZ&ÆŒ
abcdefghijklmnopqrstuvwxyz1234567890?!@$¢£
Extra Bold Italic

ABCDEFGHIJKLMNOPQRSTUVWXYZ&ÆŒ
abcdefghijklmnopqrstuvwxyz1234567890?!@$¢£
Bold

ABCDEFGHIJKLMNOPQRSTUVWXYZ&ÆŒ
abcdefghijklmnopqrstuvwxyz1234567890?!@$¢£¥
Bold Italic

ABCDEFGHIJKLMNOPQRSTUVWXYZ&ÆŒ
abcdefghijklmnopqrstuvwxyz1234567890?!@$¢£¥
Medium

ABCDEFGHIJKLMNOPQRSTUVWXYZ&ÆŒ
abcdefghijklmnopqrstuvwxyz1234567890?!@$¢£¥€
Medium Italic

ABCDEFGHIJKLMNOPQRSTUVWXYZ&ÆŒ
abcdefghijklmnopqrstuvwxyz1234567890?!@$¢£¥€
Regular

ABCDEFGHIJKLMNOPQRSTUVWXYZ&ÆŒ
abcdefghijklmnopqrstuvwxyz1234567890?!@$¢£¥€
Italic

MVB Grenadine™

Akemi Aoki
2003

Regular
Regular Italic
Medium
Medium Italic
Bold
Bold Italic
Extra Bold
Extra Bold Italic
Black
Black Italic
Ultra
Ultra Italic

MVB Fonts

MVB Peccadillo™

Holly Goldsmith & Alan Greene
2002

Eight
Eight Alternates
Twenty-Four
Twenty-Four Alternates
Ninety-Six
Ninety-Six Alternates

MVB Peccadillo Ninety-Six is a revival of a nineteenth-century metal typeface. Holly Goldsmith digitized the face, retaining the distortions caused by worn type and letterpress splat. The 'Eight' and 'Twenty-Four' sizes were then adapted by Alan Greene.

ABGHMQRS&
abefghimrstv

ABCDEFGHIJKLMNO
PQRSTUVWXYZ&ÆŒ
1234567890 AND CO ¢ $ ¢ £ F
abcdefghijklmnopq
rstuvwxyz fffifl ffl ffl ? !
ABCDEFGHIJKLMNOPQRSTUVWXYZ&ÆŒ
1234567890 § CO $¢¥ƒ€£© @ # % * { } [ ] ( )
abcdefghijklmnopqrstuvwxyz fffifl ffl ffl ? !
The quick brown fox jumps over a lazy dog. Pack
my box with five dozen liquor jugs. Crazy Frede
ricka bought many very exquisite opal jewels. J

MVB Bovine™

Mark van Bronkhorst
1993

Regular
Round

BOVINE
BOVINE

ABCDEFGHIJ
KLMNOPQR
STUVWXY&Z
1234567890

MVB Magnesium™

Mark van Bronkhorst
1992 & 2003

Regular
Condensed (new)

NO PARKING
GO AWAY
ESTATE SALE
DISCOTHEQUE

ABCDEFGHIJ
KLMNOPQR
STUVWXY&Z
1234567890
ABCDEFGHIJKL
MNOPQRSTUVX
Y&Z1234567890

info@mvbfonts.com

ABCDEFGHIJKLMNOPQRS
TUVWXYZÆŒ&1234567890
ABCDEFGHIJKLMNOPQRSTUVWXYZ
abcdefghijklmnopqrstuvwxyzæœ
ffiflffffiffl$¢¥ƒ€£@?!1234567890
ABCDEFGHIJKLMNOPQRSTUV
WXYZ&abcdefghijklmnopqrstuvwxyz?!
Semibold Bold Inline **Adornado**

WE PROMPTLY JUDGED antique
ivory buckles for the next prize
How razorback jumping frogs c
an level six piqued gymnasts Six
ty zippers were quickly picked f
rom the woven jute bag. Crazy F
redericka bought many very exq
uisite opal jewels. Jump by vow of qu
ick, lazy strength in Oxford. Pack m
y box with five dozen liquor jugs. Jac
kdaws love my big sphinx of quartz
Waltz nymph, for quick jigs vex bud.
The quick brown fox jumps over a la
zy dog. Pack my box with five dozen

MVB Celestia™ Antiqua

Mark van Bronkhorst
1993-1996

Roman
Roman Small Caps
Italic
Semibold
Bold
Inline
Adornado
Ornaments

ABCDEFGHIJKLMN
abcdefghijklmnopqrstuvwxyz1234567890
OPQRSTUVWXY&Z

Sprinkling
Rain
Wondrous

MVB Chanson d'Amour™

Kanna Aoki
1995

ABCDEFGHIJKLMNO
PQRSTUVWXYZ&ÆŒ
ABCDEFGHIJKLMNOPQRSTUVWXY&Z
abcdefghijklmnopqrstuvwxyzfiflß?!
ABCDEFGHIJKLMNOPQRS
TUVWXYZÆŒ&abcdefghijklmno
pqrstuvwxyzfiflß1234567890$¢¥£@?

WE PROMPTLY JUDGED antique iv
ory buckles for the next prize. Ho
w razorback jumping frogs can lev
el six piqued gymnasts. Sixty zip
pers were quickly picked from the
woven jute bag. Crazy Fredericka
bought many very exquisite opal je
wels. Jump by vow of quick, lazy stre
ngth in Oxford. Pack my box with five
dozen liquor jugs. Jackdaws love my bi
g sphinx of quartz. Waltz nymph, for q
uick jigs vex bud. The quick brown fox
jumps over a lazy dog. Pack my box wi

MVB Gryphius™

Otto Trace
2003

Roman
Roman Small Caps
Italic
Italic Alternates

Old type used by printer
Sebastianus Gryphius
in the early sixteenth
century.

MVB Fonts

Akemi Aoki
1996 & 2002

Roman
Semibold
Bold
Ultra (new)
Hi-Lite
Rocksie

ABCDEFGHIJ
KLMNOPQRS
TUVWXY&Z
1234567890%
abcdefghijkl
mnopqrstuvw
xyz$¢¥ƒ€£@

Semibold

Rocksie

Semibold

Hi-Lite

Dogfood
Parsnips
Ultra

Rumproast
Liverwurst
Bold

Tortilla chips
Frozen dessert
Semibold

Spreadable cheese
Disposable diapers
Roman

ABCDEFGHIJKLMNOP
QRSTUVWXYZ&1234567890
abcdefghijklmnopqrstuvwxyz
ABCDEFGHIJKLMNOP
QRSTUVWXYZ&1234567890
abcdefghijklmnopqrstuvwxyz

Café Mimi
Chocolate
Fancy Teas
Saxophones
Floribunda
Beauteous

MVB Café Mimi™

Kanna Aoki
1996 & 2003

Regular
Bold (new)

ABCDEFGHIJKLMNOPQRSTUV
abcdefghijklmnopqrstuvwxyz
ABCDEFGHIJKLMNOPQRSTUVWXYZ
abcdefghijklmnopqrstuvwxyz?!@$¢*

Dear Bob
Sweetheart
Cudgel Rat

MVB Emmascript™

Kanna Aoki
1996 & 2002

Regular
Bold (new)

ABCDEFGHIJKLMNO
PQRSTUVWXYZ&123
4567890123456789 0*
abcdefghijklmnopqrstuvwxyz
ABCEFGJMQSTV

Greymantle
HOLIDAY
Elfin shoes
Dental work
Persnickety

MVB Greymantle™

Kanna Aoki
1993

Regular
Extras

MVB Fonts

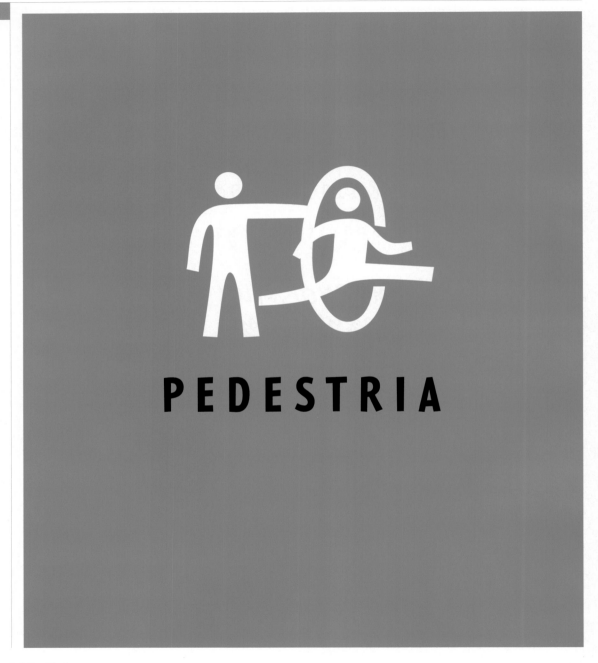

info@mvbfonts.com

ABCDEFGHIJKLMNOPQRSTUVWXY&Z
abcdefghijklmnopqrstuvwxyz1234567890
The quick brown fox jumps over a lazy dog pack

ABCDEFGHIJKLMNOPQRSTUVWXY&Z
abcdefghijklmnopqrstuvwxyz1234567890
My box with five dozen liquor jugs jaded zombies

ABCDEFGHIJKLMNOPQRSTUVWXY&Z
abcdefghijklmnopqrstuvwxyz1234567890
Acted quaintly but kept driving their oxen forwa

ABCDEFGHIJKLMNOPQRSTUVWXY&Z
abcdefghijklmnopqrstuvwxyz1234567890
Waltz, nymph, for quick jigs vex Bud jump by vow

ABCDEFGHIJKLMNOPQRSTUVWXY&Z
abcdefghijklmnopqrstuvwxyz1234567890
Of quick, lazy strength in Oxford how razorback

ABCDEFGHIJKLMNOPQRSTUVWXY&Z
abcdefghijklmnopqrstuvwxyz1234567890
Jumping frogs can level six piqued gymnasts Pack

MVB Pedestria™

Akemi Aoki
2002

Regular
Regular Italic
Medium
Medium Italic
Bold
Bold Italic
Pict One
Pict Two

NEUFVILLE DIGITAL
FUNDICIÓN TIPOGRÁFICA NEUFVILLE
BAUERSCHE GIESSEREI
LUDWIG & MAYER
FONDERIE TYPOGRAPHIQUE FRANÇAISE
FUNDICIÓN TIPOGRÁFICA NACIONAL

CLASSIC AND MODERN ORIGINAL TYPEFACES

The rich heritage of famous foundries is united in Neufville, which took over their assets in the seventies of the former century. In 1997, Neufville Digital was born as a collaboration between FT Bauer from Barcelona and Visualogik from the Netherlands. The main goal of Neufville Digital is to make this heritage available to the digital world, as well as publishing contemporary and new type designs.

The newest font fabrication technology is being used to ensure the highest level of digital quality. All fonts comply with the latest versions of current standards. Full-featured OpenType fonts, containing swashed and alternate characters, have been planned for release.

Full Latin character support - including Central European, Baltic and Turkish - is available for most of our text and display fonts. For some of them, even Greek and Cyrillic glyphs have been designed. Extended glyph sets also include genuine small caps, old style figures, and alternates.

Custom typography to suit your needs is available upon request: special glyphs, symbols, logos, extended character sets, on screen improvement, delta hinting, unusual formats, and printer support. Custom font licenses and license models can be tailored to fit your situation.

Your house style can benefit from our corporate type offerings; please feel free to ask for information.

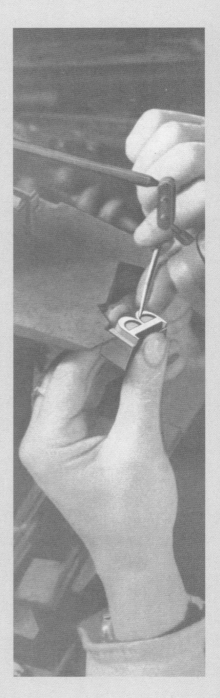

Neufville Digital fonts are available from selected font stores and directly from:

Main distributor:

Fundición Tipográfica Bauer, SL
Calle Selva de Mar, 50
E-08019 BARCELONA
España
tel.: +34 93 308 45 45
fax: +34 93 308 21 14
email: bauer@neufville.com

Manufacturer and main distributor:

Visualogik Technology & Design bv
Sint Janssingel 38   P.O. Box 1953
NL-5200 BZ 's-HERTOGENBOSCH
The Netherlands
tel.: +31 73 613 27 47
fax: +31 73 614 77 14
email: visualogik@neufville.com

Internet sales:

MyFonts
www.myfonts.com

www.neufville.com

Light

abcdefghijklmopqrstuvwxyz
ABCDEFGHIJKLMNOPQRSTUVWXYZ
0123456789
([{&.:;.,!?¿¡*%}]) €$¢£¥ƒ fifl

Futura ND

Paul Renner
1928

BAUER CLASSICS

Character sets supported:
· Windows Latin 1 · MacRoman
· Turkish · CE · Baltic

Features:
· Old Style Figures
· Genuine Small Caps
· Alternate characters

Unicode® v3.0 compliant

Light Oblique

abcdefghijklmopqrstuvwxyz
ABCDEFGHIJKLMNOPQRSTUVWXYZ
0123456789
([{&.:;.,!?¿¡*%}]) €$¢£¥ƒ fifl

Futura ND

Paul Renner
1930

BAUER CLASSICS

Book Oblique

abcdefghijklmopqrstuvwxyz
ABCDEFGHIJKLMNOPQRSTUVWXYZ
0123456789
([{&.:;.,!?¿¡*%}]) €$¢£¥ƒ fifl

Futura ND

Paul Renner
1939

BAUER CLASSICS

Futura ND

Paul Renner
1930 - 1939

BAUER CLASSICS

Light

Ce matin-là, j'étais très en retard pour aller à l'école, et j'avais grand-peur d'être grondé, d'autant que M. Hamel nous avait dit qu'il nous interrogerait sur les participes, et je n'en savais pas le premier mot.
Un moment, l'idée me vint de manquer la classe et de prendre ma course à travers champs. Le temps était si chaud, si clair! On entendait les merles siffler à la lisière du bois, et dans le pré Rippert, derrière la scierie, les Prussiens qui faisaient l'exercice. Tout cela me tentait bien plus que la règle des

Light Oblique

Ce matin-là, j'étais très en retard pour aller à l'école, et j'avais grand-peur d'être grondé, d'autant que M. Hamel nous avait dit qu'il nous interrogerait sur les participes, et je n'en savais pas le premier mot.
Un moment, l'idée me vint de manquer la classe et de prendre ma course à travers champs. Le temps était si chaud, si clair! On entendait les merles siffler à la lisière du bois, et dans le pré Rippert, derrière la scierie, les Prussiens qui faisaient l'exercice. Tout cela me tentait bien plus que la règle des

Book Oblique

Ce matin-là, j'étais très en retard pour aller à l'école, et j'avais grand-peur d'être grondé, d'autant que M. Hamel nous avait dit qu'il nous interrogerait sur les partici-pes, et je n'en savais pas le premier mot.
Un moment, l'idée me vint de manquer la classe et de prendre ma course à travers champs. Le temps était si chaud, si clair! On entendait les merles siffler à la lisière du bois, et dans le pré Rippert, derrière la scierie, les Prussiens qui faisaient l'exercice. Tout cela me tentait bien plus que la règle

Futura ND

Paul Renner
1932

BAUER CLASSICS

Character sets supported:
· Windows Latin 1 · MacRoman
· Turkish · CE · Baltic

Features:
· Old Style Figures
· Genuine Small Caps
· Alternate characters

Unicode® v3.0 compliant

Book

abcdefghijklmopqrstuvwxyz
ABCDEFGHIJKLMNOPQRSTUVWXYZ
0123456789
([{&:;.,!?¿¡*%}]) €$¢£¥ƒ fifl MMa

Futura ND

Paul Renner
1928

BAUER CLASSICS

Medium

abcdefghijklmopqrstuvwxyz
ABCDEFGHIJKLMNOPQRSTUVWXYZ
0123456789
([{&:;.,!?¿¡*%}]) €$¢£¥ƒ fifl

Futura ND

Paul Renner
1930

BAUER CLASSICS

Medium Oblique

abcdefghijklmopqrstuvwxyz
ABCDEFGHIJKLMNOPQRSTUVWXYZ
0123456789
([{&:;.,!?¿¡%}]) €$¢£¥ƒ fifl*

Futura ND

Paul Renner
1928 - 1932

BAUER CLASSICS

Book

Ce matin-là, j'étais très en retard pour aller à l'école, et j'avais grand-peur d'être grondé, d'autant que M. Hamel nous avait dit qu'il nous interrogerait sur les participes, et je n'en savais pas le premier mot.
Un moment, l'idée me vint de manquer la classe et de prendre ma course à travers champs. Le temps était si chaud, si clair!
On entendait les merles siffler à la lisière du bois, et dans le pré Rippert, derrière la scierie, les Prussiens qui faisaient l'exercice. Tout cela me tentait bien plus que la règle

Medium

Ce matin-là, j'étais très en retard pour aller à l'école, et j'avais grand-peur d'être grondé, d'autant que M. Hamel nous avait dit qu'il nous interrogerait sur les participes, et je n'en savais pas le premier mot.
Un moment, l'idée me vint de manquer la classe et de prendre ma course à travers champs. Le temps était si chaud, si clair!
On entendait les merles siffler à la lisière du bois, et dans le pré Rippert, derrière la scierie, les Prussiens qui faisaient l'exer-

Medium Oblique

Ce matin-là, j'étais très en retard pour aller à l'école, et j'avais grand-peur d'être grondé, d'autant que M. Hamel nous avait dit qu'il nous interrogerait sur les participes, et je n'en savais pas le premier mot.
Un moment, l'idée me vint de manquer la classe et de prendre ma course à travers champs. Le temps était si chaud, si clair!
On entendait les merles siffler à la lisière du bois, et dans le pré Rippert, derrière la scierie, les Prussiens qui faisaient l'exer-

sales@neufville.com

Futura ND

Paul Renner
1930

BAUER CLASSICS

Character sets supported:
· Windows Latin 1 · MacRoman
· Turkish · CE · Baltic

Features:
· Old Style Figures
· Genuine Small Caps
· Alternate characters

Unicode® v3.0 compliant

Demibold

abcdefghijklmopqrstuvwxyz
ABCDEFGHIJKLMNOPQRSTUVWXYZ
0123456789
([{&:;.,!?¿¡*%}]) €$¢£¥ƒ fifl

Futura ND

Paul Renner
1930

BAUER CLASSICS

Demibold Oblique

abcdefghijklmopqrstuvwxyz
ABCDEFGHIJKLMNOPQRSTUVWXYZ
0123456789
([{&:;.,!?¿¡%}]) €$¢£¥ƒ fifl*

Futura ND

Paul Renner
1928

BAUER CLASSICS

Bold Oblique

abcdefghijklmopqrstuvwxyz
ABCDEFGHIJKLMNOPQRSTUVWXYZ
0123456789
([{&:;.,!?¿¡*%}]) €$¢£¥ƒ fifl

Futura ND

Paul Renner
1928 - 1930

BAUER CLASSICS

Demibold

Ce matin-là, j'étais très en retard pour aller à l'école, et j'avais grand-peur d'être grondé, d'autant que M. Hamel nous avait dit qu'il nous interrogerait sur les participes, et je n'en savais pas le premier mot.
Un moment, l'idée me vint de manquer la classe et de prendre ma course à travers champs. Le temps était si chaud, si clair! On entendait les merles siffler à la lisière du bois, et dans le pré Rippert, derrière la scierie, les

Demibold Oblique

Ce matin-là, j'étais très en retard pour aller à l'école, et j'avais grand-peur d'être grondé, d'autant que M. Hamel nous avait dit qu'il nous interrogerait sur les participes, et je n'en savais pas le premier mot.
Un moment, l'idée me vint de manquer la classe et de prendre ma course à travers champs. Le temps était si chaud, si clair! On entendait les merles siffler à la lisière du bois, et dans le pré Rippert, derrière la scierie, les Prussiens qui faisaient

Bold Oblique

Ce matin-là, j'étais très en retard pour aller à l'école, et j'avais grand-peur d'être grondé, d'autant que M. Hamel nous avait dit qu'il nous interrogerait sur les partici-pes, et je n'en savais pas le premier mot.
Un moment, l'idée me vint de man-quer la classe et de prendre ma course à travers champs. Le temps était si chaud, si clair! On entendait les merles siffler à la lisière du

Futura ND

Paul Renner
1928

BAUER CLASSICS

Character sets supported:
· Windows Latin 1 · MacRoman
· Turkish · CE · Baltic

Features:
· Old Style Figures
· Genuine Small Caps
· Alternate characters

Unicode® v3.0 compliant

Bold

abcdefghijklmopqrstuvwxyz
ABCDEFGHIJKLMNOPQRSTUVWXYZ
0123456789
([{&:;.,!?¿¡*%}]) €$¢£¥ƒ fifl

Futura ND

Paul Renner
1936

BAUER CLASSICS

ExtraBold

abcdefghijklmopqrstuvwxyz
ABCDEFGHIJKLMNOPQRSTUVWXYZ
0123456789
([{&:;.,!?¿¡*%}]) €$¢£¥ƒ fifl

Futura ND

Paul Renner
1930

BAUER CLASSICS

ExtraBold Oblique

abcdefghijklmopqrstuvwxyz
ABCDEFGHIJKLMNOPQRSTUVWXYZ
0123456789
([{&:;.,!?¿¡*%}]) €$¢£¥ƒ fifl

Futura ND

Paul Renner
1928 - 1936

BAUER CLASSICS

Bold

Ce matin-là, j'étais très en retard
pour aller à l'école, et j'avais
grand-peur d'être grondé, d'autant
que M. Hamel nous avait dit qu'il
nous interrogerait sur les participes, et je n'en savais pas le premier
mot.
Un moment, l'idée me vint de manquer la classe et de prendre ma
course à travers champs. Le temps
était si chaud, si clair! On entendait
les merles siffler à la lisière du bois,

ExtraBold

Ce matin-là, j'étais très en retard
pour aller à l'école, et j'avais
grand-peur d'être grondé,
d'autant que M. Hamel nous
avait dit qu'il nous interrogerait
sur les participes, et je n'en
savais pas le premier mot. Un
moment, l'idée me vint de manquer la classe et de prendre ma
course à travers champs. Le
temps était si chaud, si clair! On
entendait les merles siffler à la

ExtraBold Oblique

Ce matin-là, j'étais très en retard
pour aller à l'école, et j'avais
grand-peur d'être grondé,
d'autant que M. Hamel nous
avait dit qu'il nous interrogerait
sur les participes, et je n'en
savais pas le premier mot. Un
moment, l'idée me vint de manquer la classe et de prendre ma
course à travers champs. Le
temps était si chaud, si clair! On
entendait les merles siffler à la

SCOsF Light

ABCDEFGHIJKLMOPQRSTUVWXYZ
UVWXYZ   0123456789

ABCDEFGHIJKLMNOPQRST
([{&:;.,!?¿¡*%}]) €$¢£¥ƒ

Futura ND

Paul Renner
1928 - 1930

BAUER CLASSICS

Character sets supported:
· Windows Latin 1 · MacRoman
· Turkish · CE · Baltic

Features:
· Old Style Figures
· Genuine Small Caps
· Alternate characters

Unicode® v3.0 compliant

SCOsF Light Oblique

ABCDEFGHIJKLMOPQRSTUVWXYZ
UVWXYZ   0123456789

ABCDEFGHIJKLMNOPQRST
([{&:;.,!?¿¡%}]) €$¢£¥ƒ*

SCOsF Book

ABCDEFGHIJKLMOPQRSTUVWXYZ
UVWXYZ   0123456789

ABCDEFGHIJKLMNOPQRST
([{&:;.,!?¿¡*%}]) €$¢£¥ƒ

Futura ND

Paul Renner
1932 - 1939

BAUER CLASSICS

SCOsF Book Oblique

ABCDEFGHIJKLMOPQRSTUVWXYZ
UVWXYZ   0123456789

ABCDEFGHIJKLMNOPQRST
([{&:;.,!?¿¡%}]) €$¢£¥ƒ*

SCOsF Medium

ABCDEFGHIJKLMOPQRSTUVWXYZ
UVWXYZ   0123456789

ABCDEFGHIJKLMNOPQRST
([{&:;.,!?¿¡*%}]) €$¢£¥ƒ

Futura ND

Paul Renner
1930

BAUER CLASSICS

SCOsF Medium Oblique

ABCDEFGHIJKLMOPQRSTUVWXYZ
UVWXYZ   0123456789

ABCDEFGHIJKLMNOPQRST
([{&:;.,!?¿¡%}]) €$¢£¥ƒ*

SCOsF Bold

ABCDEFGHIJKLMOPQRSTUVWXYZ
RSTUVWXYZ 0123456789 ([{&:;.,!?¿¡*%}]) €$¢£¥ƒ

ABCDEFGHIJKLMNOPQ

Futura ND

Paul Renner
1928

BAUER CLASSICS

SCOsF Bold Oblique

ABCDEFGHIJKLMOPQRSTUVWXYZ
RSTUVWXYZ 0123456789 ([{&:;.,!?¿¡*%}]) €$¢£¥ƒ

ABCDEFGHIJKLMNOPQ

Paul Renner
1950

BAUER CLASSICS

Character sets supported:
· Windows Latin 1 · MacRoman
· Turkish · CE · Baltic

Features:
· Old Style Figures
· Genuine Small Caps
· Alternate characters

Unicode® v3.0 compliant

Cn Light

abcdefghijklmopqrstuvwxyz ABCDEFGHIJKLMNOPQRSTUV WXYZ 0123456789 ([{&:;.,!?¿¡*%}]) €$¢£¥ƒ fi fl

Cn Light Oblique

abcdefghijklmopqrstuvwxyz ABCDEFGHIJKLMNOPQRSTUV WXYZ 0123456789 ([{&:;.,!?¿¡*%}]) €$¢£¥ƒ fi fl

Ce matin-là, j'étais très en retard pour aller à l'école, et j'avais grand-peur d'être grondé, d'autant que M. Hamel nous avait dit qu'il nous interrogerait sur les participes, et je n'en savais pas le premier mot. Un moment, l'idée me vint de manquer la classe et de prendre ma course à travers champs. Le temps était si chaud, si clair! On entendait les merles siffler à la lisière du bois, et dans le pré Rippert, derrière la scierie, les Prussiens qui faisaient l'exercice. Tout cela me tentait bien plus que la règle des participes; mais j'eus la force de résister, et je courus bien vite vers l'école.

Paul Renner
1936

BAUER CLASSICS

Cn Medium

abcdefghijklmopqrstuvwxyz ABCDEFGHIJKLMNOPQRST UVWXYZ 0123456789 ([{&:;.,!?¿¡*%}]) €$¢£¥ƒ fi fl

Cn Medium Oblique

abcdefghijklmopqrstuvwxyz ABCDEFGHIJKLMNOPQRST UVWXYZ 0123456789 ([{&:;.,!?¿¡*%}]) €$¢£¥ƒ fi fl

Ce matin-là, j'étais très en retard pour aller à l'école, et j'avais grand-peur d'être grondé, d'autant que M. Hamel nous avait dit qu'il nous interrogerait sur les participes, et je n'en savais pas le premier mot. Un moment, l'idée me vint de manquer la classe et de prendre ma course à travers champs. Le temps était si chaud, si clair! On entendait les merles siffler à la lisière du bois, et dans le pré Rippert, derrière la scierie, les Prussiens qui faisaient l'exercice. Tout cela me tentait bien plus que la règle des participes; mais j'eus la force de résister, et je courus bien vite vers

Paul Renner
1930

BAUER CLASSICS

Cn Bold

abcdefghijklmopqrstuvwxyz ABCDEFGHIJKLMNOPQRSTUV WXYZ 0123456789 ([{&:;.,!?¿¡*%}]) €$¢£¥ƒ fi fl

Cn Bold Oblique

abcdefghijklmopqrstuvwxyz ABCDEFGHIJKLMNOPQRSTUV WXYZ 0123456789 ([{&:;.,!?¿¡*%}]) €$¢£¥ƒ fi fl

Paul Renner
1936

BAUER CLASSICS

Cn ExtraBold

abcdefghijklmopqrstuvwxyz ABCDEFGHIJKLMNOPQRSTUV WXYZ 0123456789 ([{&:;.,!?¿¡*%}]) €$¢£¥ƒ fi fl

Cn ExtraBold Oblique

abcdefghijklmopqrstuvwxyz ABCDEFGHIJKLMNOPQRSTUV WXYZ 0123456789 ([{&:;.,!?¿¡*%}]) €$¢£¥ƒ fi fl

sales@neufville.com

Ce matin-là, j'étais très en retard pour aller à l'école, et j'avais grand-peur d'être grondé, d'autant que M. Hamel nous avait dit qu'il nous interrogerait sur les participes, et je n'en savais pas le premier mot.
Un moment, l'idée me vint de manquer la classe et de prendre ma course à travers champs. LE TEMPS ÉTAIT SI CHAUD, SI CLAIR! On entendait les merles siffler à la lisière du bois, et dans le pré Rippert, derrière la scierie, les Prussiens qui faisaient l'exercice. Tout cela me

Cn SCOsF Light
ABCDEFGHIJKLMOPQRSTUVWXYZ ABCDEFGHIJKLMNOPQRST UVWXYZ 0123456789 ([{&:;.,!?¿¡*%}]) €$¢£¥ƒ

Cn SCOsF Light Oblique
ABCDEFGHIJKLMOPQRSTUVWXYZ ABCDEFGHIJKLMNOPQRST UVWXYZ 0123456789 ([{&:;.,!?¿¡*%}]) €$¢£¥ƒ

Futura ND Condensed

Paul Renner
1950

BAUER CLASSICS

Character sets supported:
· Windows Latin 1 · MacRoman · Turkish · CE · Baltic

Features:
· Old Style Figures
· Genuine Small Caps
· Alternate characters

Unicode® v3.0 compliant

Ce matin-là, j'étais très en retard pour aller à l'école, et j'avais grand-peur d'être grondé, d'autant que M. Hamel nous avait dit qu'il nous inter-rogerait sur les participes, et je n'en savais pas le premier mot.
Un moment, l'idée me vint de man-quer la classe et de prendre ma course à travers champs. *Le temps était si chaud, si clair!* On entendait les merles siffler à la lisière du bois,

Cn SCOsF Medium
ABCDEFGHIJKLMOPQRSTUVWXYZ ABCDEFGHIJKLMNOPQRST UVWXYZ 0123456789 ([{&:;.,!?¿¡*%}]) €$¢£¥ƒ

Cn SCOsF Medium Oblique
ABCDEFGHIJKLMOPQRSTUVWXYZ ABCDEFGHIJKLMNOPQRST UVWXYZ 0123456789 ([{&:;.,!?¿¡*%}]) €$¢£¥ƒ

Futura ND Condensed

Paul Renner
1936

BAUER CLASSICS

Cn SCOsF Bold
ABCDEFGHIJKLMOPQRSTUVWXYZ ABCDEFGHIJKLMNOPQRST UVWXYZ 0123456789 ([{&:;.,!?¿¡*%}]) €$¢£¥ƒ

Cn SCOsF Bold Oblique
ABCDEFGHIJKLMOPQRSTUVWXYZ ABCDEFGHIJKLMNOPQRST UVWXYZ 0123456789 ([{&:;.,!?¿¡*%}]) €$¢£¥ƒ

Futura ND Condensed

Paul Renner
1930

BAUER CLASSICS

Display
abcdefghijklmopqrstuvwxyz ABCDEFGHIJKLMNOPQRST UVWXYZ 0123456789 ([{&:;.,!?¿¡*%}]) €$¢£¥ fifl

Futura ND Display

Paul Renner
1932

BAUER CLASSICS

Black
abcdefghijklmopqrstuvwxyz ABCDEFGHIJKLMNOPQR STUVWXYZ 0123456789 ([{&:;.,!?¿¡*%}]) €$¢£¥ƒ fifl

Futura ND Black

Paul Renner
1929

BAUER CLASSICS

Paris ND

Enric Crous Vidal
1953

GRAFÍA LATINA

Light

ABCDEFGHIJKLMNOPQRSTUVWXYZ
1234567890 .,:;-?!¿¡

Medium

ABCDEFGHIJKLMNOPQRSTUVWXYZ
1234567890 .,:;-?!¿¡

Bold

ABCDEFGHIJKLMNOOPQRSTUV
WXYZ 1234567890 .,:;-?!¿¡

VALENCIA

BOLOGNA

PARIS

Flash ND

Enric Crous Vidal
1953

GRAFÍA LATINA

ABCDEFGHIJKLMNOOPQRSTUV
WXYZ 1234567890 .,:;-?!¿¡

Arabescos ND

Enric Crous Vidal
1954

GRAFÍA LATINA

588   sales@neufville.com

Stage

ABCDEFGHIJKLMNOPQRSTUVW
XYZ abcdefghijklmnopqrstu
vwxyz 1234567890 -.,:;?!¿¡

Ilerda

Enric Crous Vidal
1945

GRAFÍA LATINA

W841
youth

ABCDEFGHIJKLMNOPQ
RSTUVWXYZ abcdefghij
klmnopqrstuvwxyz 1234
567890 €$¥ -.,:;?!¿¡

Gaudí ND

Ricard Girald Miracle
1962

GRAFÍA LATINA

MIDKAP

ABCDEFGHIJKLMNOPQRSTUV
WXYZ 1234567890 &$ -.,:;?!¿¡

Diagonal ND

Antoni Morillas
1970

GRAFÍA LATINA

NOVICE
NOVICE

abcdefghijklmnopqrst
uvwxyz 1234567890 €$£ -?!

Uncial Romana ND

Ricardo Rousselot
1996

GRAFÍA LATINA

def

abcdefghijklmnopqr
stuvwxyz abcdefghijklm
nopqrstuvwxyz 1234567890
& €$£ (~.,:;?!¿¡)

CarloMagno ND

Ricardo Rousselot
1997

GRAFÍA LATINA

Character sets supported:
· Windows Latin 1 · MacRoman

Features:
· Old Style Figures
· Genuine Small Caps
· Expert set containing special
  characters and ligatures

Unicode® v3.0 compliant

Aa OsF Light
abcdefghijklmopqrstuvwxyz ABCDEFGHIJKLMNOPQRST UVWXYZ   0123456789   ([{&:;.,!?¿¡*%}]) €$¢£¥ƒ   CHChch fifl

Aa OsF Light Italic
abcdefghijklmopqrstuvwxyz ABCDEFGHIJKLMNOPQRST UVWXYZ 0123456789 ([{&:;.,!?¿¡*%}]) €$¢£¥ƒ CHChchfifl

Aa SC Light
ABCDEFGHIJKLMOPQRSTUVWXYZ ABCDEFGHIJKLMNOPQRST UVWXYZ   0123456789   ([{&:;.,!?¿¡*%}]) €$¢£¥ƒ   CHChch fifl

Aa OsF Regular
abcdefghijklmopqrstuvwxyz ABCDEFGHIJKLMNOPQRST UVWXYZ   0123456789   ([{&:;.,!?¿¡*%}]) €$¢£¥ƒ   CHChch fifl

Aa OsF Regular Italic
abcdefghijklmopqrstuvwxyz ABCDEFGHIJKLMNOPQRST UVWXYZ 0123456789 ([{&:;.,!?¿¡*%}]) €$¢£¥ƒ CHChchfifl

Aa SC Regular
ABCDEFGHIJKLMOPQRSTUVWXYZ ABCDEFGHIJKLMNOPQRST UVWXYZ   0123456789   ([{&:;.,!?¿¡*%}]) €$¢£¥ƒ   CHChch fifl

Aa OsF Regular 8 pnt
El sosiego, el lugar apacible, la amenidad de los campos, la serenidad de los cielos, el murmurar de las fuentes, la quietud del espíritu son grande parte para que las musas más estériles se muestren fecundas y ofrezcan partos al mundo que le colmen de maravilla y de contento. Acontece tener un padre un hijo feo y sin gracia alguna, y el amor que le tiene le pone una venda en los ojos para que no vea sus faltas, antes

Cc OsF Regular 8 pnt
El sosiego, el lugar apacible, la amenidad de los campos, la serenidad de los cielos, el murmurar de las fuentes, la quietud del espíritu son grande parte para que las musas más estériles se muestren fecundas y ofrezcan partos al mundo que le colmen de maravilla y de contento. Acontece tener un padre un hijo feo y sin gracia alguna, y el amor que le tiene le pone una venda en los ojos para que no vea sus faltas, antes las juzga por discreciones y lindezas y las cuenta a sus amigos por agudezas y donaires. Pero yo, que,

Ee OsF Regular 8 pnt
El sosiego, el lugar apacible, la amenidad de los campos, la serenidad de los cielos, el murmurar de las fuentes, la quietud del espíritu son grande parte para que las musas más estériles se muestren fecundas y ofrezcan partos al mundo que le colmen de maravilla y de contento. Acontece tener un padre un hijo feo y sin gracia alguna, y el amor que le tiene le pone una venda en los ojos para que no vea sus faltas, antes las juzga por discreciones y lindezas y las cuenta a sus amigos por agudezas y donaires. Pero yo, que, aunque parezco padre, soy padrastro de Don Quijote, no quiero irme con la corriente del uso, ni

Fontana ND

Rubén Fontana
2001

MODERN COLLECTION
Sistema Fontana: Body Text fonts
-Cc

Character sets supported:
· Windows Latin 1 · MacRoman

Features:
· Old Style Figures
· Genuine Small Caps
· Expert set containing special
  characters and ligatures

Unicode® v3.0 compliant

Cc OsF Light

abcdefghijklmopqrstuvwxyz ABCDEFGHIJKLMNOPQRST
UVWXYZ 0123456789 ([{&:;.,!?¿¡*%}]) €$¢£¥ƒ CHChch fifl

Cc SC Light

ABCDEFGHIJKLMOPQRSTUVWXYZ ABCDEFGHIJKLMNOPQRST
UVWXYZ 0123456789 ([{&:;.,!?¿¡*%}]) €$¢£¥ƒ CHChch

Cc OsF Regular

abcdefghijklmopqrstuvwxyz ABCDEFGHIJKLMNOPQRST
UVWXYZ 0123456789 ([{&:;.,!?¿¡*%}]) €$¢£¥ƒ CHChch fifl

Cc SC Regular

ABCDEFGHIJKLMOPQRSTUVWXYZ ABCDEFGHIJKLMNOPQRST
UVWXYZ 0123456789 ([{&:;.,!?¿¡*%}]) €$¢£¥ƒ CHChch

Cc OsF Semibold

abcdefghijklmopqrstuvwxyz ABCDEFGHIJKLMNOPQRST
UVWXYZ 0123456789 ([{&:;.,!?¿¡*%}]) €$¢£¥ƒ CHChch fifl

Cc OsF Semibold Italic

abcdefghijklmopqrstuvwxyz ABCDEFGHIJKLMNOPQRST
UVWXYZ 0123456789 ([{&:;.,!?¿¡%}]) €$¢£¥ƒ CHChchfifl*

Cc SC Semibold

ABCDEFGHIJKLMOPQRSTUVWXYZ ABCDEFGHIJKLMNOPQRST
UVWXYZ 0123456789 ([{&:;.,!?¿¡*%}]) €$¢£¥ƒ CHChch fifl

Fontana ND

Rubén Fontana
2001

MODERN COLLECTION
Sistema Fontana: Body Text fonts
-Ee

Ee SC Light

ABCDEFGHIJKLMOPQRSTUVWXYZ ABCDEFGHIJKLMNOPQRST
UVWXYZ 0123456789 ([{&:;.,!?¿¡*%}]) €$¢£¥ƒCHChch

Rubén Fontana
2001

MODERN COLLECTION
Sistema Fontana: Body Text fonts
-Ee

Character sets supported:
· Windows Latin 1 · MacRoman

Features:
· Old Style Figures
· Genuine Small Caps
· Expert set containing special
  characters and ligatures

Unicode® v3.0 compliant

Ee OsF Light

abcdefghijklmopqrstuvwxyz ABCDEFGHIJKLMNOPQRST
UVWXYZ 0123456789 ([{&:;.,!?¿¡*%}]) €$¢£¥ƒ CHChch fifl

Ee OsF Regular

abcdefghijklmopqrstuvwxyz ABCDEFGHIJKLMNOPQRST
UVWXYZ 0123456789 ([{&:;.,!?¿¡*%}]) €$¢£¥ƒ CHChch fifl

Ee SC Regular

ABCDEFGHIJKLMOPQRSTUVWXYZ ABCDEFGHIJKLMNOPQRST
UVWXYZ 0123456789 ([{&:;.,!?¿¡*%}]) €$¢£¥ƒ CHCHCH

Ee OsF Semibold

abcdefghijklmopqrstuvwxyz ABCDEFGHIJKLMNOPQRST
UVWXYZ 0123456789 ([{&:;.,!?¿¡*%}]) €$¢£¥ƒ CHChch fifl

Ee SC Semibold

ABCDEFGHIJKLMOPQRSTUVWXYZ ABCDEFGHIJKLMNOPQRST
UVWXYZ 0123456789 ([{&:;.,!?¿¡*%}]) €$¢£¥ƒ CHCHCH

Ee OsF Bold

abcdefghijklmopqrstuvwxyz ABCDEFGHIJKLMNOPQRST
UVWXYZ 0123456789 ([{&:;.,!?¿¡*%}]) €$¢£¥ƒ CHChch fifl

Ee OsF Bold Italic

abcdefghijklmopqrstuvwxyz ABCDEFGHIJKLMNOPQRST
UVWXYZ 0123456789 ([{&:;.,!?¿¡%}]) €$¢£¥ƒ CHChchfifl*

Ee SC Bold

ABCDEFGHIJKLMOPQRSTUVWXYZ ABCDEFGHIJKLMNOPQRST
UVWXYZ 0123456789 ([{&:;.,!?¿¡*%}]) €$¢£¥ƒ CHCHCH

sales@neufville.com

Fontana ND

Rubén Fontana
2001

MODERN COLLECTION
Sistema Fontana: Titling fonts
-Gg

Character sets supported:
· Windows Latin 1 · MacRoman

Features:
· Expert set containing special
  characters and ligatures

Unicode® v3.0 compliant

Neufville Digital

Gg Regular

abcdefghijklmopqrstuvwxyz ABCDEFGHIJKLMNOPQRST
UVWXYZ   0123456789   ([{&:;,.!?¿¡*%}]) €$¢£¥f CHChch fifl

Gg Semibold

abcdefghijklmopqrstuvwxyz ABCDEFGHIJKLMNOPQRST
UVWXYZ   0123456789   ([{&:;,.!?¿¡*%}]) €$¢£¥f   CHChch fifl

Gg Bold

abcdefghijklmopqrstuvwxyz ABCDEFGHIJKLMNOPQRST
UVWXYZ   0123456789   ([{&:;,.!?¿¡*%}]) €$¢£¥f   CHChch fifl

Gg Black

abcdefghijklmopqrstuvwxyz ABCDEFGHIJKLMNOPQRST
UVWXYZ   0123456789   ([{&:;,.!?¿¡*%}]) €$¢£¥f   CHChch fifl

Gg Black Italic

abcdefghijklmopqrstuvwxyz ABCDEFGHIJKLMNOPQRST
UVWXYZ   0123456789   ([{&:;,.!?¿¡*%}]) €$¢£¥f   CHChchfifl

Fontana ND

Rubén Fontana
2001

MODERN COLLECTION
Sistema Fontana: Titling fonts
-Ll

Character sets supported:
· Windows Latin 1 · MacRoman

Features:
· Expert set containing special
  characters and ligatures

Unicode® v3.0 compliant

Ll Semibold

abcdefghijklmopqrstuvwxyz ABCDEFGHIJKLMNOPQRST
UVWXYZ   0123456789   ([{&:;,.!?¿¡*%}]) €$¢£¥f   CHChch fifl

Ll Bold

abcdefghijklmopqrstuvwxyz ABCDEFGHIJKLMNOPQRST
UVWXYZ   0123456789   ([{&:;,.!?¿¡*%}]) €$¢£¥f   CHChch fifl

Ll Black

abcdefghijklmopqrstuvwxyz ABCDEFGHIJKLMNOPQRST
UVWXYZ   0123456789   ([{&:;,.!?¿¡*%}]) €$¢£¥f   CHChch fifl

Character sets supported:
· Windows Latin 1 · MacRoman
· Turkish · CE · Baltic

Features:
· Old Style Figures
· Genuine Small Caps

Unicode® v3.0 compliant

Light
abcdefghijklmopqrstuvwxyz ABCDEFGHIJKLMNOPQR STUVWXYZ 0123456789 ([{&:;.,!?¿¡*%}]) €$¢£¥ƒ

Light Italic
abcdefghijklmopqrstuvwxyz ABCDEFGHIJKLMNOPQR STUVWXYZ 0123456789 ([{&:;.,!?¿¡*%}]) €$¢£¥ƒ

Regular
abcdefghijklmopqrstuvwxyz ABCDEFGHIJKLMNOPQR STUVWXYZ 0123456789 ([{&:;.,!?¿¡*%}]) €$¢£¥ƒ

Italic
abcdefghijklmopqrstuvwxyz ABCDEFGHIJKLMNOPQR STUVWXYZ 0123456789 ([{&:;.,!?¿¡*%}]) €$¢£¥ƒ

Bold
abcdefghijklmopqrstuvwxyz ABCDEFGHIJKLMNOPQR STUVWXYZ 0123456789 ([{&:;.,!?¿¡*%}]) €$¢£¥ƒ

Bold Italic
abcdefghijklmopqrstuvwxyz ABCDEFGHIJKLMNOPQR STUVWXYZ 0123456789 ([{&:;.,!?¿¡*%}]) €$¢£¥ƒ

Heavy
abcdefghijklmopqrstuvwxyz ABCDEFGHIJKLMNOPQR STUVWXYZ 0123456789 ([{&:;.,!?¿¡*%}]) €$¢£¥ƒ

Heavy Italic
abcdefghijklmopqrstuvwxyz ABCDEFGHIJKLMNOPQR STUVWXYZ 0123456789 ([{&:;.,!?¿¡*%}]) €$¢£¥ƒ

Pragma ND

Christopher Burke
2001

MODERN COLLECTION

Character sets supported:
· Windows Latin 1 · MacRoman
· Turkish · CE · Baltic

Features:
· Old Style Figures
· Genuine Small Caps

Unicode® v3.0 compliant

Neufville Digital

SCOsF Light

ABCDEGHIJKLMOPQR
STUWXYZ ABCDEG
HIJKLMOPQRSTU
0123456789
([{&:;.,!?¿i*%}])

SCOsF Light Italic

ABCDEGHIJKLMOPQR
STUWXYZ ABCDEG
HIJKLMOPQRSTU
0123456789
([{&:;.,!?¿i*%}])

Light

Dès le départ, un caractère destiné à la composition mécanique était dessiné à grande échelle pour être ensuite reporté sur plomb à l'aide d'un pantographe réducteur. Tout ce qui jusque-là faisait l'objet de nombreuses retouches manuelles de la part d'un graveur qui travaillait à son idée et selon son expérience, TOUT CELA AURAIT DÛ SE FAIRE DÈS LES DESSINS PRÉALABLES À TOUTE PRODUCTION. C'EST CE QUI NE S'EST PASSÉ. POUR

SCOsF Regular

ABCDEGHIJKLMOPQR
STUWXYZ ABCDEG
HIJKLMOPQRSTU
0123456789
([{&:;.,!?¿i*%}])

SCOsF Regular Italic

ABCDEGHIJKLMOPQR
STUWXYZ ABCDEG
HIJKLMOPQRSTU
0123456789
([{&:;.,!?¿i*%}])

Regular

Dès le départ, un caractère destiné à la composition mécanique était dessiné à grande échelle pour être ensuite reporté sur plomb à l'aide d'un pantographe réducteur. Tout ce qui jusque-là faisait l'objet de nombreuses retouches manuelles de la part d'un graveur qui travaillait à son idée et selon son EXPÉRIENCE, TOUT CELA AURAIT DÛ SE FAIRE DÈS LES DESSINS PRÉALABLES À TOUTE PRODUCTION. C'EST CE QUI NE

SCOsF Bold

ABCDEGHIJKLMOPQ
RSTUWXYZ ABCEG
HJKLMOPQRSTU
0123456789
([{&:;.,!?¿i*%}])

SCOsF Bold Italic

ABCDEGHIJKLMOPQ
RSTUWXYZ ABCEG
HJKLMOPQRSTU
0123456789
([{&:;.,!?¿i*%}])

Bold

Dès le départ, un caractère destiné à la composition mécanique était dessiné à grande échelle pour être ensuite reporté sur plomb à l'aide d'un pantographe réducteur. Tout ce qui jusque-là faisait l'objet de nombreuses retouches manuelles de la part d'un graveur qui travaillait à son IDÉE ET SELON SON EXPÉRIENCE, TOUT CELA AURAIT DÛ SE FAIRE DÈS LES DESSINS PRÉALABLES À TOUTE PRODUC-

SCOsF Heavy

ABCDEGHIJKLMPQR
STUWXYZ ABCEG
HJKLMOPQRSTU
0123456789
([{&:;.,!?¿i*%}])

SCOsF Heavy Italic

ABCDEGHIJKLMPQR
STUWXYZ ABCEG
HJKLMOPQRSTU
0123456789
([{&:;.,!?¿i*%}])

Heavy

Dès le départ, un caractère destiné à la composition mécanique était dessiné à grande échelle pour être ensuite reporté sur plomb à l'aide d'un pantographe réducteur. Tout ce qui jusque-là faisait l'objet de nombreuses retouches manuelles de la part d'un graveur qui travaillait à SON IDÉE ET SELON SON EXPÉRIENCE, TOUT CELA AURAIT DÛ SE FAIRE DÈS LES DESSINS PRÉALABLES À TOUTE

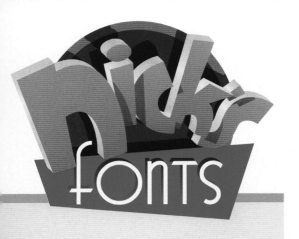

"I would attribute my love of the letterforms of yesteryear to a youth misspent hanging around in too many libraries," says award-winning type designer Nick Curtis. "As a kid, I would spend hours wandering through the stacks, devouring volumes on Currier and Ives prints, silent movies, and other visual expressions of earlier popular culture."

Nick's interest in typography began around age 13 with his discovery of a type specimen book a neighbor had discarded — a big, fat green binder filled with hundreds of fonts. Thereafter, his personal art projects were adorned with handlettering patterned after several of those fonts. Later, his influences expanded to include, among others, Push Pin Studio and the San Francisco rock poster movement.

Professionally, Nick has worked as an art director in advertising agencies, an a/v production company, and broadcast television. "In the early 80s, TV was on the leading edge of what passed for computer graphics at the time. I was fortunate enough to be at the right place at the right time to develop the technical skills that I still use to create electronic type."

Nick began creating freeware fonts in 1997, and expanded into producing commercial fonts in 2001. Two of his commercial releases that year, Jeepers ITC and Woodley Park, were recognized by the Type Directors Club as among the best new type designs of 2001. He adds to his collection of freeware fonts (now over 150) on a regular basis—available at www.nicksfonts.com—as well as his commercial endeavors (currently over 100).

Nick currently resides in the Washington, DC area, where he still hangs around in libraries. He is a registered researcher at the Library of Congress, and also regularly explores the vast virtual library that is the Internet, searching for more historical letterforms to revive and reintroduce to the world.

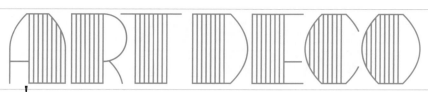

ABCDEFGHIJKLMNOPQRSTUVWXYZabcde
fghijklmnopqrstuvwxyz0123456789!?&$£¥ ÆDOÞ æßðøþ

Astoria Titling NF

Nick Curtis
2001

Influenced by Joan Trochut Blanchard, Gus Oring and Paul Carlyle.

ABCDEFGHIJKLMNOPQRSTUVWXYZABCDEFGH
IJKLMNOPQRSTUVWXYZ0123456789!?&$¢£€

Big Tent Players NF

Nick Curtis
2002

ABCDEFGHIJKLMNOPQRST
UVWXYZ0123456789!?&$¢

Boogaloo Boulevard NF

Nick Curtis
2002

Based on Harold Holland Day's version of Broadway.

ABCDEFGHIJKLMNOPQRSTUVW
XYZabcdefghijklmnopqrstuvwxyz0123

Day Tripper NF

Nick Curtis
2002

Based on Dignity Roman by Alphonso E. Tripp.

ABCDEFGHIJKLMNOPQRSTUVWXYZabcdefg
hijklmnopqrstuvwxyz0123456789!?&$¢£

Fifth Avenue Salon NF

Nick Curtis
2002

FIVE AND DIME

ABCDEFGHIJKLMNOPQRSTUVWXYZ01234567

Five and Dime NF

Nick Curtis
2002

An architectural font, great for simulating old signs.

Nick's Fonts

Gotham Rail Company NF

Nick Curtis
2002

ABCDEFGHIJKLMNOPQRSTUVWXYZA
BCDEFGHIJKLMNOPQRSTUVWXYZ012

Joost a Gigolo NF

Nick Curtis
2002

Based on the work of Dutch
comic-book artist Joost Swarte.

ABCDEFGHIJKLMNOPQR
STUVWXYZ0123456789!

La Moda NF

Nick Curtis
2002

ABCDEFGHIJKLMNOPQRSTUV
WXYZ*abcdefghijklmnopqrst*

Lance Corporal NF

Nick Curtis
2002

ABCDEFGHIJKLMNOPQRSTUV
WXYZABCDEFGHIJKLMNOPQR

Mesa Verde NF

Nick Curtis
2002

ABCDEFGHIJKLMNOPQRST
UVWXYZABCDEFGHIJKLMNO

Modern Art NF

Nick Curtis
2002

Based on the work of Dutch
comic-book artist Joost Swarte.

MODERNART
ABCDEFGHIJKLMNOPQRSTU
VWXYZ0123456789!?£-¢¥

Monte Casino NF

Nick Curtis
2002

ABCDEFGHIJKLMNOPQRSTUVW
XYZM0123456789!?&$¢€¥ÆÐ

himself@nicksfonts.com

ABCDEFGHIJKLMNOPQRSTUVWXYZO1
23456789!?&$¢£¥ÆŒØPÆßĐØÞ

Normal

ABCDEFGHIJKLMNOPQRSTUVWXYZ
0123456789!?&$¢£¥ÆŒØPÆßĐØ

Bold

ABCDEFGHIJKLMNOPQRSTUVWXYZabcdefghijklmnopq
rstuvwxyz0123456789!?&$¢£¥ÆŒØÞæßðøþ

Round Bold

ABCDEFGHIJKLMNOPQRSTUVWXYZabcdefghijklmnopqrstuvw

Square Extralight

ABCDEFGHIJKLMNOPQRSTUVW

Square Light

ABCDEFGHIJKLMNOPQRSTUVW

Square Normal

ABCDEFGHIJKLMNOPQRSTUVW

Square Bold

ABCDEFGHIJKLMNOPQRSTUVWXYZabcdef
ghijklmnopqrstuvwxyz0123456789!?&$

Oldstyle

Rocketman XV-7 NF

Nick Curtis
2001

ABCDEFGHIJKLMNOPQRSTU
VWXYZabcdefghijklmnopqr

Sabrina Zaftig NF

Nick Curtis
2002

ABCDEFGHIJKLMNO
PQRSTUVWXYZ01234567

Wagner Silhouette NF

Nick Curtis
2002

ABCDEFGHIJKLMNOPQRS
TUVWXYZabcdefghijklmnopqr

Washington Square NF

Nick Curtis
2002

ABCDEFGHIJKLMNO
PQRSTUVWXYZabcdefghijkl
mnopqrstuvwxyz0123456789!?&$¢£¥

White Tie Affair NF

Nick Curtis
2002

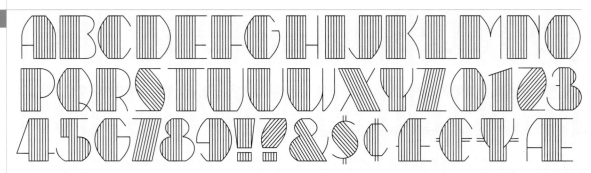

ABCDEFGHIJKLMNO
PQRSTUVWXYZ0123
456789!?&$¢£¥Æ

CLASSIC

ABCDEFGHIJKLMNOP
QRSTUVWXYZabcdefghijklmnopqrstu
vwxyz0123456789!?& $¢£¥ÆÐØÞæß

Londonderry Air NF

Nick Curtis
2002

Based on the old ATF font Canterbury.

ABCDEFGHIJKLMNOPQRSTUVW
XYZ0123456789!?&$¢£¥ÆÐØÞÆ

Persephone NF

Nick Curtis
2002

Based on the old ATF font Pericles.

ABCDEFGHIJKLMNOPQRSTUWXYZ
ÆGO0123456789!?&$¢£¥ÆÐØÞÆSS

Quadrivium NF

Nick Curtis
2002

Based on Weiss Initials II by Rudolph Weiss.

ABCDEFGHIJKLMNOPQRSTUVWX
YZabcdefghijklmnopqrstuvwxyz0123
456789!?@$¢£¥§†‡ÇÆÐØÞæßðøþ

Saturday Morning Toast NF

Nick Curtis
2001

Based on the old logotype font for *The Saturday Evening Post*.

ABCDEFGHIJKLK
LMNOPQRSTUV
WXYZabcdefghijkl
lmnopqrstuvwxyz
0123456789!?&$¢£

Slam Bang Theater NF

Nick Curtis
2002

Based on ATF Nubian, designed by Willard T. Sniffin..

DECORATIVE

Annabelle Matinee NF

Nick Curtis
2002

ABCDEFGHIJKLMNO
PQRSTUVWXYZabcdefgh
ijklmnopqrstuvwxyz012345
6789!?&$¢£€¥ÆŒØÞ æß

Bessie Mae Moocho NF

Nick Curtis
2002

ABCDEFGHIJKLMNOPQRST
UVWXYZ0123456789!?&$¢

Bo Diddlioni Stencil NF

Nick Curtis
2001

ABCDEFGHIJKLMNOPQRSTUVWXY
Zabcdefghijklmnopqrstuvwxyz012345 6

Cambridge Pinstripe NF

Nick Curtis
2002

abcdefghijklmnopqrstuvwxyz
0123456789!?&$¢£€¥ÆŒØÞß

Foo Bar Inline NF

Nick Curtis
2002

Based on the Supertipo Veloz
series by Joan Trochut
Blanchard.

ABCDEFGHIJKLMNOPQRSTUVWXYZ
0123456789!?&$¢£€¥ÆŒØÞß

Marrakesh Express NF

Nick Curtis
2002

ABCDEFGHIJKLMNOPQRS
TUVWXYZ0123456789!?&$¢

ABCDEFGHIJKLMNOPQRSTUVWX
YZabcdefghijklmnopqrstuvwxyz&

Metro Retro Redux NF

Nick Curtis

2001

Based on the typeface
Modernistic, designed by
Wadsworth A. Parker.

ABCDEFGHIJKLMNOPQRSTUVWXYZ
0123456789!?&$¢£¥ÆÐØÞÆSÐØÞ

Olbrich Display NF

Nick Curtis

2002

Based on poster lettering by
Joseph Maria Olbrich.

ABCDEFGHIJKLMNOP
QRSTUVWXYZ!?†01

Partager Caps NF

Nick Curtis

2002

ABCDEFGHIJKLMNOPQR
STUVWXYZ0123456789!

Robot Monster NF

Nick Curtis

2001

ABCDEFGHIJKLMNOPQRSTUVWXYZZ0123
456789!?&$¶¶¶S¢£¥µ¶ÆÐØÆSÐØÞ

Super Bob Triline NF

Nick Curtis

2001

Based on the Supertipo Veloz
series by Joan Trochut
Blanchard.

ABCDEFGHIJKLMNOPQRSTUVWXYZ
ABCDEFGHIJKLMNOPQRSTUVWXYZ012
3456789!?&$¢£¥ÆÐØÞ ÆSÐØÞ

Toonerville NF

Nick Curtis

2002

ABCDEFGHIJKLMNOPQRSTUV
WXYZS0123456789!?&$¢£€

Ziggy Stardust NF

Nick Curtis

2002

Nick's Fonts

Handlettering

Bergling Fantasia NF

Nick Curtis
2002

Based on handlettering by
J. M. Bergling

ABCDEFGHIJKLMNOPQRSTUVWXYZ.ab
cdefghijklmnopqrstuvwxyz0123456789!?

Bergling Fantasia Bold NF

Nick Curtis
2002

Based on handlettering by
J. M. Bergling

ABCDEFGHIJKLMNOPQRSTUVWXYZa
bcdefghijklmnopqrstuvwxyz0123456789

Bundle of Joy NF

Nick Curtis
2002

Based on handlettering by
Australian lettering artist
C. Milne

ABCDEFGHIJKLMNOPQRSTUVWX
YZabcdefghijklmnopqrstuvwxyz

Duffy's Tavern NF

Nick Curtis
2002

Based on handlettering by
E. C. Matthews.

ABCDEFGHIJKLMNOPQRSTUVWX
YZabcdefghijklmnopqrstuvwxyz012345

East Coast Frolics NF

Nick Curtis
2002

ABCDEFGHIJKLMNOPQRSTUVWX
YZabcdefghijklmnopqrstuvwxyz01

Erehwon Roman NF

Nick Curtis
2002

Based on handlettering by
J. M. Bergling.

ABCDEFGHIJKLMNOPQRST
UVWXYZabcdefghijklmnopqrstuvwx

Gasoline Alley NF

Nick Curtis
2002

Based on handlettering by
Albanis Ashmun Kelly, 1911.

ABCDEFGHIJKLMNOPQRSTU
VWXYZabcdefghijklmnopqrstuvwxy

ABCDEFGHIJKLMNOPQRSTUVWXYZabc
defghijklmnopqrstuvwxyz&01234567 8

Heberling Casual NF

Nick Curtis
2002

Based on handlettering by
Walter A. Heberling, 1922.

ABCDEFGHIJKLMNOPQRSTUVWXYZab
cdefghijklmnopqrstuvwxyz&0123456

Heberling Casual Bold NF

Nick Curtis
2002

ABCDEFGHIJKLMNOPQRSTUVWX
YZABCDEFGHIJKLMNOPQRSTUVWXYZ

Magic Lantern SW

Nick Curtis
2001

Based on handlettering by
Samuel Welo.

ABCDEFGHIJKLMNOPQRSTUVWX
YZabcdefghijklmnopqrstuvwxyz&0123

Mrs. Bathhurst FGC

Nick Curtis
2001

Based on handlettering by
Fred G. Cooper.

ABCDEFGHIJKLMNOPQRSTUV
WXYZabcdefghijklmnopqrstuvwxy

Roman Holiday Xbold NF

Nick Curtis
2001

ABCDEFGHIJKLMNOPQRSTUVWXYZ
abcdefghijklmnopqrstuvwxyz&01234

Speedball No. 1 NF

Nick Curtis
2002

Based on handlettering by
Samuel Welo.

ABCDEFGHIJKLMNOPQRS
TUVWXYZabcdefghijklmnopqrst
uvwxyz&0123456789!?$¢£€

Strongs Draughtsman NF

Nick Curtis
2001

Based on handlettering by
Lawrence Strong, ca. 1910

Nick's Fonts

Thimble Theatre NF *Nick Curtis* 2001 Based on handlettering by J. M. Bergling.	ABCDEFGHIJKLMNOPQRSTUV WXYZabcdefghijklmnopqrstuv
WHG Simpatico NF *Nick Curtis* 2002 Based on handlettering by William Hugh Gordon.	ABCDEFGHIJKLMNOPQRSTUVWXY Zabcdefghijklmnopqrstuvwxyz012345678
Whoopee Cushion SW *Nick Curtis* 2002 Based on handlettering by Samuel Welo.	ABCDEFGHIJKLMNOPQRS TUVWXYZabcdefghijklmnop
Wigwam HB *Nick Curtis* 2001 Based on handlettering by Ed and Ben Hunt.	ABCDEFGHIJKLMNOPQRSTUVWX YZABCDEFGHIJKLMNOPQRSTUVWXYZOI

All Nick's Fonts have extensive kerning, carefully and thoughtfully applied by hand.

himself@nicksfonts.com

Scripts

ABCDEFGHIJKLMNOPQRST
UVWXYZabcdefghijklmn
opqrstuvwxyz&012345678

Artemisia NF

Nick Curtis
2002

Based on Adonis by ATF.

ABCDEFGHIJKLMNOPQR
STUVWXYZabcdefghijklmn
opqrstuvwxyz&0123456789$

MargaritaVille NF

Nick Curtis
2001

ABCDEFGHIJKLMN
OPQRSTUVWXYZabcdefghi
jklmnopqrstuvwxyz&0123456789$¢

Monte Carlo Script NF

Nick Curtis
2002

Based on Médicis Script by
Deberny & Peignot.

ABCDEFGHIJKLMNOPQRSTUVW
XYZabcdefghijklmnopqrstuvwxyz&0123

Thai Foon HB NF

Nick Curtis
2001

Based on handlettering by
Ed & Ben Hunt.

Character Sets

All Nick's Fonts have complete Adobe character sets, plus the Euro symbol.

!."#$%&'()*+,-./0123456789:

;<=>?@ABCDEFGHIJKLM

NOPQ RSTUVWXYZ[\]^

_ `abcdefghijklmnopq rstuv

wxyz{|}~‚ƒ„…†‡ˆ‰Š‹Œ''""•—

—˜™š›œŸ¡¢£€¥¦§¨©ª«¬—®¯°

±²³´µ¶·¸¹º»¼½¾¿ÀÁÂÃÄÅ

ÆÇÈÉÊËÌÍÎÏÐÑÒÓÔÕÖ×Ø

ÙÚÛÜÝÞßàáâãäåæçèéêëìíî

ïðñòóôõö÷øùúûüýþÿ˘˙˚˝˛˘˙

Additional Macintosh characters

ŁłŽž≠∞≤≥µ∂∑∏π∫Ω

√≅Δ◊/⌘fifl

Text

ABCDEFGHIJKLMNOPQRSTUVWX
YZabcdefghijklmnopqrstuvwxyz&01234567
89$ƒ†‡¢£€¥!?ÆÐØÞßæðøþ™§©®µ¶

Normal

ABCDEFGHIJKLMNOPQRSTUVWXYZ
abcdefghijklmnopqrstuvwxyz&0123456789$ƒ
†‡¢£€¥!?ÆÐØÞßæðøþ™§©®µ¶

Normal Italic

ABCDEFGHIJKLMNOPQRSTUVWX
YZabcdefghijklmnopqrstuvwxyz&0123456
789$ƒ†‡¢£€¥!?ÆÐØÞßæðøþ™§©®µ¶

Bold

ABCDEFGHIJKLMNOPQRSTUVWXY
Zabcdefghijklmnopqrstuvwxyz&0123456789$
ƒ†‡¢£€¥!?ÆÐØÞßæðøþ™§©®µ¶

Bold Italic

McKenna Handletter NF

Nick Curtis
2002

Based on the eponymous text face designed by Elizabeth Colwell.

Nick's Fonts

WOODTYPE

Brazos WBW Extrabold

Nick Curtis
2001

ABCDEFGHIJKLMNOPQRST
UVWXYZABCDEFGHIJKLMNOP
QRSTUVWXYZ0123456789!?

Dime Box WBW

Nick Curtis
2001

ABCDEFGHIJKLMNOPQRS
TUVWXYZ0123456789!?

Gullywasher WBW

Nick Curtis
2001

ABCDEFGHIJKLMNOPQRSTUV
WXYZ0123456789!?&$¢£€ Æ

Jefferson Pilot WBW

Nick Curtis
2001

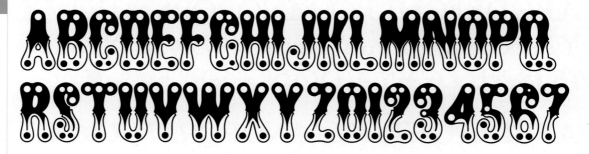

Laguna Madre WBW

Nick Curtis
2001

ABCDEFGHIJKLMNOPQRSTUVWXYZabc
defghijklmnopqrstuvwxyz0123456789!?&

ABCDEFGHIJKLMNOPQ
RSTUVWXYZ0123456789

Ouachita Way WBW

Nick Curtis
2001

ABCDEFGHIJKLMNOPQRST
UVWXYZABCDEFGHIJKLMNOP

Ozymadias Outline WBW

Nick Curtis
2001

ABCDEFGHIJKLMNOPQRS
TUVWXYZ0123456789!?

Ozymandias Solid WBW

Nick Curtis
2001

ABCDEFGHIJKLMNOPQRSTUVWX
YZ0123456789!?&$¢£¥ÆÐØÞÆSS

Pilot Point WBW

Nick Curtis
2001

ABCDEFGHIJKLMNOPQRSTUV
WXYZabcdefghijklmnopqrstuvw

Rio Grande WBW

Nick Curtis
2001

ABCDEFGHIJKLMNOPQ
RSTUVWXYZabcdefghijkl

Spaghetti Western WBW

Nick Curtis
2001

ABCDEFGHIJKLMNOPQRSTUVWXYZ012
3456789!?&$ƒ†‡$¶¢£¥©®ÆÐØÞSS

Spindletop WBW

Nick Curtis
2001

Nick's Fonts

I felt bad because I had no shoes until I met a man who had no Bodoni

No Bodoni Typography
http://www.nobodoni.com
support@nobodoni.com

No Bodoni is a small, independent type design company, inspired by Giambattista Bodoni's dedication and drive to create unique types for his time. No Bodoni believes that a typeface is a functional aesthetic object, designed to signify—rather than represent—meaning, emotion and belief. Typefaces are transcendent as well as historical and cultural. They not only carry information about the text they represent, but about the designer who uses them, the culture they come from, and commentary about the medium of typography itself.

No Bodoni's types are not the tired revivals of standard classics, nor smudged, degraded letterforms missing half the character set. They are not mere fonts, but unique, usable types that are personal responses to putting information on a page.

No Bodoni Typography is a project of George Everet(t) Thompson.

No Bodoni typefaces are available from Myfonts.com

ITC Oldrichium is available from the International Typeface Corp.

www.itcfonts.com

Claudium

AåBbÇçDdÈÉFfGgHhIiJjKkLlMmÑñÖÔP
pQqRrSsTtÛüVvWwXxYyZz&{}()[]«€1
23456789»$¢£¥%‰?!¿¡.,:;*"'/'"¶‹ŒœØø
Æœfiflß›°·@©®™ ſ∫≠≤-›÷=±‹+≥≈ᵒª·§‡†

Claudium Bold

ÅBÇDÈFGHÍJKMÑÖPQRSTÛVWXYZã
bçdêfghijklmnòpqrstúvwxyz&{}()[]
«€123456789»$¢£¥%‰?!¿j.,:;*"'/'"¶
‹ŒœØøÆœfiflß›°·@©®™

Claudium Italic

ÅBÇDÈFGHIJKLMÑÔPQRSTÜVWXYZ
åbçdèfghíjklmñöpqrstûvwxyz&{}()
[]«€123456789»$¢£¥%‰?!¿j.,:;*"'/'"¶
‹ŒœØøÆœfiflß›°·@©®™

Claudium

George Everet(t) Thompson
2002

Claudium started as an attempt to create a sans serif version of Garamond, but as time went on, it became a meditation on the nature of French typography from Garamond to Excoffon. A cursive italic was designed, based in Garamond's Greek forms. The original drawings were done in marker on tracing paper with about a nine inch body height. This was done to make them as gestural and flowing as possible. Only the lowercase italic letters were designed and then mated to the Regular caps like Griffo's original italic.

No Bodoni

Claudium 11/12

In 1833, John Calhoun came from Buffalo, New York, to become the first printer in Chicago. Calhoun had heard about the boom in Chicago from a friend, and so he shipped printing equipment from Buffalo, then followed by boat. His boat was run

Claudium Bold 11/12

In 1833, John Calhoun came from Buffalo, New York, to become the first printer in Chicago. Calhoun had heard about the boom in Chicago from a friend, and so he shipped printing equipment from Buffalo, then followed by boat.

Claudium Italic 11/12

In 1833, John Calhoun came from Buffalo, New York, to become the first printer in Chicago. Calhoun had heard about the boom in Chicago from a friend, and so he shipped his printing equipment from Buffalo,

George Everet(t) Thompson
2001

ITC Oldrichium is based on the calligraphy and typefaces of Czech designer Oldrich Menhart. I'm very enamored of his work, especially his calligraphy, which is much looser and rougher than his type designs. I wanted to design a face with the spirit of both his type and his lettering. I lettered forms in Menhart's style, using his Manuscript face as a beginning guide. The resulting type was too calligraphic, so I redrew it and made the forms more styled. The incised version was based on his Parliament type, which is more elegant and less calligraphic than Oldrichium.

ITC Oldrichium Regular

åbçdèfghijklmñôpqrstüvwxyz1234567890.,:;?!¿¡[]{}()
ÅBÇÉDFGHÌJKLMÑÖPQRSTÛVWXYZæÆœŒfiflß

Pick-Up on Noon Street

A Carrot is as Close as a Rabbit Gets to a Diamond

ITC Oldrichium Demi Italic

åbçdèfghijklmñôpqrstüvwxyz1234567890.,:;?!¿¡[]{}()
ÅBÇÉDFGHÌJKLMÑÖPQRSTÛVWXYZæŒæÆfifl

ITC Oldrichium Light

åbçdèfghijklmñôpqrstüvwxyz1234567890.,:;?!¿¡[]{}()
ÅBÇÉDFGHÌJKLMÑÖPQRSTÛVWXYZæŒæÆfiflß

The Mothers of Invention

If on a winter's night a traveler

ITC Oldrichium Bold

åbçdèfghijklmñôpqrstüvwxyz1234567890.,:;?!¿¡[]()
ÅBÇÉDFGHÌJKLMÑÖPQRSTÛVWXYZæÆœŒfifl

Regular 11/12

In 1833, John Calhoun came from Buffalo, New York, to become the first printer in Chicago. Calhoun had heard about the boom in Chicago from a friend, and so he shipped his printing equipment from Buffalo, then followed by boat. His

Italic 11/12

In 1833, John Calhoun came from Buffalo, New York, to become the first printer in Chicago. Calhoun had heard about the boom in Chicago from a friend, and so he shipped printing equipment from New York, then followed by boat. His boat

Demi 11/12

In 1833, John Calhoun came from Buffalo, New York, to become the first printer in Chicago. Calhoun had heard about the boom in Chicago from a friend, and so he shipped his printing equipment from Buffalo, then followed by boat. His

ITC Oldrichium Italic

åbçdèfghijklmñôpqrstüvwxyz1234567890.,:;?!¿¡[]{}()
ÅBÇÉDFGHÌJKLMÑÖPQRSTÛVWXYZŒœÆæßflfi

ITC Oldrichium Demi

åbçdèfghijklmñôpqrstüvwxyz1234567890.,:;?!¿¡[]{}()
ÅBÇÉDFGHÌJKLMÑÖPQRSTÛVWXYZŒœÆæßfl

Captain Beefheart & His Magic Band
Trouble is My Business

ITC Oldrichium Light Italic

åbçdèfghijklmñôpqrstüvwxyz1234567890.,:;?!¿¡[]{}()
ÅBÇÉDFGHÌJKLMÑÖPQRSTÛVWXYZŒœÆæßflfi

ITC Oldrichium Engraved

åbçdèfghijklmñôpqrstüvwxyz1234567890.,:;?!¿¡[]
ÅBÇÉDFGHÌJKLMÑÖPQRSTÛVWXYZŒœÆæßfl

DM Bob & the Deficits
The Castle of Crossed Destinies

Demi Italic 11/12

In 1833, John Calhoun came from Buffalo, New York, to become the first printer in Chicago. Calhoun had heard about the boom in Chicago from a friend, and so he shipped printing equipment from Buffalo, then followed by boat. His boat was run

Light 11/12

In 1833, John Calhoun came from Buffalo, New York, to become the first printer in Chicago. Calhoun had heard about the boom in Chicago from a friend, and so he shipped printing equipment from Buffalo, then followed by boat. His boat was run

Light Italic 11/12

In 1833, John Calhoun came from Buffalo, New York, to become the first printer in Chicago. Calhoun had heard about the boom in Chicago from a friend, and so he shipped printing equipment from Buffalo, then followed by boat. His boat was run

Tinman

George Everet(t) Thompson
2002-2003

Tinman is a humanist sans based on Goudy's University of California Oldstyle.

Tinman

ABCDEFGHIJKLMNOPQRSTUVWXYZ?!&@
abcdefghijklmnopqrstuvwxyzl234567890()

Tinman Demibold

ABCDEFGHIJKLMNOPQRSTUVWXYZ?!&
abcdefghijklmnopqrstuvwxyz123456789

Tinman Bold

ABCDEFGHIJKLMNOPQRSTUVWXYZ&
abcdefghijklmnopqrstuvwxyzl23456789

Tinman, DemiBold, Bold

Largo Desolato
Largo Desolato
Largo Desolato
Eyes of a Blue Dog
Eyes of a Blue Dog
Eyes of a Blue Dog

Tinman Italic

ABCDEFGHIJKLMNOPQRSTUVWXYZ&()@
abcdefghijklmnopqrstuvwxyz1234567890?!

Tinman DemiBold Italic

ABCDEFGHIJKLMNOPQRSTUVWXYZ@
abcdefghijklmnopqrstuvwxyz01234567890

Tinman Bold Italic

ABCDEFGHIJKLMNOPQRSTUVWXYZ&@
abcdefghijklmnopqrstuvwxyz123456789?!

Tinman Italic, DemiBold Italic, Bold Italic

Largo Desolato

Largo Desolato

Largo Desolato

Eyes of a Blue Dog

Eyes of a Blue Dog

Eyes of a Blue Dog

Sleep Tickets

George Everet(t) Thompson
2002-2003

Sleep Tickets is a sans serif based on Georg Trump's Delphin which was based on Francesco Griffo's original italic. Griffo designed the italic only as a lowercase with no capitals, and used the Bembo capitals with it.

Sleep Tickets

ABCDEFGHIJKLMNOPQRSTUVWXYZ
abcdefghijklmnopqrstuvwxyz
1234567890

Sleep Tickets Bold

ABCDEFGHIJKLMNOPQRSTUVWXYZabcdefghijklmnopqrstuvwxyz
1234567890

Sleep Tickets

Life During Wartime

Yellow Back Radio Broke Down

Sleep Tickets Bold

Pattern Recognition

Tours of the Black Clock

support@nobodoni.com

Floridium

George Everet(t) Thompson
1999-2002

Floridium grew out of an affection for the old wood types of the 1800s. Painters Roman (Issued by both Page and Wells wood type companies. See *American Wood Type: 1828-1900* by Rob Roy Kelly for more information) was the initial inspiration. It was the source for the "banana" and "snake head" serifs. But the design, released by Adobe as Juniper, was too quirky to be very useful. I tried to create a type that was more sophisticated and modern, while keeping the original personality of the 19th century type. A bold weight and an italic, which weren't part of the original wood type, were designed as well.

DAVIES BROTHERS,
COAL AND WOOD,

162 East 23d Street,

And at the offices of the Mutual District Messenger Co.

COAL and WOOD put in your CELLAR at ONE HOUR'S NOTICE.

PRESENT PRICES, DECEMBER 1st, 1891

Lehigh Coal

Stove or Range,	-	-	-	$5.25
Nut,	5.25	Egg,	-	5.25
Furnace,	-	-	-	5.25
American Cannel	-	-	-	12.00
INCE HALL English Cannel,			-	16.00

Per ton of 2000 lbs., delivered on the Sidewalk

Floridium

ABCDEFGHIJKLMNOPQRSTUVWXYZ,.;:&@
abcdefghijklmnopqrstuvwxyz123456789

Floridium

ABCDEFGHIJKLMNOPQRSTUVWXYZ,.;:&@
abcdefghijklmnopqrstuvwxyz1234567890

Floridium

ABCDEFGHIJKLMNOPQRSTUVWXYZ,.;:
abcdefghijklmnopqrstuvwxyz123456

No Bodoni

George Everet(t) Thompson
2002-2003

Dog Butter is based on an old Barnhart Brothers & Spindler script type variously called Oliphant or Advertisers Upright Script. The original BB&S design was clearly based on some hand lettering which was very inconsistent. Some characters were very nice, but others were dull as dirt. I wanted to make all the characters equally interesting and light-hearted, while making it a monotone script so there could be a wide variety of weights.

Of Grammatology

A Sign is Just a Sign

Travels in Hyper Reality

Semiotics and Structuralism

Course in General Linguisitcs

Perspectives in Zoosemiotics

The Raw & the Cooked

The Name of the Rose

The Jealous Potter

Mythologies

Dog Butter ExtraLight

abcdefghijklmnopqrstuvwxyz ABCDEFGHIJKLMN
OPQRST UVWXYZ1234567890?$&

Dog Butter

abcdefghijklmnopqrstuvwxyz ABCDEFGHIJK
LMNOPQRST UVWXYZ123456789?

support@nobodoni.com

Dog Butter Medium

abcdefghijklmnopqrstuvwxyzABCDEFGHIJK
LMNOPQRSTUVWXYZ123456789?

Dog Butter DemiBold

abcdefghijklmnopqrstuvwxyzABCDEFGHIJK
LMNOPQRSTUVWXYZ123456789?

Dog Butter Bold

abcdefghijklmnopqrstuvwxyzABCDEFGHI
JKLMNOPQRSTUVWXYZ123456

Charles Peirce

Jacques Derrida

Roman Jakobson

Claude Levi Strauss

Ferdinand de Sassure

Dog Butter (cont.)

George Everet(t) Thompson
2002-2003

No Bodoni

George Everet(t) Thompson
1994-2000

Isbellium is a sans serif version of Dick Isbell's Americana type, the last type cut in metal by the American Type Founders Co. (ATF). Isbell's Americana is an elegant face with a wide stance, and Isbellium tries to maintain that elegance. This is more difficult to achieve in a sans serif than a serif type. It has some of the flair of the serif, but with a quieter voice and a polite authority.

Isbellium is a display face with a Roman and Italique in five weights: Regular, Medium, DemiBold, Bold and ExtraBold. Small caps versions for each weight are also in progress.

Endless, Nameless
Heart-Shaped Box
Verse Chorus Verse
Smells Like Teen Spirit
Radio Friendly Unit Shifter

Isbellium Italique

åbçdèfghijklmñôpqrstüvwxyz1234567890.,:;?![]{}()
ÅBÇÉDFGHÌJKLMÑÖPQRSTÛVWXYZœŒæÆfifiß

Isbellium Medium

åbçdèfghijklmñôpqrstüvwxyz1234567890.,:;?![]{}()
ÅBÇÉDFGHÌJKLMÑÖPQRSTÛVWXYZœŒæÆfifiß

Isbellium Demibold Italique

åbçdèfghijklmñôpqrstüvwxyz1234567890.,:;?!()[]
ÅBÇÉDFGHÌJKLMÑÖPQRSTÛVWXYZœŒæÆ

Isbellium Bold

åbçdèfghijklmñôpqrstüvwxyz1234567890.,?!()
ÅBÇÉDFGHÌJKLMÑÖPQRSTÛVWXYZæÆœŒ

Isbellium ExtraBold Italique

åbçdèfghijklmñôpqrstüvwxyz1234567890?![]
ÅBÇÉDFGHÌJKLMÑÖPQRSTÛVWXYZœÆœ

support@nobodoni.com

Swordfishtrombones
Invitation to the Blues
Murder in the Red Barn
Emotional Weather Report
House Where Nobody Lives

Isbellium

åbçdèfghijklmñôpqrstüvwxyz1234567890.,:;?!¿¡()[]{}
ÅBÇÉDFGHÌJKLMÑÖPQRSTÛVWXYZŒœÆæßfifi

Isbellium Medium Italique

åbçdèfghijklmñôpqrstüvwxyz1234567890?![]{}
ÅBÇÉDFGHÌJKLMÑÖPQRSTÛVWXYZŒœÆœßfi

Isbellium DemiBold

åbçdèfghijklmñôpqrstüvwxyz1234567890?!()
ÅBÇDÉDFGHÌJKLMÑÖPQRSTÛVWXYZŒœÆ

Isbellium Bold Italique

åbçdèfghijklmñôpqrstüvwxyz1234567890?!
ÅBÇDÉDFGHÌJKLMÑÖPQRSTÛVWXYZŒœÆ

Isbellium ExtraBold

åbçdèfghijklmñôpqrstüvwxyz1234567890?!
ÅBÇDÉDFGHÌJKLMÑÖPQRSTÛVWXYZŒœÆ

Ms Kitty

George Everet(t) Thompson
2002

Some scribbles on a bar napkin, a note from a cute girl passed in history class—what is there to say but "why not a typeface?" Actually, it's that late night, "Let's get this typeface done!" madness that causes these flights of fancy. Anything to relieve the boredom of doing all those kerning pairs. Or maybe it's sunspots?

Ms Kitty is all uppercase letterforms with two versions of each letter, one in the cap position, the other in the lowercase position. There are myriad kerning pairs to allow the dots to overlap for better spacing.

Besides the regular and bold weights, there are a bolder and much bolder weight in the works. And perhaps there will be a "too bold to be believed" version. Depends on the sunspots.

Ms Kitty

AABBCCDDEEFFGGGHHIIIJJKK
LLMMNNOOPPQQRRSSTTUU
VVWWXXYYZZ1234567890?!

Ms Kitty Bold

AABBCCDDEEFFGGGHHIIIJJK
KLLMMNNOOPPQQRRSSTT
UUVVWWXXYYZZ1234567

Ms Kitty

MARDER & LUSE

Ms Kitty Bold

FREIBERGER, GERING & KRANZ

Ms Kitty

FUST AND SCHOEFFER

Ms Kitty Bold

SWEYNHEIM & PANNARTZ

628   support@nobodoni.com

ABCDEFGHIJKLMNOPQRSTUVWXYZa
bcdefghijklmnopqrstuvwxyz1234567890?!

ABCDEFGHIJKLMNOPQRSTUVWXYZ
abcdefghijklmnopqrstuvwxyz123456789

ABCDEFGHIJKLMNOPQRSTUVWXYZ
abcdefghijklmnopqrstuvwxyz1234567

ABCDEFGHIJKLMNOPQRSTUVWXY
Zabcdefghijklmnopqrstuvwxyz12345

Jim Hurtibise Billy Vukuvich

Eddie Sachs • *Roger McCluskey* • *Gordon Johncock* • Roger Ward

Troy Ruttman *Mario Andretti*

Dick Rathman • **Jim McElreath** • A. J. Foyt • *Tommy Hinnerschitz*

Dick Rathman Jim McElreath

Jim Hurtibise • **Billy Vukuvich** • Troy Ruttman • *Mario Andretti*

A. J. Foyt *Tommy Hinnerschitz*

Tommy Hinnerschitz • **Eddie Sachs** • *Jim Hurtibise* • Roger Ward

Eddie Sachs *Roger McCluskey*

Dick Rathman • **Jim McElreath** • A. J. Foyt • *Tommy Hinnerschitz*

Gordon Johncock Roger Ward

Parma Typewriter

George Everet(t) Thompson
1995-2000

Parma is a typewriter-style face with the form and elegance of a Bodoni. Functional beauty was the aim of mating the two ideas in one typeface, creating a utilitarian design with graceful features—unlike most typewriter faces, which have a mechanical feel. This avoids that inelegant, klugey appearance, and makes it possible to have an attractive italic version.

I'm converting the keys on my beloved old Olivetti portable to type in Parma. And then I'm going to get a Lambretta scooter to go zipping around in, and maybe one of those front-opening Fiats for drives in the countryside.

No Bodoni

Estiennium Regular

åbçdèfghijklmñôpqrstüvwxyz1234567890.,:;?!¿¡[]{}()
ÅBÇÉÐFGHÌJKLMÑÖPQRSTÛVWXYZœÆœŒfifiß

Estiennium Italique

åbçdèfghijklmñôpqrstüvwxyz1234567890.,:;?!¿¡[]{}()
ÅBÇÉÐFGHÌJKLMÑÖPQRSTÛVWXYZœÆœŒfifiß

Estiennium DemiBold

åbçdèfghijklmñôpqrstüvwxyz1234567890.,:;?!¿¡[]{}()
ÅBÇÉÐFGHÌJKLMÑÖPQRSTÛVWXYZœŒœÆfifi

Estiennium DemiBold Italique

åbçdèfghijklmñôpqrstüvwxyz1234567890.,:;?!¿¡[]{}()
ÅBÇÉÐFGHÌJKLMÑÖPQRSTÛVWXYZœŒœÆfifiß

Estiennium Bold

åbçdèfghijklmñôpqrstüvwxyz1234567890.,:;?!¿¡[]
ÅBÇÉÐFGHÌJKLMÑÖPQRSTÛVWXYZœÆœŒfifi

Smokestack Lightnin'
DUST MY BROOM
Standin' at the Crossroads
What's the matter with the mill?

Estiennium ExtraBold

åbçdèfghijklmñôpqrstüvwxyz1234567890,;?!¿¡[]{}()
ÅßÇÉÐFGHÌJKLMÑÖPQRSTÛVWXYZœÆœŒfifiß

Estiennium ExtraBold Italique

åbçdèfghijklmñôpqrstüvwxyz1234567890?![]{}()
ÅßÇÉÐFGHÌJKLMÑÖPQRSTÛVWXYZœÆœŒfifiß

Estiennium Black

åbçdèfghijklmñôpqrstüvwxyz1234567890?![]{}()
ÅßÇÉÐFGHÌJKLMÑÖPQRSTÛVWXYZœŒœÆfifi

Estiennium Black Italique

åbçdèfghijklmñôpqrstüvwxyz1234567890?![]{}()
ÅßÇÉÐFGHÌJKLMÑÖPQRSTÛVWXYZœŒœÆfifiß

Estiennium Bold Italique

åbçdèfghijklmñôpqrstüvwxyz1234567890.,:;?!¿¡[]
ÅßÇÉÐFGHÌJKLMÑÖPQRSTÛVWXYZœÆœŒfifi

Key to the Highway
LEVEE CAMP MOAN
Rollin' and Tumblin'
Keep your hands off her

PAR
KIN
SON

PARKINSON TYPE DESIGN

PARKINSON TYPE DESIGN

Jim Parkinson specializes in the design
of typefaces and typographic logos.
He has designed over 100 typefaces. Half
are exclusives for font companies including
The Font Bureau, Adobe, Agfa/Monotype,
ITC, FontShop and Chank.
The others, shown here, are available from
Parkinson Type Design, Phil's Fonts and MyFonts.

email: parkinson@typedesign.com
visit the website: typedesign.com

PAR KIN SON

*People who love ideas must have a love of words,
and that means, given a chance, they will take
a vivid interest in the clothes which words wear.*
    – Beatrice Warde

ABCDEFGHIJKLMNOPQRSTUVWXYZ
abcdefghijklmnopqrstuvwxyz &12345

ABCDEFGHIJKLMNOPQRSTUVWXYZ
abcdefghijklmnopqrstuvwxyz &12345

ABCDEFGHIJKLMNOPQRSTUVWXY
abcdefghijklmnopqrstuvwxyz &12345

ABCDEFGHIJKLMNOPQRSTUVWXY
abcdefghijklmnopqrstuvwxyz &12345

We use the letters of our alphabet every day with the utmost ease & unconcern, taking them almost as much for granted as the air we breathe. We do not realize that each of these letters is at our service today only as the result of a long & laboriously slow process of evolution in the age-old art of writing. Douglas C. McMurtrie

Azuza

Jim Parkinson
2001

Medium
Medium Italic
Bold
Bold Italic

Parkinson

Balboa Family

Jim Parkinson
2001-2003

Extra Condensed
Condensed
Light
Medium
Bold
Extra Bold
Black
Wide Light
Wide Medium
Wide Bold
Wide Extra Bold
Wide Black

THREE AMBULANCES TAKE BLAST VICTIM TO HOSPITAL

Cops Halt Doughnut Shop Robbery

Missouri Woman Big Winner at Hog Show

Stolen Painting Found by Tree

DEAD MAN GETS JOB BACK

Something Went Wrong in Jet Crash, Expert Says

STEALS CLOCK, FACES TIME

Man Disputes Government Claim He's Dead

PANTS MAN TO EXPAND AT THE REAR

Unwanted Workers Get Shot at Jobs

TWO SOVIET SHIPS COLLIDE, ONE DIES

TREES CAN BREAK WIND

parkinson@typedesign.com

ABCDEFGHIJKLMNOPQRSTUVWXYZ
abcdefghijklmnopqrstuvwxyz & 12345

Wisconsin Bill Would Permit Blind to Hunt Deer

ABCDEFGHIJKLMNOPQRSTUVWXYZ
abcdefghijklmnopqrstuvwxyz & 12345

HOSPITAL SUED BY 7 FOOT DOCTORS

ABCDEFGHIJKLMNOPQRSTUVWXYZ
abcdefghijklmnopqrstuvwxyz & 12345

Iowa Cemeteries Are Death Traps

ABCDEFGHIJKLMNOPQRSTUVWXYZ
abcdefghijklmnopqrstuvwxyz & 12345

RAINS DELAY UMBRELLA SHOW

Parkinson

ABCDEFGHIJKLMNOPQRSTUVWXYZ
abcdefghijklmnopqrstuvwxyz & 12345

Art Causes School Evacuation

ABCDEFGHIJKLMNOPQRSTUVWXYZ
abcdefghijklmnopqrstuvwxyz & 1234

Dead Man Found in Cemetery

ABCDEFGHIJKLMNOPQRSTUVWX
abcdefghijklmnopqrstu & 1234

Apart from the cutters of
GRAVESTONES
the most conservative people in
TYPOGRAPHY
are newspaper people.   W.A. Dwiggins

ABCDEFGHIJKLMNOPQRSTUVWXYZ
abcdefghijklmnopqrstuvwxyz & 12345
Dinosaur Faces Grand Jury Probe

ABCDEFGHIJKLMNOPQRSTUVWXYZ
abcdefghijklmnopqrstuvwxyz & 12345

ABCDEFGHIJKLMNOPQRSTUVWXYZ
abcdefghijklmnopqrstuvwxy & 12345
London Man Slain With Turnip

ABCDEFGHIJKLMNOPQRSTUVWXYZ
abcdefghijklmnopqrstuvw & 12345

ABCDEFGHIJKLMNOPQRSTUV
abcdefghijklmnopqrs & 12345
HIGH-SPEED TRAIN
Could Reach Valley in Five Years

Balboa Wide

Jim Parkinson
2003

Light
Medium
Bold
Extra Bold
Black

Parkinson

Sutro

Jim Parkinson
2003

Light
Medium
Bold
Extra Bold

ABCDEFGHIJKLMNOPQRSTUVW
abcdefghijklmnopqrstuvwxy &12345

ABCDEFGHIJKLMNOPQRSTUV
abcdefghijklmnopqrstuvw &12345

ABCDEFGHIJKLMNOPQRSTU
abcdefghijklmnopqrstuv &12345

ABCDEFGHIJKLMNOPQRSTU
abcdefghijklmnopqrstuv &12345

The graphic signs called letters are so completely
blended with the stream of written thought that
their presence therein is as unperceived as the
ticking of a clock in the measurement of time.
Only by an effort of attention does the layman
discover that they exist at all. It comes to him as
a surprise that these signs should be a matter
of concern to any one of the crafts of men.
But to be concerned with the shapes of letters is
to work in an ancient and fundamental material.
The qualities of letter forms at their best are the
qualities of a classic time: order, simpicity, grace.
W.A.Dwiggins

parkinson@typedesign.com

ABCDEFGHIJ
KLMNOPQRST
UVWXYZ & 123
SATURDAY & SUNDAY
MAY 2 & 3

Sutro Black Initials

Jim Parkinson
2003

Caps, figures, accents
& puncuation

ABCDEFGHIJK
LMNOPQRSTU
VWXYZ & 12345
HOT MINERAL
SPRINGS

Sutro Shaded Initials

Jim Parkinson
2003

Caps, figures, accents
& puncuation

Parkinson

ABCDEFGHIJKLMNOPQRSTUVWXYZ
ABCDEFGHIJKLMNOPQRSTUVWXYZ &12345

THE HUMAN PROJECTILE

ABCDEFGHIJKLMNOPQRSTUVWXYZ
ABCDEFGHIJKLMNOPQRSTUVWX & 12345

SHOT THROUGH SPACE

ABCDEFGHIJKLMNOPQRS
ABCDEFGHIJKLMNOP & 12345

AT HIGH VELOCITY

ABCDEFGHIJKLMNOPQRSTUVWXYZ
ABCDEFGHIJKLMNOPQRSTUVWXYZ & 12345

FROM A MONSTER CANNON

parkinson@typedesign.com

ABCDEFGHIJKLMNOPQRSTUVW
ABCDEFGHIJKLMNOPQRSTU &12345
YOU WILL BE AMAZED

Modesto Regular

Jim Parkinson
2001

ABCDEFGHIJKLMNOPQRS
ABCDEFGHIJKLMNOPQ &12345
BRING THE FAMILY

Modesto Expanded

Jim Parkinson
2001

ABCDEFGHIJK
LMNOPQRSTU
VWXYZ &1234
PICNIC

Modesto Inline

Jim Parkinson
2003

Caps, figures, accents
& puncuation

Parkinson

Benicia Medium

Jim Parkinson
2003

ABCDEFGHIJKLMNOPQRSTUVWXYZ
abcdefghijklmnopqrstuvwxyz & 12345

Harmonious Typeface Designs

Benicia Italic

Jim Parkinson
2003

ABCDEFGHIJKLMNOPQRSTUVWXYZ
abcdefghijklmnopqrstuvwxyz & 12345

For Advertising & Publications

Benicia Bold

Jim Parkinson
2003

ABCDEFGHIJKLMNOPQRSTUVWXY
abcdefghijklmnopqrstuvwxyz & 12345

Harmonious Typeface Designs

Benicia Bold Italic

Jim Parkinson
2003

ABCDEFGHIJKLMNOPQRSTUVWXYZ
abcdefghijklmnopqrstuvwxyz & 12345

For Advertising & Publications

parkinson@typedesign.com

We are type designers, punch cutters, wood cutters, type founders, compositors, printers, **and book-binders from conviction and** with passion, not because we *are insufficiently talented* for other higher things, but *because to us the highest* **things stand in closest** *kinship to our own crafts.*

RUDOLF KOCH

Richmond Family

Jim Parkinson
2003

Condensed Light
Condensed Medium
Condensed Bold
Condensed Extra Bold
Light
Light Italic
Medium
Medium Italic
Bold
Bold Italic
Inlined Initials

Parkinson

Jim Parkinson
2003

Light
Medium
Bold
Extra Bold

ABCDEFGHIJKLMNOPQRSTUVWXYZ
abcdefghijklmnopqrstuvwxyz &12345

ABCDEFGHIJKLMNOPQRSTUVWXYZ
abcdefghijklmnopqrstuvwxyz &12345

ABCDEFGHIJKLMNOPQRSTUVWXYZ
abcdefghijklmnopqrstuvwxyz &12345

ABCDEFGHIJKLMNOPQRSTUVWXYZ
abcdefghijklmnopqrstuvwxyz &12345

Geometry can produce legible letters,
but art alone makes them beautiful.
Art begins where geometry ends,
and imparts to letters a character
transcending mere measurement.
Paul Standard

parkinson@typedesign.com

ABCDEFGHIJKLMNOPQRSTUVWXYZ
abcdefghijklmnopqrstuvwxyz & 12345

Typography is a servant –

ABCDEFGHIJKLMNOPQRSTUVWXYZ
abcdefghijklmnopqrstuvwxyz & 12345

the servant of thought and

ABCDEFGHIJKLMNOPQRSTUVWXYZ
abcdefghijklmnopqrstuvwxyz & 12345

language to which it gives

ABCDEFGHIJKLMNOPQRSTUVWXYZ
abcdefghijklmnopqrstuvwxyz & 12345

visible existence.　　*T.M. Cleland*

Parkinson

ABCDEFGHIJKLMNOPQRSTUVWXYZ
abcdefghijklmnopqrstuvwxyz &12345
Letters are things,

ABCDEFGHIJKLMNOPQRSTUVWXYZ
abcdefghijklmnopqrstuvwxyz &12345
not pictures of things.

ABCDEFGHIJKLM
NOPQRSTUVWXY
& 1234567890
ERIC GILL

AABCDEFGHIJKKLMMNNOPQRSSTUVWXYZ & 12345

FLINSTONE VILLAGE

AABBCDEEFFGGHHIJKKLMM
NNOPPQQRRSTUU & 1234567

CHICKEN WINGS

AABCDEFGHIJKLMNOPQRSSTUVW
XYZ & 1234567890

LIBERACE MUSEUM

ABCDEFGHIJKLMNOPQRST
abcdefghijklmnopq *and* 12345
WIGWAG IS HERE

Parkinson

The Sherwood Type Collection evolved by way of
a letterpress printing background.

The fonts are available at
www.sherwoodtype.com

Albion easy pickings for Claudius of Rome

THE EMPEROR CLAUDIUS was lame in one leg, and stuttered when he spoke. Though the scion of a family which had produced many great generals, he could claim no military victories to his own name. It came as no surprise to anyone that he chose to conquer Albion. After all, everyone in Rome knew it was high time the distant island in the north was brought into the civilized world. It proved easy enough. Four legions under the command of Aulus Plautius made a landing in the summer of A.D. 43 and marched through the south-east, routing the army of the brother of the impudent chief Caractacus, whose own force they smashed a few days later. As soon as he heard that all was well, Claudius arrived, bringing a train of awe-inspiring elephants. His military triumph assured, he stayed on the island for only sixteen days.

ABCDEFGHIJKLMNOPQRSTUVW
XYZabcdefghijklmnopqrstuvwxyz&ctst
1234567890ÆæŒœfifffflffiffl?!¶§¶†()⁊{}.,:
@#/%;--*·_+

- Edward Rutherfurd: Sarum (Crown Publishers Inc., N.Y.), 1987

Albion

Ted Staunton
2002

Albion ("white") was the name used by the Romans for the island of Britain, so called because of the white chalk cliffs of Dover, as seen from the English Channel on the approach from Gaul.

Sherwood

Teutonic blood flows in John Bull's veins

When the Romans withdrew from England in the fifth century, conquerors from the north appeared, the tall, fair-haired, blue-eyed barbarians known in history as Germans, or Teutons. They still occupy the best parts of Britain, for the Englishman of today is their descendant. The pirate Teuton has in the course of history become the modern 'John Bull,' the typical Englishman. He is ruddy, broad-shouldered, in every way solid, a plain man, well-to-do, fond of his own comfort. Though he cares little for intellectual things, he is honest, resolute, and loyal, anxious to do his duty, and good-natured, though sometimes irritable and unreasonable. The classes which have led in English life have never been dwellers in towns. Except for a few months in the London season, they still prefer the country, and they relieve the monotony of rural life by outdoor pastimes. English youth play boisterous games, and the hardy pleasures of the hunting field have many devotees.

- George M. Wrong: The British Nation (1916)

ABCDEFGHIJKLMNOPQRSTUVW
XYZabcdefghijklmnopqrstuvwxyzctstfifl
ffiffl1234567890!@#$%&*()_+⁊{};:'",.//?–©®†

Albion Italic

Ted Staunton
2003

A companion to the above, with modified lowercase characteristics.

Mayflower

Ted Staunton / Other source
2002

This font was based on Roman type used for headings in a "Breeches Bible" of 1610 (the text was printed in blackletter), probably the version carried by the Pilgrims to the New World.

The Pilgrims had heard that flight to the Netherlands meant "freedome of Religion for all men." Yet flight involved suffering.

THE PILGRIMS had to escape by stealth and pay a shipmaster to transport them illegally. In 1607, they set out on foot for the small coastal town of Boston. After a few days' delay, the ship to carry them abroad arrived o>shore. After collecting his fees, the shipmaster turned them over to the local authorities, first to be paraded in public, then thrown in jail, and finally sent back home. In 1608 they made another attempt at freedom, but the Dutch ship that was supposed to pick them up ran aground. Half the company were on board, the other on land, when an armed mob of locals arrived on the scene to harass them. A furious gale then developed, blowing the ship out into the North Sea and almost all the way across to Norway.*

ABCDEFGHIJKLMNOPQRSTUVWXY
Zabcdefghijklmnopqrstuvwxyz1234567890&.,:;-
áàâäãåçéèêßÆæŒœfffiflffi‡·|~‹›‹‹››
/∏()?!@#$

*Norman K. Risjord: Representative Americans: The Colonists (D.C. Heath & Co., Lexington, 1981)

Mayflower Italic

Ted Staunton / Other source
2002

Works well for restaurant menus, wedding invitations, certificates, etc., where swash letters can be used to good effect.

Carrying 42 Puritan 'Saints' and 60 'Strangers,' the Mayflower set sail from Southampton September 6, 1620, reaching Cape Cod November 9.

The Mayflower, measuring 113 by 26 feet, was not a small ship for her day, but she was not built for the load of humanity that jammed her decks. The crew of 30 occupied the forecastle on the main deck; food and drink filled the hold. The only place for the 102 passengers to sleep was between decks, and it must have been indescribably crowded. Fierce storms came roaring out of the west. For days at a time it was impossible to carry a yard of sail, the ship drifting under bare poles with the helmsman desperately trying to hold her into the wind as she wallowed through mountainous seas ... the pounding of heavy seas opened up many seams in the deck and superstructure, letting cascades of icy water down upon the ill and frightened passengers curled up in their narrow bunks below.*

ABCDEFGHIJKLMNOPQRSTUV
WXYZabcdefghijklmnopqrstuvwxyz123456789&o()
EtStkia_e_h_n_r_t_vy}llisasssisssbshslßstspffifflffiffssl
ThYᵉ K⁺N Rh.,:;

*George F. Willison: Saints and Strangers (Reynal & Hitchcock, N.Y., 1945)

1-800-722-5080

1722 Roman

Ted Staunton
2002

From a book of the same period, when printers made their own ink from soot and glue derived from boiled animal bones. The ink was applied to the face of the hand-cast type with wooden-handled leather pads stuffed with wool and horsehair.

Sherwood

The Testimony of Dr. Stevens, Gentleman.

I live in Covent Garden. On St. Paul's Day in the Evening, I went with my Daughter to visit a friend in Silver-street. About Eleven I sent for a Hackney Coach, for as I expected to stay late I had discharged my own Chariot. We went down Pater-noster-Row, and in Ave-Mary-Lane, the Coach was stopp'd. A Man came to the Coach-door, and holding a Pistol to my Daughter's Head, he said, Don't be frightened Madam! but God damn you if you squawl, I'll shoot you thro' the Head! I had a Purse with 10 Guineas in it, which I secur'd, and gave him only a half Guinea, and a Spanish Dollar, which were loose in my Pocket. God damn you, says he, you have more! No I ha'nt, says I, you shall search me if you will. My Daughter gave him her Purse; he ask'd her what was in it? She said, Not above 3 or 4 Guineas. And then he bid the Coachman drive on.*

ABCDEFGHIJKLMNOPQRSTUVWXYabcd
efghijklmnopqrstuvwxyz1234567890!?&@N°&
O[];:"'''''⟨ornaments⟩
fiffflffiffl∫∫b∫h∫h∫k∫∫t st ct<>.,·/—*

1722 Italic

Ted Staunton
2002

Effective for period applications – an antique look on packaging, magazine spreads, book covers, etc.

The Testimony of Jonathan Dickenson, Watchman.

As I called Two o'Clock in Marlborough-street, I found a Bar of some Pallisades bent, and looking farther I found another in the same Condition. Upon this I thought there was some Roguery going forward; so I planted my Lanthern in the middle of Blenheim-street, that my Inhabitants might see I was upon my Duty, and then I went aside and stood upon the Watch, and presently I heard a cry of Stop Thief. Says I to my Brother Watch, do you go down Tyler-street, and I'll go down Little Marlborough-street, and so we did. I met the Prisoner running with his drawn Sword (for he is a Soldier) and I knocked him down. My Liberty has lately been very much robbed, which is a sign that it is pestered with Rogues: I have lost a great deal of Iron and Lead — not that it was my own, but my Inhabitants; and as several Attempts have been made, they had lost a great deal more if it had not been for the Care of the Watch, which is a Sign that the Watch have not neglected their Duty; and if the Watch should sink, by consequence my Inhabitants cannot stand. And therefore, pray, my Lord, stand by the Watch whatever you do, or else my People will be undone; they will be robbed, and have their Throats cut and their Houses burnt about their Ears.*

ABCDEFGHIJKLMNOPQRSTUVWXYZ&!?
abcdefghijklmnopqrstuvwxyz1234567890@O[]:·,·/
fiffflffiffl∫∫b∫h∫iffl∫t st ct st as is Uk

*From the Sessions of Peace, and Oyer and Terminer for the City of London and the County of Middlesex, 1732 - 1733.

Mercian

Ted Staunton
2003

Designed for continuous text setting.

King's coinage - and rule - set the standard

In eighth century England, one of the difficulties encountered by traders was the scarcity of market towns with facilities for the safe storage, display and sale of their goods. Only the king could grant the right to hold a market, in which properly established weights and measures were used. Offa, king of Mercia, controlled all the smaller English kingdoms south of the Humber, and was able to standardize the coinage being used. By 795 Offa's silver pennies had become the only recognized currency, and were so handsomely designed that they set a fashion in coinage that persisted in England for the next 500 years. Offa presided over councils of churchmen and nobles, foreshadowing a time when there would be only one king in England who would preside over councillors from every part of the land. His reputation stood so high that he was treated as an equal by the emperor Charlemagne. Offa's Dike, a great ditch and rampart, was constructed to mark the boundary between Mercia and Wales, vestiges of which still remain.

ABCDEFGHIJK
LMNOPQRSTU
VWXYZÆŒ
abcdefghijklmnopq
rstuvwxyzſtctæœ
1234567890
&!?@#$*(),.,;:'"""fifffflffiffl

ROMAN EMPIRE LEAVES PERMANENT MARKS

AFTER OCCUPYING BRITAIN IN THE FIRST CENTURY, THE ROMANS SOON ESTABLISHED A NETWORK OF HIGHWAYS ACROSS THE LAND, WITH MILITARY CAMPS AT STRATEGIC POINTS. ONE OF THESE WAS AT LINDUM COLONIS (LINCOLN). REMAINS OF A STONE WALL ENCLOSING THE TOWN STILL EXIST, AND ITS ROADS AND GATEWAYS ARE STILL IN USE.

ABCDEFGHIJKLMNO
PQRSTUVWXYZÆŒ
1234567890O&$?!()/"""""

Lindum

Ted Staunton
2000

A serif/sans serif hybrid, designed as a titling font to be used in display sizes.

Tudor queen ordered burning of godly men

HUGH LATIMER, born c. 1485 at Mountsorrel, Leicestershire, was born again while a student at Cambridge. A fearless preacher of the Gospel, he was persecuted by enemies within the church, but, after voicing support for Henry VIII's divorce from Catherine of Aragon, was protected by the king and appointed Bishop of Worcester. However, when Henry's daughter Mary, an avowed Catholic, came to the throne in 1553, Latimer was arrested as a leading Protestant and condemned to death.
"The prisoners Latimer and Ridley were brought forth together on the 16th of October, 1555. Then the smith took a chain of iron and fastened it about both Ridley's and Latimer's middle to one stake. A bag of gunpowder was tied about the neck of each. Then they brought a faggot kindled with fire, and laid it down at Ridley's feet, to whom Latimer then spake in this manner: "Be of good comfort, master Ridley, and play the man; we shall this day light such a candle, by God's grace, in England, as I trust shall never be put out."
- Foxe, Book of Martyrs

Latimer

Ted Staunton
2002

One of a series exploring a convergence of Gothic and Roman influences.

ABCDEFGHIJKLMNOPQRSTUVWXYZ
abcdefghijklmnopqrstuvwxyz1234567890fiflß
&@™#%^*_±+(){}[]:?|!$£¢$†‡¶©®·'""""

Stratford Theatre presents

A Midsummer
by William
Shakespeare

Night's Dream

You spotted snakes with double tongue,
Thorny hedgehogs, be not seen;
Newts and blind-worms, do no wrong;
Come not near our fairy queen.

Weaving spiders, come not here;
Hence, you long-legg'd spinners, hence!
Beetles black, approach not near;
Worm or snail, do no offence.

ABCDEFGHIJKLMNOPQRSTUVWXYZ
abcdefghijklmnopqrstuvwxyz
1234567890!#$&*()[]:;",,?

Traditional Pantomime at Burr Theatre

Mother Goose
by Ellie King

Come and cheer Boy Blue and the Fairy Queen! Boo the Demon
King, hiss at Squire Nastiman! Laugh with Bo Peep, Simple Simon,
Mr. Tweedle & Mr. Dee, Georgie Porgie and Mary Mary! Groan at
the corny jokes! Clap and sing along to the music!

ABCDEFGHIJKLMNOPQRSTUVWXYZabcd
efghijklmnopqrstuvwxyz1234567890!?&@#$%
ctstch_m_n_r_t*()-_-=+[]{};:'"<>/.,

Wooden warship comes under enemy fire

The din of battle continued. Grape and canister shot were pouring through our port-holes like leaden rain, carrying death in their train. The large shot came against the ship's side like iron hail, shaking her to the very keel, or passing through her timbers, and scattering terrific splinters, which did a more appalling work than even their own death-giving blows. Grape shot is formed by seven or eight balls confined to an iron and tied in a cloth. Canister shot is made by filling a powder canister with balls, each as large as two or three musket balls; these also scatter with direful effect when discharged. What, then, with splinters, cannon-balls, grape, and canister poured incessantly upon us, the reader may be assured that the work of death went on in a manner which must have been satisfactory even to the King of Terrors himself.

Samuel Leech: Life of a Sailor-Boy (1843)

ABCDEFGHIJKLMNOPQRSTUVW
XYZabcdefghijklmnopqrstuvwxyz
1234567890&stſctfiifflffifflfl$?!O.,@#:;'''""

Sherwood

Unknown
2002

Reproduced from a font of unusually small wood poster type (5-line, or 60pt). An interesting feature of the font is the long "s," which went out of use in the late 17th century; the font is, therefore, likely at least 200 years old. Proofs were taken of each character on a letterpress platen machine and digitized.

Sherwood

Stray bullet finds its mark in wooden biplane

I had longed to fly. Now I sat among flying men and was one of them. It was sheer bliss. We flew BE2C's. The observer sat between the pilot and the engine, surrounded by struts and stays and cross-bracing wires. He had around him several metal pegs and was supposed in the heat of combat, while the machine dived and banked, to fight off the enemy by transferring the machine-gun from the one to the other and then firing through the small apertures left by the struts and wires. It was like fighting from an animated parrot's cage . . . We circled round and round, lower and lower, trying to plot the line to the last remnant of trench and shell-hole. I was hit where you would expect to be hit if you were sitting down and being fired at from below.

Douglas Reed: Insanity Fair (1938)

Founders

Ted Staunton
2002

ABCDEFGHIJKLMNOPQRSTUVWXYZ
abcdefghijklmnopqrstuvwxyz
1234567890&!?@#$%*(){}-;:'"|.,/

Sparrow

Ted Staunton
2001

The "blobby" look is the result of varying pressure on a sharply pointed crow-quill pen nib.

Tears fall at the death of a pet sparrow

(Written by John Skelton, tutor to Henry VIII)

Pla ce bo,
Who is there, who?
Di le xi,
Dame Margery;
Fa, re, my, my,
Wherefore and why, why?
For the sowle of Phyllyp
    Sparowe,

That was late slayn at Carowe,
Among the nones blake,
For that sweet soules sake,
And for all sparowes soules,
Set in our bederolls,
Pater noster qui,
With an Ave Mari,
And with the corner of a Crede
The more shalbe your mede.
I wept and I wayled,
The tearys downe hayled;

But nothing it auayled
To call Phylyp agayne,
Whom Gyb our cat
    hath slayne.
Kyrie, eleison,
Christe, eleison,
Kyrie, eleison!
For Phylyp Sparowes soule
Set in our bederoll
Let vs now whysper
A Pater noster . . .

ABCDEFGHIJKLMNOPQRSTUVWXYZ
abcdefghijklmnopqrstuvwxyz1234567890
&?!@#$%*()[]{};:.,/"''"

Father mourns the death of a promising son

Successive generations of the Oglander family lived at Nunwell on the Isle of Wight for over 800 years. Following is an extract from the diary of Sir John Oglander (1585 - 1655), concerning the loss of his eldest son, who died from smallpox in France in 1632.

On the 21st July, being at Newport, and there busy in many things concerning the good of our Island, I heard a murmuring and sadness amongst the gentlemen and clergy and the rest. Mr. Price of Calbourne told me he hoped the ill news that was come to town was not true. Then I, becoming suspicious, demanded whether he had heard any ill news of any of my family. And he, finding my ignorance, converted it to a loss of the King of Sweden's army. Many more overtures I had, but knew nothing until I was putting my foot in the stirrup. Then Sir Robert Dillington and Sir Edward Dennys came unto me and told me of a flying report, brought by a bark off Weymouth, lately come from France, that my eldest son George was very sick – if not dead.
With my tears instead of ink I write these last lines. O George, my beloved George, is dead, and with him most of my terrestrial comforts, although I acknowledge I have good and dutiful sons left. Only with my tears and a foul pen was this written.

ABCDEFGHIJKLMNOPQRSTUVWXYZ
abcdefghijklmnopqrstuvwxyz123456789&0

Indians Sold into Slavery

Roanoke Script

Ted Staunton
2002

Sherwood

As Indian captives – men, women, and children – continued to pour into Plymouth, all were sold into slavery, some to local planters, the majority in the West Indies. All the Wampanoag lands were seized and sold "so as to settle plantations thereon in an orderly way to promote the publick worship of God, and our owne publicke good."

"The design of Christ in these last days is not to extirpate nations but to gospelize them," exclaimed John Eliot in bitter protest against these and similar acts throughout the United Colonies. "To sell souls for money seemeth to me a dangerous merchandise."

– George F. Willison: Saints and Strangers

ABCDEFGHIJKLMNOP
QRSTUVWXYZabcdefghijklmnopqrstu
vwxyz1234567890&.,()!?/:·@ij

Shakespeare, Austen popularize romantic love

Let me not to the marriage of true minds
Admit impediments.
Love is not love which alters when it alteration finds,
Or bends with the remover to remove: –
O no! it is an ever-fixed mark
That looks on tempests, and is never shaken;
It is the star to every wandering bark,
Whose worth's unknown, although his height be taken.

— *William Shakespeare*

"Engagement!" cried Marianne, "there has been no engagement."
"No engagement?"
"No, he is not so unworthy as you believe him. He has broken no faith with me."
"But he told you that he loved you?"
"Yes – no – never absolutely. It was every day implied, but never professedly declared. Sometimes I thought it had been – but it never was."

— *Jane Austen*

ABCDEFGHIJKLMNOPQRST
UVWXYZabcdefghijklmnopqrstuvwxyz
1234567890?!@#$%&*()/;:""

Burns eulogizes love beside a Scottish stream

Flow gently, sweet Afton, among thy green bræs,
Flow gently, I'll sing thee a song in thy praise.
My Mary's asleep by thy murmuring stream,
Flow gently, sweet Afton, disturb not her dream.

Thou stock-dove whose echo resounds thro' the glen
Ye wild whistling blackbirds, in yon thorny den
Thou green-crested lapwing thy screaming forbear
I charge you, disturb not my slumbering Fair.

How lofty, sweet Afton, thy neighbouring hills
Far mark'd with the course of clear, winding rills
There daily I wander as noon rises high,
My flocks and my Mary's sweet cot in my eye.

How pleasant thy banks and green valleys below,
Where, wild in the woodlands, the primroses blow;
There oft, as mild Ev'ning weeps over the lea
The sweet-scented birk shades my Mary and me.

The Afton rises near Cumnock in south-western Scotland and travels only eight miles before emptying into the River Nith. The poem was written by Robert Burns in 1789.

ABCDEFGHIJKLMNOPQRSTU
VWXYZabcdefghijklmnopqrstuvwxyz
ctst?!$&1234567890fiflffffffiffle h m n

Wordsworth had lovely vision in Lake District

I wandered lonely as a cloud
That floats on high o'er vales and hills,
When all at once I saw a crowd,
A host of golden daffodils,
Beside the lake, beneath the trees,
Fluttering and dancing in the breeze.

Continuous as the stars that shine
And twinkle on the Milky Way,
They stretched in never-ending line
Along the margin of the bay;
Ten thousand saw I at a glance,
Tossing their heads in sprightly dance.

The waves beside them danced, but they
Outdid the sparkling waves in glee;
A poet could not but be gay,
In such a jocund company;
I gazed - and gazed - but little thought
What wealth to me the show had brought.

For oft, when on my couch I lie,
In vacant or in pensive mood,
They flash upon that inward eye
Which is the bliss of solitude,
And then my heart with pleasure fills,
And dances with the daffodils.

ABCDEFGHIJKL
MNOPQRSTUVWXYZ
abcdefghijklmnopqrstuvwxyz
1234567890

a 6 b bd d dd e e g g ff fi fl ffi ffl g h k k k l ll l m n
r r s t tt v w w y & st æ B D L P R S T Th W
& & ✠ ↄ ae ¶ ↄ ↄ ↄ ↄ ↄ ↄ ↄ

Ted Staunton
2000

One of a series exploring a
convergence of Gothic and Roman
influences.

They bought his books - only to burn them

WILLIAM TYNDALE was born in Gloucestershire, England between 1490 and 1495. As a young man he attended both Oxford and Cambridge universities. A follower of the 'new learning' being propagated by such scholars as Colet and Erasmus, he wished to translate the Bible into English, but was forced to leave England to do so. Large numbers of his New Testament, printed in Holland, were bought up in England by the Bishop of London - not for distribution, but that they might be burned! The income provided Tyndale with enough capital to begin working on a new translation of the Old Testament, but he was betrayed from his hiding place among the merchants of Antwerp and strangled at the stake October 6, 1536.

It is estimated that about 90 per cent of the King James Authorized Version of 1611 is Tyndale's work.

ABCDEFGHIJK
LMNOPQRSTU
VWXYZ
abcdefghijklmno
pqrstuvwxyz
1234567890
&.,;:'"[]{}()!@#$%^*fifl‡ÆÆæŒœ

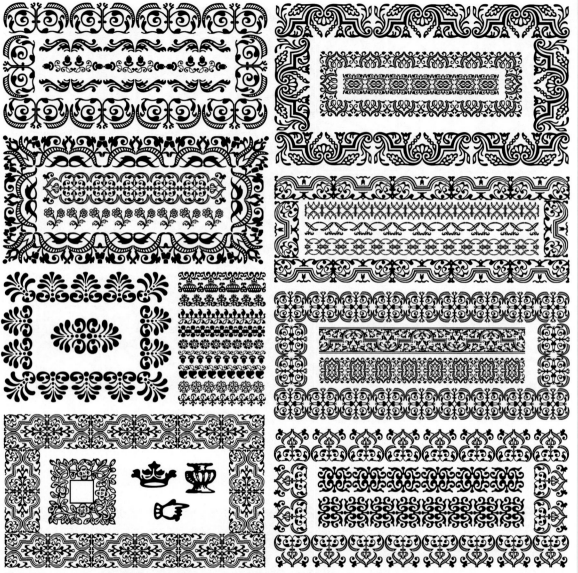

Tyndale Xtras

Ted Staunton / Other sources
2002

Arabesque and other ornaments from printed books of the 17th and 18th centuries, plus extra ligatures for the Tyndale font.

Sherwood

Initials in the Victorian style, plus
a selection of wood-engraved
blanks from the 18th century,
artist unknown.

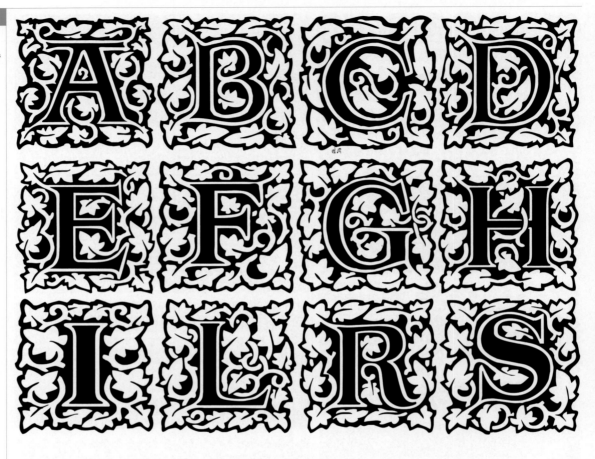

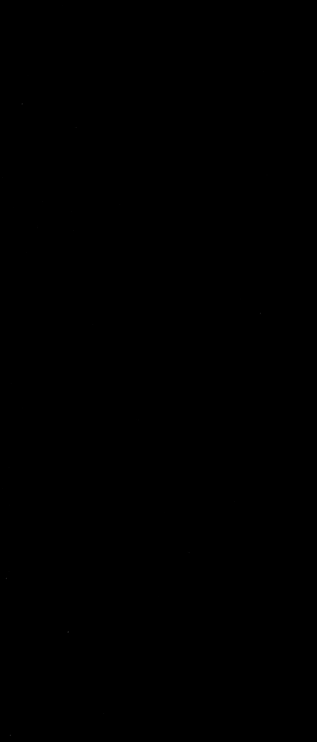

Mark Simonson

STUDIO

Mark Simonson Studio is a one-person operation offering, among other things, lettering and type design services. Several of Mark's fonts were licensed by FontHaus beginning in 1992, the most popular thus far being Felt Tip Roman,™ based on his own messy handwriting. In 2000, after a several-year break, he resumed typeface design and production in earnest. Many of the typefaces shown here are recent releases.

The M.S.S. collection is eclectic, offering original vintage and contemporary styles for both display and text. All fonts are of high quality with complete character sets (including European accents), careful spacing and extensive kerning tables for care-free setting. Every font is available for both Macintosh or Windows in PostScript™ Type 1 and TrueType formats.

M.S.S. typefaces are available from several different vendors, online and off, or direct from the source. See www.ms-studio.com for details.

In addition to the retail fonts shown here, M.S.S. offers custom font design and development services. Custom lettering for any purpose is also available. Scripts are Mark's specialty. Call or write for details.

Mark Simonson Studio

www.ms-studio.com
mark@ms-studio.com

1496 Raymond Avenue
Saint Paul, Minnesota 55108 USA

651-649-0553

MADCAP CAFÉ

WESTERN UNION TELEGRAPH OFFICE

NICK DANGER SILVER SCREEN

THE GHOST OF THE WHITE ROOM AND MANY MORE EXCITING STORIES

1934

CLIMB MT. KILIMANJARO!

GOLDEN AGE OF COMEDY

FAMOUS SUPERHERO COMICS

DEMOLITION MAN WAR!

BEEZLE BUMBLE MAKES HIS DEBUT IN THIS ISSUE!

ARMY & NAVY COFFEE BEANS

PABLO PICASSO EH?

CHICKEN SALAD SANDWICH FOR ONLY $29.99

Blakely

Mark Simonson
2000–2003

Blakely Light is based on a custom font created in 1994 for the Signals mail order catalog. It is more restrained than other similar Art Deco typefaces, avoiding the typical high- or low-waisted cross bars. The Bold and Black weights are recent additions.

Mark Simonson Studio

Blakely Light

ABCDEFGHIJKLMNOP
QRSTUVWXYZ 12345678
90 &*$¢£.,:;!?''""«»()

Blakely Bold

ABCDEFGHIJKLMN
OPQRSTUVWXYZ 12
34567890 &*$.,:;!?(

Blakely Black

ABCDEFGHIJKLM
NOPQRSTUVWX
YZ 1234567890&

Mark Simonson
2001

Coquette is a hybrid of 1920s-era sans serif faces (Erbar, Kabel, Futura) and traditional French Civilité-inspired scripts (Typo Upright Script, Gando). The result is a face that is original yet familiar. It retains many script-like details and flows like a script, but remains disconnected.

Botticelli
2004
Florida Everglades
Eh?
Holiday Packages
Carriage
Guys
Transportation
Parade

Radio
Arts Décoratifs & Industriels Modernes
World Movie Premiere
·
Lumiere
Le Più Belle Confezioni Per La Donna
Ziegfield Follies of 1933
Azure Sky
Beans Roasted Fresh Daily

Coquette Light

ABCDEFGHIJK
LMNOPQRSTU
VWXYZ abcdefg
hijklmnopqrstuvwxyz
1234567890 &*$¢£.,:;
!?""" «»( )[ ]{ }@©®/%

Coquette Regular

ABCDEFGHIJK
LMNOPQRSTU
VWXYZ abcdefg
hijklmnopqrstuvwxyz
1234567890 &*$¢£.,:;
!?""" «»( )[ ]{ }@©®/%

Coquette Bold

ABCDEFGHIJK
LMNOPQRSTU
VWXYZ abcdefgh
ijklmnopqrstuvwxyz
1234567890 &*$¢£.,:;
!?""" «»( )[ ]{ }@©®/%

mark@ms-studio.com

Goldenbook

Mark Simonson
2003

Goldenbook is based on the logotype of a literary magazine from the late 1920s called *The Golden Book Magazine*. It is meant to be used large, and includes both ranging and lining numerals.

FITZGERALD

San Francisco

EL PUEBLO DE NUESTRA SENORA LA REINA DE LOS ANGELES DE PORCIUNCULA

CHICAGO

Admiral

City

NEW YORK SUBWAY

VIDEO MELIORA PROBOQVE DETERIORA SEQVOR

WINE &

DINE QUARTERLY / SEPTEMBER 2003

WORLD

Mr.

LITERARY GUILD

Fortune

BRIDGE

AN ALTERNATIVE TO THE USUAL MOVIE TITLE

VIRTUE

Rig

Goldenbook Light

ABCDEFGHIJKLM
NOPQRSTUVWXY
Z 1234567890 abcdef
ghijklmnopqrstuvwxyz
1234567890(&*$.,:;!?'')

Goldenbook Regular

ABCDEFGHIJKLM
NOPQRSTUVWXY
Z 1234567890abcdef
ghijklmnopqrstuvwxyz
1234567890(&*$.,:;!?)

Goldenbook Bold

ABCDEFGHIJKLM
NOPQRSTUVWXY
Z 1234567890abcdef
ghijklmnopqrstuvwxyz
1234567890(&*$.,:;!?)

Mark Simonson
2001

Mostra was inspired by Italian Art Deco posters from the 1920s and '30s. It is a caps-only design, but has up to three alternate forms for many characters, providing a range of looks from the conventional to the more stylized.

RISTORANTE

WIZARD

RISK

SIGARETTE

HA!

GRAN PARADISO

A&E

CAPPUCCINO & ESPRESSO

ROMA

MOSTRA DELLA LUCE

COFFEE

FLORAL ARRANGEMENTS

PRELUDE ON THE AFTERNOON OF A FAUN

SIMPLICITY

BETWEEN THE WARS

MAGAZINE

CIOCCOLATO CARAMELLE & CONFETTVRE

WHAT?

Mostra Light

AAABCCDEEFFGGG
HIJKKLMNOPQQRR
SSSTUVWXYYZ 1234
567890 &*$¢£.,;:!?
'''""«»()/%@©®⅄◦†‡

Mostra Regular

AAABCCDEEFFGGG
HIJKKLMNOPQQRR
SSSTUVWXYYZ 1234
567890 &*$¢£.,;:!?
'''""«»()/%@©®⅄◦†

Mostra Bold

AAABCCDEEFFGG
GHIJKKLMNOPQ
QRRSSSTUVWXYYZ
1234567890 &*$¢£
.,;:!?'''""«»()/%@©

mark@ms-studio.com

ACCIDENTAL
APPLICAZIONI ELETTRICHE MODERNE
SOAP
LA CAMICIA CHE PORTA QUESTI MARCHI
WAR & PEACE
POUR AVOIR DES CHEVEUX MAGNIFIQUES
SARSAPARILLA

2001
1928
37
396
$4,568.99

Mostra Heavy

AAABCCDEEFFGG
GHIJKLMNOPQQ
RRSSSTUVWXYYZ
1234567890 &*$¢£
.,;:"!?'"""«»()/%@

Mostra Black

AAABCCDEEFFG
GGHIJKLMNOPQ
QRRSSSTUVWXY
YZ1234567890 &
*$¢£.,;:"!?'"""()/%

Metallophile Sp 8

ABCDEFGHIJKLMNOPQRSTUVWXYZ
abcdefghijklmnopqrstuvwxyz 1234567890
&.,;:!?<>"""«»-—=+()[]{}%*#@ $¢£¥©®
åœÆøœéíûñ™fifl¶ºⁿ/

Metallophile Sp 8 Italic

ABCDEFGHIJKLMNOPQRSTUVWXYZ
abcdefghijklmnopqrstuvwxyz 1234567890
&.,;:!?<>"""«»-—=+()[]{}%#@ $¢£¥©®*
åéüœÆøœéíûñ™fifl¶ºⁿ/

HOW IS ONE TO ASSESS AND EVALUATE a type face in terms of its esthetic design? Why do the pace-makers in the art of printing rave over a specific face of type? What do they see in it? Why is it so superlatively pleasant to their eyes? Good design is always practical design. And what they see in a good type design is, partly, its excellent practical fitness to perform its work. It has a "heft" and balance in all of its parts just right for its size, as any good tool has. Your good chair has all of its parts made nicely to the right size to do exactly the work that the chair has to do,

HOW IS ONE TO ASSESS AND EVALUATE a type face in terms of its esthetic design? Why do the pace-makers in the art of printing rave over a specific face of type? What do they see in it? Why is it so superlatively pleasant to their eyes? Good design is always practical design. And what they see in a good type design is, partly, its excellent practical fitness to perform its work. It has a "heft" and balance in all of its parts just right for its size, as any good tool has. Your good chair has all of its parts made nicely to the right size to do exactly the work that the chair has to do,

Metallophile Sp 8

Mark Simonson
2002

Metallophile Sp 8 is a faithful facsimile of an 8 point sans serif typeface as set on a 1940s vintage hot metal typesetting machine. The effect is very different from its modern cousins, which are drawn more rigidly, and use one design for all sizes. Metallophile Sp 8 is best if used at or near 8 points. This is the first font in a series.

Refrigerator

Mark Simonson
1987, 2000-2003

Refrigerator is based on a style of lettering that was in wide use in the mid-twentieth century. The genre has rarely been translated into the typographic medium without "improvements" intended either to give more warmth and less rigidity to the forms, or to update it in various ways. The Light and Heavy weights are recent additions.

WRENCH

Rice

Easy Assembly Instructions

PUBLISHING INDUSTRY ICON

CANYON

ASTERISK

Mig

Science & Mechanics

POSSIBLE

CYBERNETICS

NO!

DO BLENDERS DREAM OF ELECTRIC CLOCKS?

Kitchen Appliance

Refrigerator Light

ABCDEFGHIJKLMNOPQ
RSTUVWXYZ abcdefg
hijklmnoprstuvwxyz
1234567890 &*$.,:;!
?'"""@#%( )<>=+--—

Refrigerator Bold

ABCDEFGHIJKLMNO
PQRSTUVWXYZ abcd
efghijklmnoprstuvw
xyz 1234567890 &
*$.,:;!?'"""@#%( )<>=

Refrigerator Heavy

ABCDEFGHIJKLMN
OPQRSTUVWXYZ
abcdefghijklmnop
rstuvwxyz 12345
67890 &*$.,:;!?'"

mark@ms-studio.com

MÏX do androids dream of electric sheep?

TERMINAL

trek

MILLENNIUM

DANGER: EXPLOSIVE BOLTS

earth2

RED

doomsday

IDENTITY AFFIRMED: PROCEDURE: 033-03

ACCESS DENIED

SURROGATE INPUT CONTRARY TO ESTABLISHED NORMS

RETROGRAM

BEGIN DATA DUMP *.*/A5:DE:03:05:B1:11:CC:C0:C0:A3:6A:FF:FE:87:$

Euforia Light

AaBbCcDdEeFfGg
HhIiJjKkLlMmNnOp
PqQrRsStTuUvWx
YyZ 1234567890
(&$¢£€%* --.,;;!?'' "" /)

Euforia Regular

AaBbCcDdEeFfGg
HhIiJjKkLlMmNnOp
PqQrRsStTuUvWx
YyZ 1234567890
(&$¢£€%* --.,;;!?'' "" /)

Euforia Bold

AaBbCcDdEeFfGg
HhIiJjKkLlMmNnOp
PqQrRsStTuUvWx
YyZ 1234567890
(&$¢£€%* --.,;;!?'' "" /)

Euforia Stencil

AaBbCcDdEeFfGg
HhIiJjKkLlMmNnOp
PqQrRsStTuUvWx
YyZ 1234567890
(&$¢£€%* --.,;;!?'' "" /)

Euforia Inline

AaBbCcDdEeFfGg
HhIiJjKkLlMmNnOp
PqQrRsStTuUvWx
YyZ 1234567890
(&$¢£€%* --.,;;!?'' "" /)

Sanctuary Regular

ABCDEFGHIJKLMNOPQR
STUVWXYZ 123456789
O (&$£€%-.,;;!?'' "" /*@)

Sanctuary Bold

ABCDEFGHIJKLMNOPQR
STUVWXYZ 123456789
O (&$£€%-.,;;!?'' "" /*@)

Euforia

Mark Simonson
2003

Euforia is a revival and expansion of China, a Visual Graphics Corporation typeface from the early 1970s by Stan Davis (better known as the designer of Amelia). The original design had only one weight (similar to Bold here) in all caps with a few alternates. In Euforia, many characters have been redesigned for better setting. Lowercase-style variants have been added to nearly all the uppercase forms, offering endless "unicase" combinations. Four more styles—Light, Regular, Stencil, and Inline—were added as well as full character sets and extensive kerning tables.

Sanctuary

Mark Simonson
2003

The blow-dried shopping mall dystopia of the 1976 movie *Logan's Run* featured the VGC face Huit (designed by Michel and Roselyne Besnard in 1970) for all its fake computer displays. Sanctuary is a reinterpretation of Huit based on how it looks in the film. Future-techno-kitsch, '70s style. Caps only.

Mark Simonson
2000, 2003

Sharktooth began as an attempt to create a sans serif typeface based on the general structure of Felt Tip Roman (facing page). It turned out quite different in the end, though you can still see similarities. It has an unusual structure for a sans serif, with the diagonal stress of the round elements in tension with the perpendicularity of the linear elements. This seeming contradiction gives Sharktooth a lively, unconventional texture. The Bold and Heavy weights are recent additions.

anagram

Go!

SQUARE

2,634

Eccentricity

WASHINGTON

Monster Truck Show

MYSTERIOUS

65TH ST.

Natural Dentistry

TRIG

Mondays

Oh?

Wet & Wild

Woofers & Tweeters

swatches

Fix

PRESENT

$895

Quagmire

SPEED FREAK

GIVE ME the attention of your eyes, and through this one of your senses **I will lead your thinking** into those contemplations and associations that will make the product advertised appear as a thing greatly to be desired, says the modern selling scientist, who has mastered the meaning of Psychology and knows how to apply its force in the business of causing favorable mental impressions for any article of merchandise. The writer of the successful message and the designer work together to develop an effect. They comprehend

GIVE ME the attention of your eyes, and through this one of your senses **I will lead your thinking** into those contemplations and associations that will make the product advertised appear as a thing greatly to be desired, says the modern selling scientist, who has mastered the meaning of Psychology and knows how to apply its force in the business of causing favorable mental impressions for any article of merchandise. The writer of the successful message and the designer work together to develop an

GIVE ME the attention of your eyes, and through this one of your senses I will lead your thinking into those contemplations and associations that will make the product advertised appear as a thing greatly to be desired, says the modern selling scientist, who has mastered the meaning of Psychology and knows how to apply its force in the business of causing favorable mental impressions for any article of merchandise. The writer of the successful message and the designer work to-

Sharktooth Regular

ABCDEFGHIJKLMN
OPQRSTUVWXYZ &
1234567890 abcdefg
hijklmnopqrstuvwxyz
(.,:;!?-——) [/*'"] {$@%}

Sharktooth Bold

**ABCDEFGHIJKLMN
OPQRSTUVWXYZ &
1234567890 abcdefg
hijklmnopqrstuvw
yz (.,:;!?-) [/*'"] {$@%}**

Sharktooth Heavy

**ABCDEFGHIJKLMN
OPQRSTUVWXYZ &
1234567890abcdefg
hijklmnopqrstuvwx
yz(.,:;!?-) [/*'"] {$@%}**

mark@ms-studio.com

COGITO ERGO SUM

QUOUSQUE TANDEM ABUTERE, CATALINA, patientia nostra?
quamdiu nos etiam furor iste tuus eludet? quem ad fin em
sese effrenata jactabit audacia? nihilne te nocturnum
praesidium pa latii, nihil urbis vigiliae, nihil timor populi, nihil
consensus bonorum omnium, nihil hic munitissimus habendi
senatus locos, nihil horum ora vultusque moverunt? patere tua
consilia non sentis? constrictam jam omnium horum conscientia

Ipso Facto
PLAUDITE CIVES!
gloria

Felt Tip Roman

Mark Simonson
1992, 2003

Felt Tip Roman began as an
experiment in 1989–a straight
adaptation of the designer's
handwriting. The Bold and
Heavy weights were added
recently to broaden its
usefulness.

Felt Tip Roman

ABCDEFGHIJKLMNOPQ
RSTUVWXYZ abcdef
ghijklmnoprstuvwxyz
1234567890 &*$.,:;!?"'""
@#%( )<>=+-—éàÆ¶

Felt Tip Roman Bold

ABCDEFGHIJKLMNOPQ
RSTUVWXYZ abcdef
ghijklmnoprstuvwxyz
1234567890 &*$.,:;!?"'""
@#%( )<>=+-—éàÆ¶

Felt Tip Roman Heavy

ABCDEFGHIJKLMNOP
QRSTUVWXYZ abc
defghijklmnoprstuv
wxyz 1234567890 &
*$.,:;!?"'""@#%( )<>=+

Felt Tip Woman

Mark Simonson
2003

Felt Tip Woman is based on the
handwriting of designer Patricia
Thompson. The name was
inspired by a mis-hearing of the
name "Felt Tip Roman" by a
colleague.

Felt Tip Woman

ABCDEFGHIJKLMNOPQRS
TUVWXYZ abcdefghijklmno
prstuvwxyz 1234567890 &
*$.,:;!?°'""@#%( )<>=+-

Felt Tip Woman Bold

ABCDEFGHIJKLMNOPQRS
TUVWXYZ abcdefghijklmno
prstuvwxyz 1234567890 &

ERRARE HUMANUM EST

QUOUSQUE TANDEM ABUTERE, CATALINA, patientia
nostra? quamdiu nos etiam furor iste tuus eludet? quem
ad fin em sese effrenata jactabit audacia? nihilne te
nocturnum praesidium pa latii, nihil urbis vigiliae, nihil
timor populi, nihil consensus bonorum omnium, nihil hic
munitissimus habendi senatus locos, nihil horum ora
vultusque moverunt? patere tua consilia non sentis?

Felt Tip Senior

Mark Simonson
2000

Felt Tip Senior is based on the
handwriting of Leroy Simonson,
father of the designer. It was
originally licensed exclusively to
Mr. Simonson in 1994, but was
made available to the general
public in 2000.

Felt Tip Senior

ABCDEFGHIJKLMN
OPQRSTUVWXYZ
abcdefghijklmno
prstuvwxyz 1234
567890 $*.,:;!?¿?¿‹‹
@#°%()<>=+-[]

DIEM PERDIDI

QUOUSQUE TANDEM ABUTERE, CATALINA, patientia
nostra? quamdiu nos etiam furor iste tuus eludet? quem ad fin em sese effrenata jactabit
audacia? nihilne te nocturnum praesidium pa latii,
nihil urbis vigiliae, nihil timor populi, nihil consensus
bonorum omnium, nihil hic munitissimus habendi
senatus locos, nihil horum ora vultusque moverunt?
patere tua consilia non sentis? constrictam jam

Mark Simonson Studio

Mark Simonson
1994

Kandal is a slab-serif face with oldstyle or antique qualities. Like other slab serifs, it has low contrast in weight between thicks and thins, even as it gets bolder. Its proportions are slightly condensed, and the color and texture of Kandal Book is not unlike Century Old Style. The name "Kandal" rhymes with "bundle."

BIOLOGY HAS IT THAT THE BODY OF A MAN is made up of some water, enough phosphorus to make *a couple of boxes of matches,* iron good for about two nails, lime enough to white-wash a chicken coop, and sulphur enough to kill the fleas on one dog, with a few other items for good measure. **All the component** parts of his body if disposed of for their commercial value would bring about *ninety cents* and the buyer would not get much of a bargain. If this man were literally worth his weight in gold, he would total at about $45,000, and this amount at interest of five per cent would bring in about $49.00 per week. *But the same personality* which makes one man worth his weight in gold will make another man's value many fold that sum. The personality of men is what distinguishes one from an-other. Biology has it that the body of a man is made up of some water, enough

BIOLOGY HAS IT THAT THE BODY OF A MAN is made up of some water, enough phospho-rus to make a couple of *boxes of matches,* iron good for about two nails, lime enough to white-wash a chicken coop, and sulphur enough to kill the fleas on one dog, with a few other items for good measure. **All the component** parts of his body if disposed of for their commercial value would bring about *ninety cents* and the buyer would not get much of a bargain. If this man were literally worth his weight in gold, he would total at about $45,000, and this amount at interest of five per cent would bring in about $49.00 per week. *But the same person-ality* which makes one man worth his weight in gold will make another man's value many fold that sum. The person-ality of men is what distinguishes one from another. Biology has it that the

YEARLING

Will technology force us to choose between privacy and freedom?

DAMN THE TORPEDOES

Geography

Please

WINE & ROSES

The Society for Putting One Thing on Top of Another

Kandal Book

ABCDEFGHIJKLM NOPQRSTUVWXY Z 1234567890 abc defghijklmnopqrst uvwxyz &*$.,:;!?"""

Kandal Medium

ABCDEFGHIJKLM NOPQRSTUVWX YZ 1234567890 a bcdefghijklmnop qrstuvwxyz &*$.,:

Kandal Book Italic

ABCDEFGHIJKLM NOPQRSTUVWXY Z 1234567890 abc defghijklmnopqrst uvwxyz &$.,:;!?"""*

Kandal Medium Italic

ABCDEFGHIJKLM NOPQRSTUVWX YZ 1234567890 a bcdefghijklmnop qrstuvwxyz &$.,:*

mark@ms-studio.com

SPARKLE
CONFIDENTIALITY
Cardinal

Proxima Sans

Mark Simonson
1994

Proxima Sans Black

Proxima Sans Black Oblique

ABCDEFGHIJKLM
NOPQRSTUVWX
YZ 1234567890 a
bcdefghijklmnopq
rstuvwxyz &$.,:;!?

*ABCDEFGHIJKLM
NOPQRSTUVWX
YZ 1234567890 a
bcdefghijklmnopq
rstuvwxyz &$.,:;!?*

AMONG THOSE WHO HAVE SERIOUSLY CONSIDERED the *flying saucer* as a mode of flight are aerodynamists who are oddly reluctant to accept my own interplantary explanation. Nevertheless, they have not ignored the aerodynamic qualities of a *disc-shaped aircraft.* It is said that such aircraft have been built and flown years ago—it would seem not without some success. Recently, the press has released information about a saucer-type aircraft being developed in Canada. (Plate 1.) The craft is still in the mock-up stage and is said to be *nearly forty feet in diameter.* The revolutionary feature about the plane is not so much the shape of the wing itself, but in the turbine power plant

MONOSPACED

```
clipA.loadMovie("section1.swf"); // Load a document into clipA
```

>>> T = [(1,2),(3,4)]

Code Head

OBJECT-ORIENTED PROGRAMMING

"Typewriter Quotes"

Anonymous™

```
ABCDEFGHIJKLMNOPQRSTUVWXYZ 1234567890 %°$¢£€ƒ¥
abcdefghijklmnopqrstuvwxyz (&$.,:;!?¿¡-—*«»/)
[ '"''""†‡] {@©®™∞§¶•□♀+−=≠÷±<>≤≥¬|\^#∫√≈ΩΔ∂ΣΠπ}
(áàâäãåæçéèêëíìîïñóòôöõøœúùûüÿﬁﬂÁÀÂÄÃÅÆÇÉÈÊËÍ)
```

Anonymous™

Mark Simonson
2001

Anonymous started as a 9 point Macintosh bitmap font designed by Susan Lesch and David B. Lamkins. It was intended as a more legible alternative to the Monaco system font. Mark Simonson developed the outline version shown here. The goal was to interpret the simple bit patterns of the original typographically.

ANONYMOUS
Original bitmap font
ANONYMOUS
Typographic interpretation

MOTION PICTURES AND PERSISTENCE OF VISION.--The motion picture projector is simply a projection lantern that casts a series of pictures on a screen in rapid succession. To the eye, the pictures seem to blend into one another, thus producing the illusion of continuous motion. The reason for this blending is that the impression made upon the retina of the eye by a given picture persists for about one-sixteenth of a second after the picture has been removed. Hence, when pictures are shown one after another at the rate of sixteen or more per second, the image of any one picture will not have time to fade from the retina before the next one appears. The motion projector is simply a projection lantern that casts a series of pictures on a

Raster Gothic Condensed

Mark Simonson
2003

Originally designed as a bitmap font in 1986, and loosely based on Alternate Gothic, Raster Gothic Condensed is a series of outline fonts that retain the aliased look of a bitmap font. The original was retooled for better consistency across sizes, and expanded to include two more sizes and bold for all sizes. Small caps can be made by using caps from the next size down. Perfect for on-screen use, including Flash animations, or any time anti-aliasing is not desired.

Raster Gothic 9 Condensed

ABCDEFGHIJKLMNOPQRSTUVWXYZ
abcdefghijklmnoprstuvwxyz 1234567890
&*$.,:;!?‘’“”@#%( )<>=+-–—¶§∞¢£™
¡¿•°€‹›ﬁﬂ‡°·©®†Ω≈ç√∫∆∂æœéåüøõñ÷
[]{}/|\'"ƒÅÉØÜÎÆŒÈÑ¬…˜˘˙˚¨˝¸˛ˇ

Raster Gothic 9 Bold Condensed

ABCDEFGHIJKLMNOPQRSTUVWXYZ abcdefghijklmnoprstuvwxyz 1234567890 &*$.,:;!?‘’“”@#%( )<>=+-–—¶§∞¢£™¡¿•°€‹›ﬁﬂ‡°·©®†Ω≈ç√∫∆∂æœéåüøõñ÷[]{}/|\'"ƒÅÉØÜÎÆŒÈÑ¬…˜˘˙˚¨˝¸˛ˇ

Raster Gothic 12 Condensed

ABCDEFGHIJKLMNOPQRSTUVWXYZ
abcdefghijklmnoprstuvwxyz
1234567890 &*$.,:;!?‘’“”@#%( )
<>=+-–—¶§∞¢£™¡¿•°€‹›ﬁﬂ‡°·©
®†Ω≈ç√∫∆∂éåüøõñ÷[]{}/|\'"ƒÅÉØ
ÜÎÆŒÈÑéèëêáàâäãóòôöõ¬…˜˘˙˚¨˝¸˛ˇ

Raster Gothic 12 Bold Condensed

ABCDEFGHIJKLMNOPQRSTUVWXYZ abcdefghijklmnoprstuvwxyz 1234567890 &*$.,:;!?‘’“”@#%( )<>=+-–—¶§∞¢£™¡¿•°€‹›ﬁﬂ‡°·©®†Ω≈ç√∫∆∂ÜÎÆŒÈÑéèëêáàâäã¬…˜˘˙˚¨˝¸˛ˇ

Amongst the several mechanic Arts that have engaged my attention, there is no one which I have pursued with so much steadiness and pleasure, as **that of Letter-Founding.** Having been an early admirer of the beauty of Letters, I became insensibly desirous of contributing to the perfection of them. I formed to my self Ideas of greater accuracy than had yet appeared, and have endeavoured to **produce a Sett of Types according** to what I conceived to be their true proportion. ¶ Mr. Caslon is an Artist, to whom the Republic of Learning has great obligations; his ingenuity has left a fairer copy for my emulation, than any other master. In his great variety of Characters I intend not to follow him; the Roman and Italic are all I have hitherto attempted; if in these he has left **room for improvement, it is probably** more owing to that variety which divided his attention, than to any other cause. I honor his merit, and only wish to derive some small share of Reputation, from an Art which proves accidentally to have been the object of our mutual pursuit. ¶ Amongst the several mechanic Arts that have engaged my attention, there is **no one which I have pursued** with so much steadiness and pleasure, as that of Letter-Founding. Having been an early admirer of the beauty of Letters, I became insensibly desirous of contributing to the perfection of them. I formed to myself Ideas of greater accuracy than had yet appeared, and have endeavoured to produce a Sett of Types according to what I concieved to be their true proportion. ¶ Mr. Caslon is an Artist, **to whom the Republic of Learning** has great obligations; his ingenuity has left a fairer copy for my emulation, than any other master. In his great variety of Characters I intend not to follow him; the Roman and Italic are all I have hitherto attempted; if in these he has left room for improvement, it is probably more owing to that variety which divided his attention, than to any other cause. I honor his merit, and only wish to derive some small share of Reputation, from an Art which proves accidentally to have been the object of our mutual pursuit. Amongst the several mechanic Arts that have engaged my attention, there is no one which I have pursued with so

Raster Gothic 14 Condensed

ABCDEFGHIJKLMNOPQRSTUVWXYZ abcdefghijklmnoprstuvwxyz 1234567890 &*$.,:;!?‘’“”@#%( )<>=+-–—§¶∞¢£™¡¿µñåøæüé®©¥†

Raster Gothic 14 Bold Condensed

ABCDEFGHIJKLMNOPQRSTUVWXYZ abcdefghijklmnoprstuvwxyz 1234567890 &*$.,:;!?‘’“”@#%( )<>=+-–—§¶∞¢£™¡¿µñåøæüé®©¥†

Raster Gothic 18 Condensed

ABCDEFGHIJKLMNOPQRSTUVWXYZ abcdefghijklmnoprstuvwxyz 1234567890 &*$.,:;!?‘’“”@#%( )<>=+-–—¶§∞¢£™¡¿µñ

Raster Gothic 18 Bold Condensed

ABCDEFGHIJKLMNOPQRSTUVWXYZ abcdef ghijklmnoprstuvwxyz 1234567890 &*$.,:;! ?‘’“”@#%( )<>=+-–

mark@ms-studio.com

FLEXIBLE PLAN
VIRTUAL REALITY
HEADLINE OPTION
FLUID PARAMETERS
COMPUTERIZATION
TAKE A TRIP TO EARTH
PADDED DASHBOARD
COMMERCIAL POSSIBILITY
MAGNETIC RESONANCE
ELECTRONIC PHOTOGRAPHY
DIGITAL IMAGERY PARADE
ROBOTICS REVOLUTION BEGINS
WORLD WIDE WEBMASTER
BILLIONS OF BILIOUS BARNACLES
RANDOM THOUGHTS DISPLAYED
JOHN BASKERVILLE'S APOLOGY
THANK YOU FOR READING THIS PHRASE
TINY TYPEFACE FOR TITANIC THOUGHTS

Raster Gothic 24 Condensed

ABCDEFGHIJKLMNO
PQRSTUVWXYZ abc
defghijklmnoprstu
vwxyz 12345678
90 &*$.,:;!?'''""@
#%( )<>=+-−

Raster Gothic 28 Condensed

ABCDEFGHIJK
LMNOPQRSTU
VWXYZ abcde
fghijklmnoprs
tuvwxyz 1234
567890 &*$.,
:;!?''""@#%()

Raster Gothic 24 Bold Condensed

ABCDEFGHIJKLMN
OPQRSTUVWXYZ a
bcdefghijklmnop
rstuvwxyz 1234
567890 &*$.,:;!
?'''""@#%( )<>=

Raster Gothic 28 Bold Condensed

ABCDEFGHIJKL
MNOPQRSTUV
WXYZ abcdef
ghijklmnoprst
uvwxyz 12345
67890 &*$.,:;!
?'''""@#%()<>

Raster Gothic Condensed

Mark Simonson
2003

Mark Simonson Studio

PREMIUM
No. 25
JADE TREE
REG

Raster Bank 21

ABCDEFGHIJKLMNOPQ
RSTUVWXYZ ABCDEFGHI
JKLMNOPQRSTUVWXYZ 123
4567890 &*$.,:;!?'''""@
#%()<>=+-−ÆŒ¥€Ç«»¶§£©®

Raster Bank

Mark Simonson
2003

A pixelized version of Bank Gothic, Raster Bank is an outline font that retains the aliased look of a bitmap font. Perfect for on-screen use, including Flash animations, or any time anti-aliasing is not desired.

StormType
foundry.

Storm Type Foundry was founded in Prague in 1993 with the aim to restore the values of classical typography for the benefit of digital technologies. *"Back to the roots" is a tendency which characterizes a large part of our production, inspired by the Renaissance, Baroque, and Neo-classical periods. Our catalogue includes a group of Baroque type families which have been digitized for the first time in the world, and whose shape is almost intact.* We started by drawing alphabets which could be used in book printing, then we proceeded to alphabets for film- and photosetting, and, nowadays, in the era of computers, we use the experience we have gained to make digital typefaces more human.

Our current TypoKatalog5 contains over 490 original fonts.

visit us on **www.stormtype.com**
*buy online on **www.myfonts.com***

ABCDEFGHJKLMNOPabcdefghjklmnop
qrstuvwxyzQRSTUVWXYZ&0123456789
AaBbCcDdEeFfGgHhJjKkLlMmNn
PpQqRTwYyffſtſtctſſfi&0123456789

Antique Ancienne

František Štorm
1998

Inspired by 18th-century type
specimens.

Baroque typography deserves anything else but the attribute "transitional". In the first half of the 18th-century, besides persons whose names are prominent and well-known up to the present, as was Baskerville or Caslon, there were many type founders who did not manage to publish their manuals or forgot to become famous in some other way. They often imitated the typefaces of their more experienced contemporaries, but many of them arrived at a quite strange, even weird originality, which ran completely outside the mainstream of typographical art. The prints from which we have drawn inspiration for these six digital designs come from Paris, Vienna and Prague, from the period

Antique Ancienne 11 pt.

František Štorm
1998

Inspired by 18th-century type
specimens.

Gloria patri & *filii* & *spiritui* Sancto.

Antique Moderne

František Štorm
1998

Inspired by 18th-century type
specimens.

Antique Regent: ABCDEFG
HJKLMNOPabcdefghjklmno
pqrstuvwxyzQRSTUVWXYZ
&0123456789AaBbCcDdEeFfG
gHhJjKkLlMmNnPpQqRTw
Yyffvfi&0123456789

Antique Moderne: ABCDEF
GHJKLMNOPabcdefghjklm
nopqrstuvwxyzQRSTUVW
XYZ&0123456789AaBbCcD
dEeFfGgHhJjKkLlMmNnPp
QqRTwffſtfi&0123456789

Ant. Regent & Moderne

František Štorm
1998

Inspired by 18th-century type
specimens.

Storm Type Foundry

Jannon T Moderne OT

František Štorm
2002

Regular

OpenType font with full range of features.

ABCDEFGHIJKLMNOPQRSTUVWXYZ
abcdefghijklmnopqrsßtuvwxyzfiflfkstctfIftfüfjsp
ABCDEFGHIJKLMNOPQRSTUVWXYZ0123456789
+@!?€£&,0123456789→0123456789

Jannon T Moderne OT

František Štorm
2002

Italic

ABCDEFGHIJKL MNPQR STUVWXYZ
abcdefghijklmnopqrsßtuvwxyz & Swash & Endings
ABCDEFGHIJKLMNQRSTUVWX bdfghjklpqrsßtuvwx yz
+@!?€£&,0123456789→0123456789 r s ß t u vz

Jannon T Moderne OT

František Štorm
2002

Bold

ABCDEFGHIJKLMNOPQRSTUVWXYZ
abcdefghijklmnopqrsßtuvwxyzfiflfkstctfIftfüfjsp
ABCDEFGHIJKLMNOPQRSTUVWXYZ0123456789
+@!?€£&,0123456789→0123456789

Jannon T Moderne OT

František Štorm
2002

Bold Italic

ABCDEFGHIJKLMNOPQRSTUVWXYZ
abcdefghijklmnopqrsßtuvwxyzfiflfkstctfIftfüfjsp
ABCDEFGHIJKLMNOPQRSTUVWXYZ0123456789
+@!?€£&,0123456789→0123456789

Jannon

František Štorm
1995-2002

c'est *une* occafion faite

Jannon Text 137 pt.

Jannon Text 68 pt.

pour l'amplification d'idée progreſsiste

Jannon Antiqua 32 pt.

de **Jannon.** *Jannon* redresse l'axe des hachures, supprime les

Jannon Antiqua 19 pt.

courbes et les subſtitue par les lignes droites. Il n'a pas peur d'incorporer les éléments tout à fait ſtatiques dans l'ensemble parfaitement dynamique d'antique, ce qu'eſt le cas de la plupart des majuscules. Il dessine hardiement l'italique d'une façon nouvelle avec l'angle d'inclinaison irregulier. Notre transcription digitale précédente contenait également tels annomalies, comme la minuscule „*z*" en italique, posée trop haut (ce qu'eſt peut-être une pittoresque faute de compositeur), élargissement léger de la partie moyenne des tiges verticales et quelques autres défauts. En somme: c'eſt une fonte trop beau et trop orientée vers ses origines, qui ne correſponde pas tout à fait au exigences contemporai-

nes. JANNON TEXT MODERNE SOLUTIONNE LES POINTS FAIBLES DES VERSIONS DIGITALES PRÉCÉDENTES. *Tous les traits fins sont accentués et la hauteur medium des minuscules eſt légerement plus petite en comparaison avec Jannon Text. En suivant l'eſprit cristallin et presque froid de Jannon, nous avons approché notre alphabet de baroque, mais aussi des exigeances des lecteurs contemporains. Jannon Text Moderne compte naturellement huit styles de base avec petite capitales, & en plus les chiffres non-tabulés, italiques décoratives, ligatures et vignettes d'époque. Nous éditons cette fonte comme l'alternative entre les autres répliques postgaramondiennes, convenable à toutes les genres de la littérature, qui fera digestibles même les romans gigantesques.* Jannon T Moderne OT 9 pt.

The engraver Jean Jannon ranks among the significant representatives of French typography of the first half of the 17th-century. He was born in 1580, apparently in Switzerland. He trained as punch-cutter in Paris. From 1610, he worked in the printing office of the Calvinist Academy in Sedan, where he was awarded the title "Imprimeur de son Excellence et de l'Academie Sédanoise." He began working on his own alphabet in 1615, so that he would not have to order type for his printing office from Paris, Holland, and Germany, which at that time was rather difficult. The other reason was that not only the existing typefaces, but also the respective punches, were rapidly wearing out.

Their restoration was extremely painstaking, not to mention the fact that the result would have been just a poor shadow of the original elegance. Thus, a new typeface came into existence, standing on a traditional basis, but with a life-giving sparkle from its creator. In 1621, Jannon published a Roman typeface and italics, derived from the shapes of Garamond's typefaces. As late as the start of the 20th-century, Jannon's typeface was mistakenly called Garamond, because it looked like a traditional face at first sight. Jannon's Early Baroque Roman typeface, however, differs from Garamond in contrast and in having grander forms. Jannon's italics rank among the most successful italics of all time – they are brilliantly cut and elegant.

Storm Type Foundry

Jannon T Moderne OT 42 pt.

Jannon Antiqua

Jannon Text

Jannon T Moderne

Elqa& Elqa&Elqa&

Baskerville Ten OT

František Štorm
2002

Regular

OpenType font with full range of features.

ABCDEFGHIJKLMNOPQRSTUVWXYZ
abcdefghijklmnopqrsßtuvwxyzfiflfkstctfstfüsp
ABCDEFGHIJKLMNOPQRSTUVWXYZ0123456789
+@!?€£&,0123456789→0123456789

Baskerville Ten OT

František Štorm
2002

Italic

ABCDEFGHIJKLMNOPQRSTUVWXYZ
abcdefghijklmnopqrsßtuvwxyzfiflfkstctfstfüfisp
ABCDEFGHIJKLMNOPQRSTUVWXYZ0123456789
+@!?€£&,0123456789→0123456789

Baskerville Ten OT

František Štorm
2002

Bold

ABCDEFGHIJKLMNOPQRSTUVWXYZ
abcdefghijklmnopqrsßtuvwxyzfiflfkstctfstfüsp
ABCDEFGHIJKLMNOPQRSTUVWXYZ0123456789
+@!?€£&,0123456789→0123456789

Baskerville Ten OT

František Štorm
2002

Bold Italic

ABCDEFGHIJKLMNOPQRSTUVWXYZ
abcdefghijklmnopqrsßtuvwxyzfiflfkstctfstfüsp
ABCDEFGHIJKLMNOPQRSTUVWXYZ0123456789
+@!?€£&,0123456789→0123456789

Bask | Bask

An analytical

transcription is also

to remove any potential

shortcomings of the source of inspiration

and must not take over mechanically all details of the design.

An analytical

transcription is also

to remove any potential

shortcomings of the source of inspiration

and must not take over mechanically all details of the design.

John Baskerville Original

ABCDEFGJKLMNPQR
STUVWXYZabcdefghjk
mnopqrstuwxyzABCDEFGJK
LMNOPQRSTUVWXYZ+@!?
0123456789013456789
ßfffistctftæœ&

John Baskerville

František Štorm
2000-2002

Until recently, the story of this typeface ended with mediocre digital versions, which did not get at the root of its inspiration. We selected as the most successful models for the digitalization of this typeface its Roman and italics in the size of about today's 14 points, which Baskerville used for the printing, among other things, of his folio Bible in 1763, and Vergil's works in Latin in 1757. These were large-size, stately prints on paper smoothed out by hot copper calender rollers. His engraver, John Handy, was given the task to make the typeface different from the then-fashionable Caslon, which was a surprise for a certain part of typophiles of the period. Baskerville's production in this way perhaps prepared the public also for some ideas of Bodoni and Didot, which is why nowadays everybody calls it a "transitory" phenomenon. A detailed evaluation of Baskerville's heritage, however, remains a task for historians. An analytical transcription is also needed to remove any potential shortcomings of the source of inspiration, and must not take over mechanically all details of the design. Even creators of genius, however, make mistakes sometimes, and, therefore, in spite of the fact that we officially speak about "a transcription," what was involved in the case of all complementary designs was a fairly fundamental reworking. Our aim was not so much to be reverently faithful to the original, as to preserve the spirit of the typeface and to breathe new life into it. Baskerville is a typeface with the character of a gentleman, a typeface of sober elegance and clear design. Its nature is remote from dramatic contrasts, as we know them from the Continental typography of the Late Baroque period. A project of a typeface family which includes twenty designs cannot rely on a single pair of tired eyes; that is why we are again grateful to Otakar Karlas for his valuable advice, especially when putting the finishing touches to the typeface.

Storm Type Foundry

Walbaum Text OT

František Štorm
2002

Regular

OpenType font with full range of
features.

ABCDEFGHIJKLMNOPQRSTUVWXYZ
abcdefghijklmnopqrsßtuvwxyzfiflfksťcťſſtfüfjsp
ABCDEFGHIJKLMNOPQRSTUVWXYZ0123456789
+@!?€£&,0123456789→0123456789

ABCDEFGHIJKLMNOPQRSTUVWXYZ
abcdefghijklmnopqrsßtuvwxyzfiflfksťcťſſtfüfjsp
ABCDEFGHIJKLMNOPQRSTUVWXYZ0123456789
+@!?€£&,0123456789→0123456789

ABCDEFGHIJKLMNOPQRSTUVWXYZ
abcdefghijklmnopqrsßtuvwxyzfiflfksťcťſtfüsp
ABCDEFGHIJKLMNOPQRSTUVWXYZ0123456789
+@!?€£&,0123456789→0123456789

ABCDEFGHIJKLMNOPQRSTUVWXYZ
abcdefghijklmnopqrsßtuvwxyzfiflfksťcťſtfüsp
ABCDEFGHIJKLMNOPQRSTUVWXYZ0123456789
+@!?€£&,0123456789→0123456789

J.E.W. MINOR
irregularities
& the soft
details

František Štorm
2002

Just like the teacher of calligraphy, designer of gravestones and
painter-craftsman Baskerville,
Justus Erich Walbaum also came
to typography from another
- this time much more distant
- profession. He was born in
1768 as a parson's son, and was
apprenticed to a confectioner in
his young days. From engraving
confectioner's moulds it was
only a short step to cutting type
punches and type-founder's
tools. Renaissance graphic
artists, to be sure, were fellows of
a different calibre – they started
their careers by engraving weap-
ons! Walbaum's name, however,
does not appear in any imprint
lines, because he probably never
printed books himself. The same
typefaces were used by other
printers of that period, for example, Unger or Prillwitz. Maybe
the last fine Walbaum typeface
was used to print Berthold's
Specimen Book of 1923, which
also includes a specimen text in
the size of 12 points, on which
our transcription draws.

In contradistinction to the
strictly rational Didot or the
elegant Bodoni, Walbaum, at first
sight, does not possess any features that might lead to a brief
attribute. In any case, however,
it is an outstanding work, a far
cry from chocolate wafer-cakes
or cream horns. The expression
of the typeface is robust, as if it
had been seasoned with the spicy
smell of the dung of Saxon cows
somewhere near Weimar, where
the author had his type foundry
in the years 1803-39. Its typical
features are: a firm skeleton
of the design of the individual
letters, in some cases supported
by a square scheme; daring
triangular serifs on S, s, C, and
G; K and R standing, like an old
grumblers, with one foot placed
forward; and rather conservative
italics. An especially unsuccessful
solution for its time was the
design of italic figures. Nevertheless, they were blindly taken
over by the Berthold Company
in 1919, together with the other
shortcomings.

Storm Type Foundry

Walbaum Text OT 36 pt. (above) and 10pt. (bottom)

UNSERE TEXT-WALBAUM HAT EINE KLASSIZISTISCH ANGEMESSENE MINUSKELMITTELHÖHE, IN Bezug auf die Barockexperimente mit Proportionen. Die untere Schriftlinie ist relativ lang, die obere korrespondiert mit den Versalien. *Bei den Kursiven sind die Minuskeltypen um einen geringen Grad mehr als die Versalien geneigt: dies ist eine typische Erscheinung der meisten historischen Schriften, und wir haben uns daran im Laufe der Hunderte von Jahren bereits gewöhnt.* **Feine Unregelmäßigkeiten und weiche Details** sind für angenehmes Lesen behalten. Die schon erwähnten ***Kursivenziffern*** sind zur Erhaltung des zeitgemäßen Char-akters der Schriftfamilie völlig neu bearbeitet. Alle Schriftbilder sind für kleine Schriftkegel unter 12 Punkte ausbalanciert. Diese wuchtige leibartige Schrift kann für alle Arten der schöngeistigen Literatur angewendet werden, insbesondere für deutsche Novellen der Ro-mantik aus dem ländlichen Milieu.

Underneath

THE CONTEMPORARY-LOOKING DESIGN OF BIBLON,

one can conjecture a Baroque play, with the shifting of shadows, **intentional overstatement,** *or absolute simplification of forms.*

Regular	ABDEGJKLMQRSTUWXYZabcdefghjklnopqrstuwxyz&1234567890
Italic	*ABDEGJKLMQRSTUWXYZabcdefghjklnopqrstuwxyz&1234567890*
Bold	**ABDEGJKLMQRSTUWXYZabcdefghjklnopqrstuwxyz&1234567890**
Bold Italic	***ABDEGJKLMQRSTUWXYZabcdefghjklnopqrstuwxyz&1234567890***
Small Caps	ABDEGJKLMQRSTUWXYZABCDEFGHJKLNOPQRSTUWXYZ&1234567890
Small Caps Bold	**ABDEGJKLMQRSTUWXABCDEFGHJKLNOPQRSTUWXYZ&1234567890**
Swash Italic	*ABDEGJKLMQRSTUWXYZabcdefghjklnopqrstuwxyz&1234567890*
Swash Italic Bold	***ABDEGJKLMQRSTUWXYZabcdefghjklnopqrstuwxyz&1234567890***

another
variation

on the **RENAISSANCE-BAROQUE** ROMAN FACE,

it extends the selection
of text typefaces.

Serapion **Italics** *are inspired*
partly by the Renaissance
Cancelleresca.

Storm Type Foundry

ABDEGJKLMQRSTUWYabcdefghjklnopqrstuwxyz&1234567890 — Regular

ABDEGJKLMQRSTUWXYZabcdefghijklmnopqrstuwxyz&1234567890 — Italic

ABDEGJKLMQRSTUabcdefghjklnopqrstuwxyz&1234567890 — Bold

ABDEGKLMQRSTUWXYabcdefghjklmnopqrstuwxyz&1234567890 — Bold Italic

ABDEGJKLMQRSTUabcdefghjklnopqrstuwxyz&1234567890 — Small Caps

ABDEGKLMQRSTUWabcdefghjklnopqrstuwxyz&1234567890 — Small Caps Italic

ABDEGJKLMQRabcdefghjklnopqrstuwxyz&1234567890 — Small Caps Bold

ABDEGJKLMQRTabcdefghjklnopqrstuwxyz&1234567890 — Small Caps Bold Italic

František Štorm
2001

The idea of a brand-new grotesk is certainly rather foolish – there are already lots of these typefaces in the world, and, quite simply, nothing is more beautiful than the original Gill. The sans serif chapter of typography is now closed by hundreds of technically perfect imitations of Syntax and Frutiger, which are, however, for the most part based on the cool DIN aesthetics. The only chance, when looking for inspiration, is to go very far …

A grotesk does not afford such a variety as a serif typeface; it is dull, and can soon tire the eye. This is why books are not set in sans serif faces. A grotesk is, however, always welcome for expressing different degrees of emphasis, for headings, marginal notes, captions, registers, etc.; in short for any service accompaniment of a book, including its titlings. We also often come across a text in which we want to distinguish the individual speaking or writing persons by the use of different typefaces. The condition is that such grotesk should blend in perfectly with the proportions, colour and, above all, with the expression of the basic serif typeface. In the area of non-fiction typography, what we appreciate in sans serif typefaces is that they are clamorous in inscriptions and economic in the setting. John Sans is to be a modest servant and at the same time an original loudspeaker; it wishes to inhabit libraries of educated persons and to shout from billboards.

A year ago, we completed the transcription of the typefaces of John Baskerville, whose heritage still stands out vividly in our memory. Baskerville cleverly incorporated certain constructional elements in the design of the individual letters of his typeface. These elements include, above all, the alternation of soft and sharp stroke endings. The frequency of these endings in the text and their rhythm produce a balanced impression. The anchoring of the letters on the surface varies, and they do not look monotonous when they

ABDEGJKMQRSTUWXYZabcdefghjknoprstuwxyz&123567890
ABDEGJKMQRSTUWXYZabcdefghjknoprstuwxyz&123567890
ABDEGJKMQRSTAbcdefghijklmnopqrstuvwxyz&1234567890
ABDEGJKMQRSTAbcdefghijklmnopqrstuvwxyz&1234567890

ABDEGJKMQRSTUWXYZabcdefghjknoprstuwxyz&123567890
ABDEGJKMQRSTUWXYZabcdefghjknoprstuwxyz&123567890
ABDEGJKMQRSTAbcdefghijklmnopqrstuvwxyz&1234567890
ABDEGJKMQRSTAbcdefghijklmnopqrstuvwxyz&1234567890

ABDEGJKMQRSTUWXYZabcdefghjknoprstuwxyz&123567890
ABDEGJKMQRSTUWXYZabcdefghjknoprstuwxyz&123567890
ABDEGJKMQRSTAbcdefghijklmnopqrstuvwxyz&1234567890
ABDEGJKMQRSTAbcdefghijklmnopqrstuvwxyz&1234567890

ABDEGJKMQRSTUWXYZabcdefghjknoprstuwxyz&123567890
ABDEGJKMQRSTUWXYZabcdefghjknoprstuwxyz&123567890
ABDEGJKMQRSTAbcdefghijklmnopqrstuvwxyz&1234567890
ABDEGJKMQRSTAbcdefghijklmnopqrstuvwxyz&1234567890

Can **John** *survive* **without** *SERIFS?*

mail@stormtype.com

ABDEGJKMQRSTUWXYZabcdefghjknoprstuwxyz&123567890
ABDEGJKMQRSTUWXYZabcdefghjknoprstuwxyz&123567890
ABDEGJKMQRSTUWXYZabcdefghjknoprstuwxyz&123567890
ABDEGJKMQRSTUWXYZabcdefghjknoprstuwxyz&123567890

ABDEGJKMQRSTUWXYZ ABCDEFGHJKNOPRSTUWXYZ&123567890
ABDEGJKMQRSTUWXYZ ABCDEFGHJKNOPRSTUWXYZ&123567890
ABDEGJKMQRSTUWXYZ ABCDEFGHJKNOPRSTUWXYZ&123567890
ABDEGJKMQRSTUWXYZ ABCDEFGHJKNOPRSTUWXYZ&123567890

ABDEGJKMQRSTUWXYZabcdefghjknoprstuwxyz&123567890
ABDEGJKMQRSTUWXYZabcdefghjknoprstuwxyz&123567890
ABDEGJKMQRST ABCDEFGHIJKLMNOPQRSTUVWXYZ&1234567890
ABDEGJKMQRST ABCDEFGHIJKLMNOPQRSTUVWXYZ&1234567890

ABDEGJKMQRSTUWXYZabcdefghjknoprstuwxyz&123567890
ABDEGJKMQRSTUWXYZabcdefghjknoprstuwxyz&123567890
ABDEGJKMQRST ABCDEFGHIJKLMNOPQRSTUVWXYZ&1234567890
ABDEGJKMQRST ABCDEFGHIJKLMNOPQRSTUVWXYZ&1234567890

Baskerville Ten OT

John Sans

John Sans

František Štorm
2003

are read. We attempted to use these tricks also in the creation of a sans-serif typeface. Except that, if we wished to create a genuine "Baroque grotesk," all the decorativeness of the original would have to be repeated, which would result in a parody. On the contrary, to achieve a mere contrast with the soft Baskerville, it is sufficient to choose any other hard grotesk and not take a great deal of time designing a new one. Between these two extremes, we chose a path starting with the construction of an almost monolinear skeleton, to which the elements of Baskerville were carefully attached. After many tests of the text, however, some of the flourishes had to be removed again. Anything that is superfluous or ornamental is against the substance of a grotesk typeface. The monolinear character can be impinged upon in those places where any consistency would become a burden. The fine shading and softening is for the benefit of both legibility and aesthetics. The more marked incisions of all crotches are a characteristic feature of this typeface, especially in the bold designs. The colour of the Text, Medium and Bold designs is commensurate with their serif counterparts. The White and X-Black designs already exceed the framework of book graphics, and are suitable for use in advertisements and magazines.

Also, the inclusion of non-aligning figures in the basic designs and aligning figures in the small caps serves the purpose of harmonization of the sans serif families with the serif types. Non-aligning figures link up better with lowercase letters in the text.
If John Sans looks like many other modern typefaces, it is just as well. It certainly is not to the detriment of a Latin typeface as a means of communication, if different typographers in different places of the world arrive in different ways at a similar result.

František Štorm
1995

The whole family contains 60 styles

The warm character of
DynaGrotesk *&Italic*

DynaGrotesk*&Italic*DynaGrotesk*&Italic*DynaGrotesk*&Italic*DynaGrotesk*&Italic*
DynaGrotesk*&Italic*DynaGrotesk*&Italic*DynaGrotesk*&Italic*DynaGrotesk*&Ita*
*lic*DynaGrotesk*&Italic*DynaGrotesk*&Italic*DynaGrotesk*&Italic*DynaGrotesk*&Italic*
DynaGrotesk*&Italic*DynaGrotesk*&Italic*DynaGrotesk*&Italic*DynaGrotesk*&Italic*
DynaGrotesk*&Italic*DynaGrotesk*&Italic*DynaGrotesk*&Italic*DynaGrotesk*&Italic*
DynaGrotesk*&Italic*DynaGrotesk*&Italic*DynaGrotesk*&Italic*DynaGrotesk*&Italic*DynaGrot
esk*&Italic*DynaGrotesk*&Italic*DynaGrotesk*&Italic*DynaGrotesk*&Italic*DynaGrotesk*&Italic*

derives from **early** sans-serif typefaces,
those *which appeared* before *Helvetica.*

AaáBbCcčDdEeěFf
GgH*hJjKkLl*MmNn
*ňOoôPp*QqRrřSss̆
Ttt̆UuůVvWwX*xYy*
*ýZz̧z̆&*123456789

mail@stormtype.com

The overall.
expression
of Mramor is vertical.
It is a tranquil, contemplative and intimate typeface. It is not suitable for inscriptions which are supposed to shout out of the surface. *However, in larger sizes, the nakedness of the letters results in a strange, wistful tone.*

ABDFGHJKLMNPQRSTUWXYZabcdefghjklnopqrstuwxyz&1234567890

ABDFGHJKLMNPQRSTUWXYZabcdefghjklnopqrstuwxyz&1234567890

ABDFGHJKLMNPQRSTUWXYZabcdefghjklnopqrstuwxyz&1234567890

ABDFGHJKLMNPQRSTUWXYZabcdefghjklnopqrstuwxyz&1234567890

ABDFGHJKLMNPQRSTUWXYZabcdefghjklnopqrstuwxyz&1234567890

ABDFGHJKLMNPQRSTUWXYZabcdefghjklnopqrstuwxyz&1234567890

ABDFGHJKLMNPQRSTUWXYZabcdefghjklnopqrstuwxyz&1234567890

ABDFGHJKLMNPQRSTUWXYZabcdefghjklnopqrstuwxyz&1234567890

Mramor Text Regular, *Italic*, **Bold** and ***BoldItalic*** are balanced for small point sizes.

Mramor

František Štorm
1994

Mramor arose (about 1988) from the narrowing of Roman capitals. It has uniform width proportions and, above all, original lowercase letters and picturesque italics. The text designs are suitable only for the printing of shorter texts, because the artistic singularity of the typeface soon makes the reader tired. Altogether, Mramor has 14 designs, each of them appropriate for posters. The uppercase letters used in a simple inscription have absolute mastery of the entire area of the page, whereas the arabesques of the lowercase italics play an uncommon decorative accord in it. Were we to look deeper into the "nooks" of this alphabet, we would behold florally-modelled serifs and stems with a very delicate entasis; the curves seem to follow, on the one hand, the merging of palm trunks, on the other, a succession of rugged ridges.

Storm Type Foundry

Teuton

František Štorm
2002

Inspired by a gravestone lettering, suitable for communicatin systems, posters, and technical literature.

Kaufmann *nicht* *unter* 25 Jahre alt, mit Kenntnissen der *doppelten* *Buchführung* und Korrespondenz, für Metallwarenfabrik zum *Eintritt per 15.* Januar 1906 gesucht. Bewerbungen mit Gehaltsforderungen unter K 25 an die Expedition. **Teuton** hat 14 Schriftschnitte.

Plagwitz

František Štorm
2000

Plagwitz is a part of Leipzig, where the ATypI congress in 2000 was held.

Zwei Herzen in Dreivierteltakt aus Plagwitz zusammen gebracht ABCFGRST@℞℔&0123456 78ßfff

Monarchia

František Štorm
1996

Modelled freely after Rodolf Koch's Frühling.

Eine Schwalbe macht kein Sommer (oder Frühling). ABCDabcd@&123456789ffi

Juvenis

Josef Týfa and František Štorm
2002

Under the name Juvenis, Josef Týfa published an original concept of a sans serif typeface in the past half-century. It had a large x-height, space-saving proportions, and daring semi-serifs. Later, in 2001, Týfa came with numerous new sketches and refreshing variations. In summer 2002, we made extra bold versions, interpolated weights, and new italics. The result is a contemporary typeface with good legibility. Juvenis definitely exceeds its original intention as type for children's literature, and it can be used for longer texts and periodicals.

AaBbCcDdEeFfGgHhIiJjKkLlMmNnOoPpQqRrSsTtUuVvWwXxYyZzf

iflfk!?€£&0123456789

LightEFGHIJKLMPQRSTUabcdefghjklnopqrstuwxyz&1234567890
ABCDEFGHIJKLMPQRSTUabcdefghjklnopqrstuwxyz&1234567890
ABCDEFGJKLMPQRSTabcdefghjklnopqrstuwxyz&1234567890
ABCDEFGJKLMPQRSTabcdefghjklnopqrstuwxyz&1234567890
BookEFGHIJKLMPQRSTUabcdefghjklnopqrstuwxyz&1234567890
ABCDEFGHIJKLMPQRSTUabcdefghjklnopqrstuwxyz&1234567890
ABCDEFGJKLMPQRSabcdefghjklnopqrstuwxyz&1234567890
ABCDEFGJKLMPQRSabcdefghjklnopqrstuwxyz&1234567890
TextEFGJKLMPQRSTUabcdefghjklnopqrstuwxyz&1234567890
ABCDEFGJKLMPQRSTabcdefghjklnopqrstuwxyz&1234567890
ABCDEFGJKLMPQabcdefghjklnopqrstuwxyz&1234567890
ABCDEFGJKLMPQabcdefghjklopqrstuwxyz&1234567890
MediumGJKLMPQRSabcdefghjklnopqrstuwxyz&1234567890
ABCDEFGJKLMPQRSabcdefghjklnopqrstuwxyz&1234567890
ABCDEFGJKLMPabcdefghjklopqrstuwxyz&1234567890
ABCDEFGJKLQabcdefghjklnopqrstuwxyz&1234567890

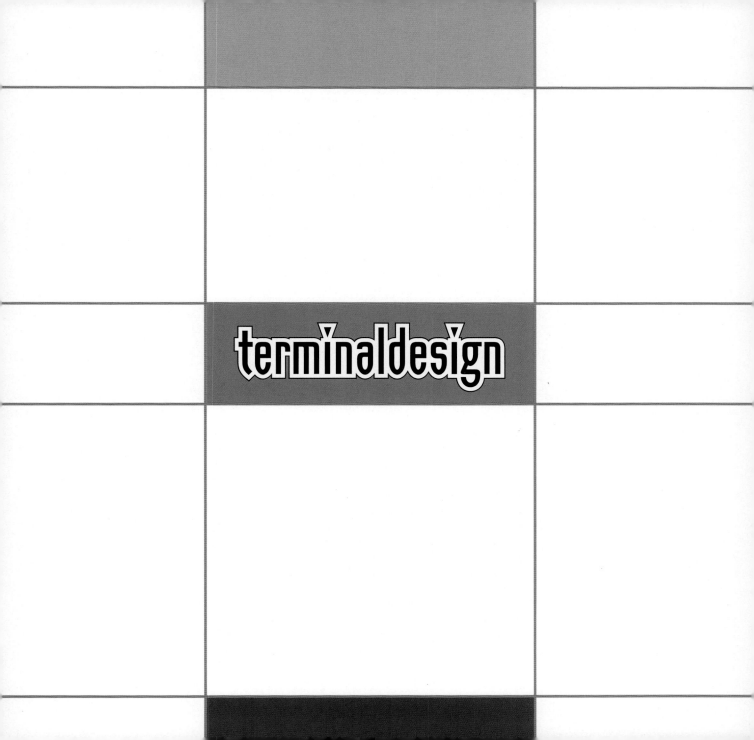

Terminal Design, Inc., is an independent type design and lettering studio, creating original and custom work for advertising, editorial, corporate, publishing and government clients. Our work ranges from complex road guide sign type systems and custom font development to magazine logo and book jacket lettering. We are particularly interested in developing large, legible type families that can be applied over a broad range of applications. Our library of retail fonts is growing, and licenses are available for any installation.

Terminal Design, Inc.
125 Congress Street Brooklyn, NY 11201
V: 718-246-7069 • F: 718-246-7085
www.terminaldesign.com • type@terminaldesign.com

Started by James Montalbano in 1990, Terminal Design, Inc., is currently located on the terminal moraine in Brooklyn, NY. Montalbano's professional career began as a public school graphic arts teacher, trying to get his young students interested in letterpress, offset and silk screen printing. When told he would also have to teach wood shop, he went off to graduate school and taught graphic arts to college students along the way. Seeing no real difference between teaching 8th grade or college undergraduates, he returned to NYC and found work in the wild world of type shops and magazine art departments. It was during this time that he took a lettering course with Ed Benguiat, which changed everything. Montalbano's career continued as a magazine art director, then as the design director responsible for 20 trade magazines (whose subject matter no one should be required to remember). He tried his hand at designing pharmaceutical packaging, but that only made him ill. When his nausea subsided, he started Terminal Design, Inc., and hasn't been sick since.

Featured text:
A Descent into the Maelstrom
by Edgar Allan Poe

We had now reached the summit of the loftiest crag. For some minutes the old man seemed too much exhausted to speak. "Not long ago," said he at length, "and I could have guided you on this route as well as the youngest of my sons; but, about three years past,

Giacomo Light

James Montalbano
2002

OpenType: Contains Tabular & Oldstyle Figures, Fractions, Superior & Inferior Figures and Ligatures.

There happened to me an event such as never happened before to mortal man, or at least such as no man ever survived to tell of, and the six hours of deadly terror which I then endured have broken me up body and soul. You suppose me a very old man,

Giacomo Light Italic

James Montalbano
2002

OpenType: Contains Tabular & Oldstyle Figures, Fractions, Superior & Inferior Figures and Ligatures.

But I am not. It took less than a single day to change these hairs from a jetty black to white, to weaken my limbs, and to unstring my nerves, so that I tremble at the least exertion, and am frightened at a shadow. Do you know I can scarcely look over this little cliff

Giacomo Regular

James Montalbano
2002

OpenType: Contains Tabular & Oldstyle Figures, Fractions, Superior & Inferior Figures and Ligatures.

Without getting giddy?" The "little cliff," upon whose edge he had so carelessly thrown himself down to rest that the weightier portion of his body hung over it, while he was only kept from falling by the tenure of his elbow on its extreme and slippery edge, this

Giacomo Regular Italic

James Montalbano
2002

OpenType: Contains Tabular & Oldstyle Figures, Fractions, Superior & Inferior Figures and Ligatures.

Terminal Design

Giacomo Medium

James Montalbano
2002

OpenType: Contains Tabular
& Oldstyle Figures, Fractions,
Superior & Inferior Figures
and Ligatures.

"Little cliff" arose, a sheer unobstructed precipice of black shining rock, some fifteen or sixteen hundred feet from the world of crags beneath us. Nothing would have tempted me to be within half a dozen yards of its brink. In truth so deeply was I

Giacomo Medium Italic

James Montalbano
2002

OpenType: Contains Tabular
& Oldstyle Figures, Fractions,
Superior & Inferior Figures
and Ligatures.

Excited by the perilous position of my companion, that I fell at full length upon the ground, clung to the shrubs around me, and dared not even glance upward at the sky, while I struggled in vain to divest myself of the idea that the very foundations

GiacomoBold

James Montalbano
2002

OpenType: Contains Tabular
& Oldstyle Figures, Fractions,
Superior & Inferior Figures
and Ligatures.

Of the mountain were in danger from the fury of the winds. It was long before I could reason myself into sufficient courage to sit up and look out into the distance. "You must get over these fancies," said the guide, "for I have brought you

Giacomo Bold Italic

James Montalbano
2002

OpenType: Contains Tabular
& Oldstyle Figures, Fractions,
Superior & Inferior Figures
and Ligatures.

Here that you might have the best possible view of the scene of that event I mentioned, and to tell you the whole story with the spot just under your eye. We are now," he continued, in that particularizing manner which distinguish him,

"We are now close upon the Norwegian coast, in the sixty-eighth degree of latitude, in the great province of Nordland, and in the dreary district of Lofoden. The mountain upon whose top we sit is Helseggen, the Cloudy. Now raise

Giacomo Heavy

James Montalbano
2002

OpenType: Contains Tabular & Oldstyle Figures, Fractions, Superior & Inferior Figures and Ligatures.

Yourself up a little higher, hold on to the grass if you feel giddy so, and look out, beyond the belt of vapor beneath us, into the sea." I looked dizzily, and beheld a wide expanse of ocean, whose waters wore so inky a hue as to bring at

Giacomo Heavy Italic

James Montalbano
2002

OpenType: Contains Tabular & Oldstyle Figures, Fractions, Superior & Inferior Figures and Ligatures.

Once to my mind the Nubian Geographer's account of the Mare Tenebrarum. A pano-rama more deplorably desolate no human imagination can conceive. To the right and left, as far as the eye could reach, there lay

Giacomo Black

James Montalbano
2002

OpenType: Contains Tabular & Oldstyle Figures, Fractions, Superior & Inferior Figures and Ligatures.

Out stretched, like ramparts of the world, lines horridly black and beetling cliff, whose character of gloom was but the more forc-ibly illustrated by the surf which reared high up against it, its white and ghastly

Giacomo Black Italic

James Montalbano
2002

OpenType: Contains Tabular & Oldstyle Figures, Fractions, Superior & Inferior Figures and Ligatures.

Terminal Design

Rawlinson Regular

James Montalbano
2002

OpenType: Contains Tabular,
Proportional & Oldstyle Figures,
Fractions, Superior & Inferior
Figures, Ligatures.

Crest, howling and shrieking forever. Just opposite the promontory upon whose apex we were placed, and at a distance of some five or six miles out at sea, there was visible a small, bleak-looking island; or, more properly, its position was discernible

Rawlinson Italic

James Montalbano
2002

OpenType: Contains Tabular,
Proportional & Oldstyle Figures,
Fractions, Superior & Inferior
Figures, Ligatures.

Through the wilderness of surge in which it was enveloped. About two miles nearer the land, arose another of small size, hideously craggy and barren, and encompassed at various intervals by a cluster of dark rocks. The appearance of the ocean, in the space

Rawlinson Medium

James Montalbano
2002

OpenType: Contains Tabular,
Proportional & Oldstyle Figures,
Fractions, Superior & Inferior
Figures, Ligatures.

Between the more distant island and the shore, had something very unusual about it. Although, at the time, so strong a gale was blowing landward that a brig in the remote offing lay to under a double reefed trysail, and constantly plunged her

Rawlinson Med Italic

James Montalbano
2002

OpenType: Contains Tabular,
Proportional & Oldstyle Figures,
Fractions, Superior & Inferior
Figures, Ligatures.

Whole hull out of sight, still there was here nothing like a regular swell, but only a short, quick, angry cross dashing of water in every direction, as well in the teeth of the wind as otherwise. Of foam there was little except in the immediate vicinity of the

Rocks. "The island in the distance," resumed the old man, "is called by the Norwegians Vurrgh. The one midway is Moskoe. That a mile to the northward is Ambaaren. Yonder are Islesen, Hotholm, Keildhelm, Suarven, and Buckholm.

Further off, between Moskoe and Vurrgh, are Otterholm, Flimen, Sandflesen, and Stockholm. These are the true names of the places, but why it has been thought necessary to name them at all, is more than either you or I can understand.

Do you hear anything? Do you see any change in the water?" We had now been about ten minutes upon the top of Helseggen, to which we had ascended from the interior of Lofoden, so that we had caught no glimpse of the sea until it had

Burst upon us from the summit. As the old man spoke, I became aware of a loud and gradually increasing sound, like the moaning of a vast herd of buffaloes upon an American prairie; and at the same moment I perceived that what

Rawlinson Bold

James Montalbano
2002

OpenType: Contains Tabular, Proportional & Oldstyle Figures, Fractions, Superior & Inferior Figures, Ligatures.

Rawlinson Bold Italic

James Montalbano
2002

OpenType: Contains Tabular, Proportional & Oldstyle Figures, Fractions, Superior & Inferior Figures, Ligatures.

Rawlinson Heavy

James Montalbano
2002

OpenType: Contains Tabular, Proportional & Oldstyle Figures, Fractions, Superior & Inferior Figures, Ligatures.

Rawlinson Heavy Italic

James Montalbano
2002

OpenType: Contains Tabular, Proportional & Oldstyle Figures, Fractions, Superior & Inferior Figures, Ligatures.

Terminal Design

Rawlinson Cn Regular

James Montalbano
2002

OpenType: Contains Tabular,
Proportional & Oldstyle Figures,
Fractions, Superior & Inferior
Figures, Ligatures.

Seamen termed the chopping character of the ocean beneath us, was rapidly changing into a current which set to the eastward. Even while I gazed, this current acquired a monstrous velocity. Each moment added to its speed, to its head long impetuosity. In five minutes the whole sea, as far

Rawlinson Cn Italic

James Montalbano
2002

OpenType: Contains Tabular,
Proportional & Oldstyle Figures,
Fractions, Superior & Inferior
Figures, Ligatures.

As Vurrgh, was lashed into ungovernable fury, but it was between Moskoe and the coast that the main uproar held its sway. Here the vast bed of the waters, seamed and scarred into a thousand conflicting channels, burst suddenly into phrensied convulsion, heaving, boiling, hissing, gyrating in gigantic and

Rawlinson Cn Medium

James Montalbano
2002

OpenType: Contains Tabular,
Proportional & Oldstyle Figures,
Fractions, Superior & Inferior
Figures, Ligatures.

Innumerable vortices, and all whirling and plunging on to the eastward with a rapidity which water never elsewhere assumes, except in precipitous descents. In a few minutes more, there came over the scene another radical alteration. The general surface grew somewhat more smooth,

Rawlinson Cn Med Italic

James Montalbano
2002

OpenType: Contains Tabular,
Proportional & Oldstyle Figures,
Fractions, Superior & Inferior
Figures, Ligatures.

And the whirlpools, one by one, disappeared, while prodigious streaks of foam became apparent where none had been seen before. These streaks, at length, spread out to a great distance, and entering into combination, took unto themselves the gyratory motion of the subsided vortices,

718-246-7069

And seemed to form the germ of another more vast. Suddenly, very suddenly, this assumed a distinct and definite existence, in a circle of more than a mile in diameter. The edge of the whirl was represented by a broad belt of gleaming spray; but no particle of this slipped into the

Rawlinson Cn Bold

James Montalbano
2002

OpenType: Contains Tabular, Proportional & Oldstyle Figures, Fractions, Superior & Inferior Figures, Ligatures.

Mouth of the terrific funnel, whose interior, as far as the eye could fathom it, was a smooth, shining, and jet-black wall of water, inclined to the horizon at an angle of some forty-five degrees, speeding dizzily round and round with a swaying and sweltering motion, and sending forth to

Rawlinson Cn Bold Italic

James Montalbano
2002

OpenType: Contains Tabular, Proportional & Oldstyle Figures, Fractions, Superior & Inferior Figures, Ligatures.

The winds an appalling voice, half shriek, half roar, such as not even the mighty cataract of Niagara ever lifts up in its agony to Heaven. The mountain trembled to its very base, and the rock rocked. I threw myself upon my face, and clung to the scant herbage in

Rawlinson Cn Heavy

James Montalbano
2002

OpenType: Contains Tabular, Proportional & Oldstyle Figures, Fractions, Superior & Inferior Figures, Ligatures.

An excess of nervous agitation. "This," said I at length, to the old man, "this can be nothing else than the great whirlpool of the Maelstrom. So it is sometimes termed," said he. "We Norwegians call it the Moskoe-strom, from the island of Moskoe in the Midway."

Rawlinson Cn Hvy Italic

James Montalbano
2002

OpenType: Contains Tabular, Proportional & Oldstyle Figures, Fractions, Superior & Inferior Figures, Ligatures.

Terminal Design

The ordinary account of this vortex had by no means prepared me for what I saw. That of Jonas Ramus, which is perhaps the most circumstantial of any, cannot impart the faintest conception either of the magnificence, or of the

Horror of the scene or of the wild bewildering sense of the novel which confounds the beholder. I am not sure from what point of view the writer in question surveyed it, nor at what time; but it could neither have been

From the summit of Helseggen, nor during a storm. There are some passages of his description, nevertheless, which may be quoted for their details, although their effect is exceedingly feeble in conveying

An impression of the spectacle. "Between Lofoden and Moskoe," he says, "the depth of the water is between thirty-six and forty fathoms; but on the other side, toward Ver (Vurrgh) this depth

Decreases so as not to afford a convenient passage for a vessel, without the risk of splitting on the rocks, which happens even in the calmest weather. When it is flood, the stream runs up the

Country between Lofoden and Moskoe with boisterous rapidity; but the roar of its impetuous ebb to the sea is scarce equalled by the loudest and most dreadful cataracts; the

Noise being heard several leagues off, and the vortices or pits are of such an extent and depth, that if a ship comes within its attraction, it is inevitably absorbed and carried

Down to the bottom, and there beat to pieces against the rocks; and when the water relaxes, the fragments there of are thrown up again. But these intervals of

Tranquillity are only at the turn of the ebb and flood, and in calm weather, and last but a quarter of an hour, its violence gradually returning. When the stream is most boisterous, and its fury heightened by a storm, it is dangerous

ClearviewOne XThin Ital

James Montalbano, Donald Meeker, Chris O'Hara
1999

Tabular, Proportional & Oldstyle figures

To come within a Norway mile of it. Boats, yachts, and ships have been carried away by not guarding against it before they were carried within its reach. It likewise happens frequently, that whales come too near the

ClearviewOne Thin Ital

James Montalbano, Donald Meeker, Chris O'Hara
1997

Tabular, Proportional & Oldstyle figures

Stream, and are overpowered by its violence; and then it is impossible to describe their howlings and bellowings in their fruitless struggles to disengage themselves. A bear once, attempting to swim from Lofoden

ClearviewOne Light Ital

James Montalbano, Donald Meeker, Chris O'Hara
1997

Tabular, Proportional & Oldstyle figures

To Moskoe, was caught by the stream and borne down, while he roared terribly, so as to be heard on shore. Large stocks of firs and pine trees, after being absorbed by the current, rise again broken

ClearviewOne Book Ital

James Montalbano, Donald Meeker, Chris O'Hara
1997

Tabular, Proportional & Oldstyle figures

And torn to such a degree as if bristles grew upon them. This plainly shows the bottom to consist of craggy rocks, among which they are whirled to and fro. This stream is regulated by

ClearviewOne Med Ital

James Montalbano, Donald Meeker, Chris O'Hara
1997

Tabular, Proportional & Oldstyle figures

The flux and reflux the sea it being constantly high and low water every six hours. In the year 1645, early in the morning of Sexagesima Sunday, it raged with such noise and impetuosity

ClearviewOne Bold Ital

James Montalbano, Donald Meeker, Chris O'Hara
1997

Tabular, Proportional & Oldstyle figures

That the very stones of the houses on the coast fell to the ground." In regard to the depth of the water, I could not see how this could have been ascertained at all in the

ClearviewOne Hvy Ital

James Montalbano, Donald Meeker, Chris O'Hara
1997

Tabular, Proportional & Oldstyle figures

Immediate vicinity of the vortex. The "forty fathoms" must have reference only to portions of the channel close upon the shore either of Moskoe or Lofoden. The depth in

ClearviewOne Black Ital

James Montalbano, Donald Meeker, Chris O'Hara
1999

Tabular, Proportional & Oldstyle figures

Terminal Design

ClearviewOne XThin Cn

James Montalbano,
Donald Meeker, Chris O'Hara
1999

Tabular & Proportional figures

The centre of the Moskoe-strom must be unmeasurably greater; and no better proof of this fact is necessary than can be obtained from even the sidelong glance into the abyss of the whirl which may be had from the highest crag of Helseggen. Looking

ClearviewOne Thin Cn

James Montalbano,
Donald Meeker, Chris O'Hara
1997

Tabular & Proportional figures

Down from this pinnacle upon the howling Phlegethon below, I could not help smiling at the simplicity with which the honest Jonas Ramus records, as a matter difficult of belief, the anecdotes of the whales and the bears, for it appeared to me,

ClearviewOne Light Cn

James Montalbano,
Donald Meeker, Chris O'Hara
1997

Tabular & Proportional figures

In fact, a self-evident thing, that the largest ships of the line in existence, coming within the influence of that deadly attraction, could resist it as a feather the hurricane, and must disappear bodily and at once. The attempts to account for

ClearviewOne Book Cn

James Montalbano,
Donald Meeker, Chris O'Hara
1997

Tabular & Proportional figures

The phenomenon, some of which I remember, seemed to me sufficiently plausible in perusal, now wore a very different and unsatisfactory aspect. The idea generally received is that this, as well as three smaller vortices

ClearviewOne Med Cn

James Montalbano,
Donald Meeker, Chris O'Hara
1997

Tabular & Proportional figures

Among the Ferroe Islands, "have no other cause than the collision of waves rising and falling, at flux and reflux, against a ridge of rocks and shelves, which confines the water so that it precipitates itself like

ClearviewOne Bold Cn

James Montalbano,
Donald Meeker, Chris O'Hara
1997

Tabular & Proportional figures

A cataract; and thus the higher the flood rises, the deeper must the fall be, and the natural result of all is a whirlpool or vortex, the prodigious suction of which is sufficiently known by lesser

ClearviewOne Heavy Cn

James Montalbano,
Donald Meeker, Chris O'Hara
1997

Tabular & Proportional figures

Experiments." These are the words in the Encyclopaedia Britannica. Kircher and others imagine that in the centre of the channel of the maelstrom is an abyss penetrating the globe, and

ClearviewOne Black Cn

James Montalbano,
Donald Meeker, Chris O'Hara
1997

Tabular & Proportional figures

Issuing in some very remote part the Gulf of Bothnia being somewhat decidedly named in one instance. This opinion, idle in itself, was the one to which, as I gazed, my imagina-

Most readily assented; and, mentioning it to the guide, I was rather surprised to hear him say that, although it was the view almost universally entertained of the subject by the Norwegians, it nevertheless was not his own. As to the former notion he confessed his

Inability to comprehend it; and here I agreed with him for, however conclusive on paper, it becomes altogether unintelligible, and even absurd, amid the thunder of the abyss. "You have had a good look at the whirl now," said the old man, "and if

You will creep round this crag, so as to get in its lee, and deaden the roar of the water, I will tell you a story that will convince you I ought to know something of the Moskoe-strom." I placed myself as desired, and he proceeded. "Myself and

My two brothers once owned a schooner, rigged smack of about seventy tons burthen, with which we were in the habit of fishing among the islands beyond Moskoe, nearly to Vurrgh. In all violent eddies at sea there is good

Fishing, at proper opportunities, if one has only the courage to attempt it; but among the whole of the Lofoden coastmen, we three were the only ones who made a regular business of going out to the

Islands, as I tell you. The usual grounds are a great way lower down to the southward. There fish can be got at all hours, without much risk, and therefore these places are preferred. The choice spots

Over here among the rocks, however, not only yield the finest variety, but in far greater abundance; so that we often got in a single day, what the more timid of the craft could not scrape

Together in a week. In fact, we made it a matter of desperate speculation, the risk of life standing instead of labor, and courage answering for capital. "We kept the smack in a cove

Terminal Design

ClearviewOne XThin Cp

James Montalbano,
Donald Meeker, Chris O'Hara
1999

Tabular & Proportional figures

About five miles higher up the coast than this; and it was our practice, in fine weather, to take advantage of the fifteen minutes' slack to push across the main channel of the Moskoe-strom, far above the pool, and then drop down upon anchorage somewhere near Otterhoim, or Sandflesen, where the eddies are not

ClearviewOne Thin Cp

James Montalbano,
Donald Meeker, Chris O'Hara
1997

Tabular & Proportional figures

So violent as elsewhere. Here we used to remain until nearly time for slack-water again, when we weighed and made for home. We never set out upon this expedition without a steady side wind for going and coming, one that we felt sure would not fail us before our return, and we seldom

ClearviewOne Light Cp

James Montalbano,
Donald Meeker, Chris O'Hara
1997

Tabular & Proportional figures

Made a miscalculation upon this point. Twice, during six years, we were forced to stay all night at anchor on account of a dead calm, which is a rare thing in deed just about here; and once we had to remain on the grounds nearly a week, starving to death, owing to a gale

ClearviewOne Book Cp

James Montalbano,
Donald Meeker, Chris O'Hara
1997

Tabular & Proportional figures

Which blew up shortly after our arrival, and made the channel too boisterous to be thought of. Upon this occasion we should have been driven out to sea in spite of everything (for the whirlpools threw us round and round so violently, that, at length,

ClearviewOne Med Cp

James Montalbano,
Donald Meeker, Chris O'Hara
1997

Tabular & Proportional figures

We fouled our anchor and dragged it), if it had not been that we drifted into one of the innumerable cross currents, here today and gone tomorrow, which drove us under the lee of Flimen, where, by good luck, we brought up. "I could not tell

ClearviewOne Bold Cp

James Montalbano,
Donald Meeker, Chris O'Hara
1997

Tabular & Proportional figures

You the twentieth part of the difficulties we encountered 'on the ground', it is a bad spot to be in, even in good weather, but we made shift always to run the gauntlet of the Moskoe-strom itself without accident; although at

ClearviewOne Heavy Cp

James Montalbano,
Donald Meeker, Chris O'Hara
1997

Tabular & Proportional figures

Times my heart has been in my mouth when we happened to be a min-ute or so behind or before the slack. The wind sometimes was not as strong as we thought it at starting, and then we made rather less way

ClearviewOne Black Cp

James Montalbano,
Donald Meeker, Chris O'Hara
1999

Tabular & Proportional figures

Than we could wish, while the current rendered the smack unmanageable. My eldest brother had a son eighteen years old, and I had two stout boys of my own. These would have

Been of great assistance at such times, in using the sweeps as well as afterward in fishing, but somehow, although we ran the risk ourselves, we had not the heart to let the young ones get into the danger for, after all said and done, it was a horrible danger, and that is the truth. "It is now within a few days of three

ClearviewOne XThn Cp It

James Montalbano,
Donald Meeker, Chris O'Hara
1999

Tabular & Proportional figures

Years since what I am going to tell you occurred. It was on the tenth of July, a day which the people of this part of the world will never forget, for it was one in which blew the most terrible hurricane that ever came out of the heavens. And yet all the morning, and indeed until late in

ClearviewOne Thin Cp It

James Montalbano,
Donald Meeker, Chris O'Hara
1997

Tabular & Proportional figures

The afternoon, there was a gentle and steady breeze from the southwest, while the sun shone brightly, so that the oldest seaman among us could not have foreseen what was to follow. "The three of us, my two brothers and myself, had crossed over to the islands

ClearviewOne Lt Cp It

James Montalbano,
Donald Meeker, Chris O'Hara
1997

Tabular & Proportional figures

About two o'clock p.m., and soon nearly loaded the smack with fine fish, which, we all remarked, were more plenty that day than we had ever known them. It was just seven, by my watch, when we weighed and started for home, so as to make the worst of the

ClearviewOne Book Cp It

James Montalbano,
Donald Meeker, Chris O'Hara
1997

Tabular & Proportional figures

Strom at slack water, which we knew would be at eight. "We set out with a fresh wind on our starboard quarter, and for sometime spanked along at a great rate, never dreaming of danger, for indeed we saw not the slightest reason to appre-

ClearviewOne Med Cp It

James Montalbano,
Donald Meeker, Chris O'Hara
1997

Tabular & Proportional figures

Hend it. All at once we were taken aback by a breeze from over Helseggen. This was most unusual something that had never happened to us before, and I began to feel a little uneasy, without exactly knowing why. We put

ClearviewOne Bold Cp It

James Montalbano,
Donald Meeker, Chris O'Hara
1997

Tabular & Proportional figures

The boat on the wind, but could make no headway at all for the eddies, and I was upon the point of proposing to return to the anchorage, when, looking astern, we saw the whole horizon covered with a singular

ClearviewOne Hvy Cp It

James Montalbano,
Donald Meeker, Chris O'Hara
1997

Tabular & Proportional figures

Copper-colored cloud that rose with the most amazing velocity. "In the meantime the breeze that had headed us off fell away and we were dead becalmed, drifting about in every direction.

ClearviewOne Blk Cp It

James Montalbano,
Donald Meeker, Chris O'Hara
1999

Tabular & Proportional figures

Terminal Design

ClearviewOne XThin SC

James Montalbano,
Donald Meeker, Chris O'Hara
1997

Tabular, Proportional &
Oldstyle figures

THIS STATE OF THINGS, HOWEVER, DID NOT LAST LONG ENOUGH TO GIVE US TIME TO THINK ABOUT IT. IN LESS THAN A MINUTE THE STORM WAS UPON US, IN LESS THAN TWO THE SKY WAS ENTIRELY OVERCAST AND WHAT WITH THIS AND THE DRIVING SPRAY, IT

ClearviewOne Thin SC

James Montalbano,
Donald Meeker, Chris O'Hara
1997

Tabular, Proportional &
Oldstyle figures

BECAME SUDDENLY SO DARK THAT WE COULD NOT SEE EACH OTHER IN THE SMACK. "SUCH A HURRICANE AS THEN BLEW IT IS FOLLY TO ATTEMPT DESCRIBING. THE OLDEST SEAMAN IN NORWAY NEVER EXPERIENCED ANY THING LIKE IT. WE HAD LET OUR SAILS

ClearviewOne Light SC

James Montalbano,
Donald Meeker, Chris O'Hara
1997

Tabular, Proportional &
Oldstyle figures

GO BY THE RUN BEFORE IT CLEVERLY TOOK US; BUT, AT THE FIRST PUFF, BOTH OUR MASTS WENT BY THE BOARD AS IF THEY HAD BEEN SAWED OFF, THE MAIN-MAST TAKING WITH IT MY YOUNGEST BROTHER, WHO HAD LASHED HIMSELF TO IT

ClearviewOne Book SC

James Montalbano,
Donald Meeker, Chris O'Hara
1997

Tabular, Proportional &
Oldstyle figures

FOR SAFETY. "OUR BOAT WAS THE LIGHTEST FEATHER OF A THING THAT EVER SAT UPON WATER. IT HAD A COMPLETE FLUSH DECK, WITH ONLY A SMALL HATCH NEAR THE BOW, AND THIS HATCH IT HAD ALWAYS BEEN OUR CUSTOM

ClearviewOne Med SC

James Montalbano,
Donald Meeker, Chris O'Hara
1997

Tabular, Proportional &
Oldstyle figures

TO BATTEN DOWN WHEN ABOUT TO CROSS THE STROM, BY WAY OF PRE-CAUTION AGAINST THE CHOPPING SEAS. BUT FOR THIS CIRCUMSTANCE WE SHOULD HAVE FOUNDERED AT ONCE, FOR WE LAY ENTIRELY BURIED FOR

ClearviewOne Bold SC

James Montalbano,
Donald Meeker, Chris O'Hara
1997

Tabular, Proportional &
Oldstyle figures

SOME MOMENTS. HOW MY ELDER BROTHER ESCAPED DESTRUCTION I CANNOT SAY, FOR I NEVER HAD AN OPPORTUNITY OF ASCERTAINING. FOR MY PART, AS SOON AS I HAD LET THE FORESAIL RUN, I THREW

ClearviewOne Heavy SC

James Montalbano,
Donald Meeker, Chris O'Hara
1999

Tabular, Proportional &
Oldstyle figures

MYSELF FLAT ON DECK, WITH MY FEET AGAINST THE NARROW GUN-WALE OF THE BOW, AND WITH MY HANDS GRASPING A RING-BOLT NEAR THE FOOT OF THE FOREMAST. IT WAS MERE INSTINCT THAT

ClearviewOne Black SC

James Montalbano,
Donald Meeker, Chris O'Hara
1999

Tabular, Proportional &
Oldstyle figures

PROMPTED ME TO DO THIS, WHICH WAS UNDOUBTEDLY THE VERY BEST THING I COULD HAVE DONE, FOR I WAS TOO MUCH FLURRIED TO THINK. "FOR SOME MOMENTS WE WERE COMPLETELY DELUGED,

718-246-7069

Chicago Lakefront 54

Chicago Lakefront 54

ClearviewHwy 6W & 6B

*James Montalbano
Donald Meeker, Chris O'Hara
2002*

For large, bifurcated road guide sign applications.

Sarasota Tampa St Pete

Sarasota Tampa St Pete

ClearviewHwy 5W & 5B

*James Montalbano
Donald Meeker, Chris O'Hara
2002*

FHWA approved alternate to Highway Gothic Series E Modified

Hohokus Saddle River Rd

Hohokus Saddle River Rd

ClearviewHwy 4W & 4B

*James Montalbano
Donald Meeker, Chris O'Hara
2002*

FHWA approved alternate to Highway Gothic Series E

Forty-Fifth Parallel 9 miles

Forty-Fifth Parallel 9 miles

ClearviewHwy 3W & 3B

*James Montalbano
Donald Meeker, Chris O'Hara
2002*

FHWA approved alternate to Highway Gothic Series D

Brooklyn-Queens Expressway 30

Brooklyn-Queens Expressway 30

ClearviewHwy 2W & 2B

*James Montalbano
Donald Meeker, Chris O'Hara
2002*

FHWA approved alternate to Highway Gothic Series C

United Nations Restaurant & Parking

United Nations Restaurant & Parking

ClearviewHwy 1W & 1B

*James Montalbano
Donald Meeker, Chris O'Hara
2002*

FHWA approved alternate to Highway Gothic Series B

Terminal Design

Underware

*is a (typo)graphic designstudio focusing on designing and producing
typefaces. These are published for retail sale or are specially tailor-made.
The studios are based in Den Haag, Amsterdam and Helsinki.*

Dolly™ and Sauna™ are trademarks of Underware.

The stories which are shown here can be more extensively read in
the original type specimens. The *Dolly* and *Sauna* fonts are also fully
shown in a more extensive way in these two type specimens.

   Dolly, a book typeface with flourishes contains many different
stories about the dog Dolly, written by many different people like
Markus Brilling, Somi Kim, Michael Rock, Ewan Lentjes, Anne
Knopf, Guy Tavares, Edwin Smet, Eike Menijn, Wilbert Leering &
Lennart Wienecke. The preface is written by Erik Spiekermann.
The book is designed by Faydherbe/de Vringer (Wout de Vringer).

   Read naked is a sauna proof book which doesn't only contain
stories about sauna's, but can also be read inside the sauna.
Even better, some stories only become visible inside the sauna at 80
degrees Celsius or higher. The preface is written by Henrik Birkvig.
The book is designed by Piet Schreuders in cooperation with
Underware.

   The book *Dolly, a book typeface with flourishes* (ISBN 90-76984-
01-8) and the book *Read naked* (ISBN 90-76984-03-4) are available
in specialized bookshops.

Underware
Schouwburgstraat 2
2511 VA Den Haag
the Netherlands

T +31-(0)70 42 78 117
F +31 (0)70 42 78 116
E info@underware.nl
www.underware.nl

Dolly

a book typeface
with flourishes

Underware
2001

Dolly Roman is neutral and useful for long texts. It has old-style figures.

Dolly Italic is narrower and lighter in colour than the roman, and so it can be used to emphasize words within roman text.

Dolly Bold is also useful for emphasizing words within roman text. It also works well as a display type.

Dolly Small Caps are intended for setting whole words or strings of characters, while roman capitals are used only for the first letter in a word. They match the roman in weight and have figures that align with the x-height.

5.10 If you put on the dog, you behave in an unpleasant, grand way that suggests you think that you are much more important or intelligent than anyone else; used in informal American English. **5.11** If you say that something is going to the dogs (thanks to *The Boys*; if you don't understand this, just put the cd which is included in the Dolly book in your cd-player, pump up the volume and there you go!), you mean that it is losing the good qualities that it had. EG. *This country is going to the dogs!* **5.12** · To fight like cat and dog: see cat. · raining cats and dogs: see rain. **6** See also dogged.

dogcart, dogcarts; often spelled with a hyphen (thanks Robin). A dogcart is a light cart with two wheels pulled by a horse, which people can ride in.

dog-eared. A book or piece of paper that is dog-eared has been used so much that the corners of the pages are turned down or torn.

dogfight, dogfights. A dogfight is **1** A fight between fighter planes, in which they fly close to one another and manoevre very fast. **2** A fight between dogs, especially one that has been organized by human beings for entertainment, although in The Hague this is illegal.

dogged means showing determination to continue with something however difficult it is. EG. *...his dogged refusal to admit defeat... ...dogged determination.* · doggedly. EG. They persisted doggedly in their campaign against the law. · doggedness.

doggerel is poetry which is silly or funny, often written quickly and not intended to be serious. EG. *She wrote some doggerel on the subject in 1883.*

doggie paddle; also spelled with a hyphen. The doggie paddle or dog paddle is a swimming stroke in which the arms and legs are moved up and down rapidly, with short strokes under the water; an informal term. The doggie paddle is often used by children who are learning to swim.

doggo. If you lie doggo, you lie still and keep very quiet so that people will not find you; an informal expression. EG. *I lay doggo in my tent in Norway at my own lake (thanks Ietje).*

doggone is an informal American word that's used to emphasize what you are saying. EG. *It's a doggone shame.*

doggy, doggies. See doggie.

dog-house. If you are in the dog-house, you are in disgrace and people are annoyed with you; an informal expression. EG. *Poor Martin Gaus is in the dog-house.*

dogma, dogmas. A dogma is a belief or a system of beliefs which is accepted as true and which people are expected to accept, without questioning it. EG. *He had no time for political or other dogmas... ...Christianity in the early days when there was less dogma.*

dogmatic. Someone who is dogmatic is convinced that they are right and gives their personal opinions without looking at the evidence and without considering that other opinions might be justified. EG. *He was so dogmatic about it that I almost believed what he was saying... His friends were all intensely dogmatic political theoreticians... She was not impressed by his dogmatic assertions.* · dogmatically. EG. *'This stone,' he said dogmatically, 'is far older than the rest.'*

dogmatism is a strong and confident assertion of opinion, which is made without looking at the evidence and without considering that different opinions might be justified. EG. *His education has taught him a distrust of dogmatism.* · Dogmatist. EG. *England inherited the worst dogmas and dogmatists of the women's movement from America.*

do-gooder, do-gooders. A do-gooder is someone who does things which they think will help other people, although others think they are interfering; used showing disapproval.

dog paddle means the same as doggie paddle.

dogsbody, dogsbodies. A dogsbody is a person who had to do all the unpleasant or boring jobs that nobody else wants to do; an informal British word. EG. *He was employed as a general dogsbody on the project.*

dog-tired. If you are dog-tired, you are extremely tired; used in informal English. EG. *Joeri and Ilone were dog-tired that evening.*

doings. Someone's doings are their activities at a particular time. EG. *Bas gave an admiring account of Sami's doings.*

do-it-yourself. See d.i.y. EG. *You can't get this font from good do-it-yourself shops.*

dole, doles, doling, doled. In Britain, the dole is money that is given by the government to people who are unemployed. It is given at regular intervals, for example every two weeks. EG. *How much is the dole now, 20 quid?... There was no dole for farm labourers.* · Someone who is on the dole is registered as unemployed and receives money regularly from the government. EG. *They made him redundant but he wouldn't go on the dole... He's spent the last year on the dole.*

doleful. A doleful expression, manner, voice, etc is depressing and miserable. EG. *'Things are getting desperate,' he said in a doleful monotone.* › used of people. EG. *...his rapid transformation from senator to doleful night-club comic.* · dolefully. EG. *Hogan nodded dolefully.*

doll, dolls, dolling, dolled. A doll is **1** A smart child's toy which looks like a small person or baby. **2** A girl or young woman, especially one who is pretty; used especially in informal American English. EG. *Who's the doll over there?*

doll up. If a woman dolls herself up, she puts on smart or fashionable clothes in order to try and look attractive for a particular occasion; used in informal British English. EG. *She dolled herself up to meet her new boyfriend.* · dolled up. EG. *She was all dolled up in the latest fashion.*

dollar, dollars. A dollar is a unit of money used in the USA, Canada, and other countries, which is divided into one hundred smaller units called cents. EG. *They spent half a million dollars on the font... The pound fell more than 25 percent against the dollar.*

dolly, dollies. **1** Dolly is a child's word for a doll. **2** A dolly or dolly bird is a young woman who is considered to be very pretty but not very intelligent. EG. *He was too busy chasing the teenage dollies of Paris.* **3** A little very ugly french bulldog, always angry, never satisfied, originally from The Hague, loves to play with Martin Gaus (thanks Edgar).

dolphin, dolphins. A dolphin is a mammal which lives in the sea and looks like a large fish with a pointed mouth. 7,5/9 pts.

dolt, dolts. A dolt is a stupid person. EG. *You would have to be a*

OVER THE COURSE OF FOUR OR FIVE MONTHS, Dolly started to limp. I couldn't really find any reason for it, no thorn in her paw, for instance, or improperly executed manicure. One day she simply stopped walking on her right hind leg altogether. She would hold it daintily an inch or so off the ground and lope along on three legs.

Dolly tended to be a long-suffering girl, and never would she actively complain about some malady. She would bear her pain in silence, occasionally tossing a watery-eyed glance my way to indicate her general misery. Finally the situation seemed dire enough to warrant a visit to the veterinarian and the ensuing x-ray revealed a *displaced knee-cap* that required surgery to repair it. Her convalescence involved three months in a bright purple cast which held her leg straight out to the side like a chicken wing and out of the end of which her little tuft of a foot stuck like a tribal fetish.

When her cast was finally removed, her little leg was revealed, completely atrophied and as spindly as a toothpick. Dolly tentatively touched her foot 9/10,5 pts.

to the ground, looked up in disgust and went right on limping along on all-threes. Well, this limping went on all Fall, and each day her useless little leg grew increasingly soft and ineffectual. I was growing concerned and every morning I would draw her foot, which was now covered with long fur from lack of friction, to the pavement and rub her uncalloused pad on the ground to remind her of the sensation.

One day on our morning walk, in frustration, I called out in a gruff voice: '*Dolly, would you please walk on that leg!*' 11/13 pts.

Dolly

Underware
2001

All Dolly fonts have Adobe Standard Encoding and a full Western European character set.

Underware

Dolly is no ordinary émigré. She is a jindo, the indigenous breed prized as Korea's Natural Treasure No. 53, a symbol of national pride (an abundant Korean resource). When I flew back from Seoul to L.A. with a jindo pup, my husband and I had no idea what lay ahead. To our dismay, Dolly was embraced by the Kim side of the family as a surrogate grandchild and a direct link to a deceased aunt. We attempted to distance ourselves emotionally from our canine ward by giving her a different surname. We chose a flower: *Dolly Dahlia.* No confusing interspecies hyphenation for us. Some have accused us of latent hippiedom, but that is so not true. 12/15 pts.

Dolly

These texts are parts of stories published in the book 'Dolly, a book typeface with flourishes'. These stories are written by many different people.

Korean Angelenos like to frequent the hilly trails of Griffith Park. Rarely do we pass them without triggering exclamatory superlatives: "*Oh-hoh! Jindo-gae! Best dog in the world!*" Clearly Koreans esteem the jindo above all other dogs. But one person's esteem is another's tasty treat. An encyclopedic jindo web site states: "*Even though Korea still has a custom of eating dogs, there is a strict distinction of pet dogs and dogs for eating.*" Best… tasting? 15/18 pts.

Dolly

Dolly

Underware
2001

These four fonts provide a good basis for the most of the problems of book typography. If you meet a particular problem that could be solved by adding to or adapting these fonts, then please contact Underware.

MAYBE WE HAD SAVED **Dolly** from a savory end. Jindos are notable for their loyalty and borderline domestication. The latter alarmed us as novice dog handlers. *Dolly was like a little bucking bronco the first times we tried to leash her.* Sometimes in the early weeks Markus and I would look at each other 36/42 pts.

bored &

lazy dog

& FAT ?

bulldog

Underware
2001

Dolly is designed to be set in very small sizes. Because of this purpose, the font has a low contrast. However, the font contains also many subtle details which are not visible at small sizes. The example here is set at 120 points.

Underware

» THE CHAPTERS IN THIS SPREAD are from **Marja Jalava's** whole article *'Getting intellectual'* in *Read naked* -book. » More about *Read naked* -book on Underware's website » www.underware.nl

SAUNA HAS BEEN SACRED – restricted and isolated – spatially, temporally and **socially**. This has been evident already in the way the sauna has been built apart from the everyday sphere. Nor has the sauna been entered on a whim, since the heating of traditional stoves has taken hours as well as skill passed from generation to generation. Taking off one's clothes before going into the hot sauna is besides an obvious necessity also a sign of passing into a sacred place. Along with the clothes, the bather symbolically removes his social roles and gets **a temporary relief** from their demands. Furthermore, baring one's body is a display of trust toward the fellow bathers. Even nowadays, bathers often have in common a rare feeling of equality and consensus. In public saunas, this makes possible a spontaneous, at times even very downright personal exchange of thoughts between complete strangers. […]

Sauna

Underware
2002

Sauna – A typeface for all sizes.

Sauna has a warm and comfortable feeling. The straight lines and sharp corners work as a contrast to round forms; they give a dynamic kick and make the round forms look even rounder.

shown on this page:
Sauna Dingbats (multi-colour)
Sauna-Black
Sauna-BoldItalicSwash
Sauna-Bold
Sauna-SmallCaps
Sauna-Roman
Sauna-Italic

Sauna

A typeface for all sizes.

IN THE OLD AGRICULTURAL SOCIETY sauna has marked out the borders between everyday life and **Sundays**, and the turning points of an individual's life-span and the four seasons. In the sauna, babies were born, brides were bathed, corpses were washed, spells were recited, magic was made and the sick were healed. In these rituals, the sauna represented **the borderline between this life and the hereafter**, the microcosm and the macrocosm. *Löyly*, the steam rising from the hot stove stones, was what especially joined the bathers with the afterlife. In addition to signifying this special type of steam, in many Finno-Ugric languages the word *löyly* has stood for a power of life associated with breathing. Fundamentally, this power has been **ambivalent**, at the same time reforming and destroying human life. It brought relief to the tired and the sick, but it could also cause incurable diseases and ailments. This is referred to by the expression *löylynlyömä* (hit by *löyly*), used in vernacular speech as a synonym for mental illness or retardation. ¶

Sauna

Underware
2002

The Sauna family contains three weights. Every weight has two italics: a standard italic and a fancy swashy italic. On this page the lightest weight is shown. This weight can also be used for small size and can be combined with the bold weight (previous spread). The lightest weight contains small caps.

shown on this page:
Sauna-Roman
Sauna-Italic
Sauna-ItalicSwash
Sauna-SmallCaps

Sauna Dingbats-Solo

My dear grandfather *used to challenge* his fellow saunamen *into a competition.*

IF IT ENDED LIKE IT USUALLY DID, *that he won and was the last man in the sauna,* HE WENT DOWN ON THE FLOOR, *into the cool space under the benches, and threw* ANOTHER PAILFUL OF WATER ON THE STONES, YELLING:

"*Now it's* time *to* steam up!"

His companions were in an awe, thinking Grandpa was still sitting on the top bench. *Perkele!*

¶ Jussi Karjalainen (27), a player of cardboard box drum, performs in Helsinki, Finland.

+31 (0)70 4278117

The tolerance varies;

During a sauna session one of our company's foreign workers was asking: 'Is it a part of the experience to black-out?'.

{We carried him outside to recover.}

¶ Ville Repo (31), a construction worker lifting heavy objects at Nastola, Finland.

Sauna

Underware
2002

The bold weight, which is shown on this page, can be combined with the lightest weight (opposite page) in small sizes. Of course, it also works as a display font.

shown on this page:
Sauna-Bold
Sauna-BoldItalic
Sauna-BoldItalicSwash

Underware

Sauna

Underware
2002

The black weight is designed for display use, for big and extremely big sizes. Therefore, it's individual, and can't be combined with regular and bold weights in small sizes.

shown on this page:
Sauna-Black

Always, when I'm visiting my parents, going to sauna is a polite way to escape their over'enthusiasm.

+31 (0)70 4278117

Sauna

Underware
2002

shown on this page:
Sauna-BlackItalic

Underware

I just switch the sauna on,
wait for half an hour
and I've got
a perfect
excuse
to spend an hour
only with my boyfriend.

¶ Agnes Magnusson (24), a student/cheerleader in the University of Uppsala, Sweden.

One time I pee on the rocks and it smelt ten times worse than normal pee smell…

¶ Ashley Ringrose (21), a game programmer in Sydney, Australia.

Don't tell me more, please.

Sauna

Underware
2002

Scale it bigger, and you get even more details!

Each Sauna italic swash font contains a set of 26 ligatures, including the double 'l' shown on this page. All light weight ligatures are shown below.

shown on this spread:
Sauna-BlackItalicSwash
Sauna Ligatures-BlackItalicSw

Underware

Th Qu Qu
fb ff fh fi fj
fk fl ft ffi ffl
Ch Ck Cl Ct
Sh Sk Sl St
kk ll ss tt zz

Sauna Ligatures-ItalicSwash

Ten basic Sauna fonts are shown briefly on this page. A set of 26 ligatures is provided for the swashy fonts in every weight. The previous page and our website has information about Sauna Ligatures.

All Sauna fonts have Adobe Standard Encoding and a full Western European character set.

This set of fonts fits for a flexible range of text and display typography.

Ollahan iliman pyyhkeitä.
¶ May I ask you to take your clothes off? Sauna-Roman 22/20 pts

Elikkä ilkialasti.
¶ In other words: reveal your beautiful belly. Sauna-Italic 22/20 pts

Löylyn heitto ainoostaan napoolla.
¶ Only use the scoop to throw water, please. Sauna-ItalicSwash 22/20 pts

SITÄ EI TRENKÄÄ KOSKAAN KIELTÄÄ.
¶ DON'T DENY IF SOMEONE IS STEAMING UP. Sauna-SmallCaps 22/20 pts

Vaan tulee siirtyä alalauteelle.
¶ No guts to stay? Take a step down. Sauna-Bold 22/20 pts

Akkaan ja kakarootteen sekahan.
¶ To down between the wives and babies. Sauna-BoldItalic 22/20 pts

Lauteella ei sovi viheltää.
¶ Whispering is strictly forbidden. Sauna-BoldItalicSwash 22/20 pts

Eikä muutoonkaan tehdä kiusantekoo.
¶ Behave yourself. Sauna-Black 22/20 pts

Kuten puhaltelua naapurin selekään.
¶ Don't blow air on your fellows back. Sauna-BlackItalic 22/20 pts

Puhuta muuta eiku aikuusten asiaa.
¶ Think twice before your speak. Sauna-BlackItalicSwash 22/20 pts

Sauna Dingbats

Underware
2002

The Sauna family contains 26
dingbat illustrations. They can be
set as a single colour illustrations
or as a multi-layer illustrations,
like the ones on this page.

Constructing a four layer
illustration in your layout program
is really easy! The layers switch
automatically on top of eachother,
and they behave like one
character; so you can edit your
text, and the dingbat flows along
in the text field. More information
about dingbats can be found on
our website: www.underware.nl

UNIONFONTS.COM · BUY AND DOWNLOAD 24 - 7

maqma

maqma

maqma

Magma Light

buckets and spoons dug trenches of thought into hard luck stories where cars ignore the laybys and whys because in clanking madness the hissing fury controls no past no future disrupts the present with grinders of steam and rivets of fire and no one around except the sky and the ground bare beauty of thought

Magma Light Condensed

buckets and spoons dug trenches of thought into hard luck stories where cars ignore the laybys and whys because in clanking madness the hissing fury controls no past no future disrupts the present with grinders of steam and rivets of fire and no one around except the sky and the ground bare beauty of thought in fields of yellow.

Magma Regular

buckets and spoons dug trenches of thought into hard luck stories where cars ignore the laybys and whys because in clanking madness the hissing fury controls no past no future disrupts the present with grinders of steam and rivets of fire and no one around except the sky and the ground bare beauty of thought in fields of

Magma Condensed

buckets and spoons dug trenches of thought into hard luck stories where cars ignore the laybys and whys because in clanking madness the hissing fury controls no past no future disrupts the present with grinders of steam and rivets of fire and no one around except the sky and the ground bare beauty of thought in fields of yellow.

Magma Bold

buckets and spoons dug trenches of thought into hard luck stories where cars ignore the laybys and whys because in clanking madness the hissing fury controls no past no future disrupts the present with grinders of steam and rivets of fire and no one around except the sky and the ground bare beauty of thought in fields of yellow.

Magma Bold Condensed

buckets and spoons dug trenches of thought into hard luck stories where cars ignore the laybys and whys because in clanking madness the hissing fury controls no past no future disrupts the present with grinders of steam and rivets of fire and no one around except the sky and the ground bare beauty of thought in fields of yellow.

Headroom Regular

HEADROOM

Headroom Bold

HEADROOM

Headroom Hard Regular

HEADROOM

Headroom Hard Bold

HEADROOM

Headroom Regular 24pt

BUCKETS AND SPOONS DUG TRENCHES OF THOUGHT INTO HARD LUCK

Headroom Regular 18pt

BUCKETS AND SPOONS DUG TRENCHES OF THOUGHT INTO HARD LUCK STORIES WHERE CARS IGNORE

Headroom Regular 12pt

BUCKETS AND SPOONS DUG TRENCHES OF THOUGHT INTO HARD LUCK STORIES WHERE CARS IGNORE THE LAYBYS AND WHYS BECAUSE IN CLANKING

Headroom Regular 12pt

BUCKETS AND SPOONS DUG TRENCHES OF THOUGHT INTO HARD LUCK STORIES WHERE CARS IGNORE THE LAYBYS AND WHYS BECAUSE IN CLANKING MADNESS THE HISSING FURY CONTROLS NO PAST NO

Chube Thin

chube

buckets and spoons dug trenches of thought into hard luck stories where cars ignore the laybys and whys because in clanking madness the hissing fury controls no past no future disrupts the present with grinders of steam and rivets of fire and no one around except the sky and the ground bare beauty of thought in fields of yellow.

Chube Thin Italic

chube

buckets and spoons dug trenches of thought into hard luck stories where cars ignore the laybys and whys because in clanking madness the hissing fury controls no past no future disrupts the present with grinders of steam and rivets of fire and no one around except the sky and the ground bare beauty of thought in fields of yellow.

Chube Fat

chube

buckets and spoons dug trenches of thought into hard luck stories where cars ignore the laybys and whys because in clanking madness the hissing fury controls no past no future disrupts the present with grinders of steam and rivets of fire and no one around except the sky and the ground bare beauty of thought in fields of yellow.

Chube

Lee Fasciani
2003

Lee created Chube by formalising his handwriting.

Chube Fat Italic

chube

buckets and spoons dug trenches of thought into hard luck stories where cars ignore the laybys and whys because in clanking madness the hissing fury controls no past no future disrupts the present with grinders of steam and rivets of fire and no one around except the sky and the ground bare beauty of thought in fields of yellow.

Chube Tubby

chube

buckets and spoons dug trenches of thought into hard luck stories where cars ignore the laybys and whys because in clanking madness the hissing fury controls no past no future disrupts the present with grinders of steam and rivets of fire and no one around except the sky and the ground bare beauty of thought in fields of yellow.

Chube Tubby Italic

chube

buckets and spoons dug trenches of thought into hard luck stories where cars ignore the laybys and whys because in clanking madness the hissing fury controls no past no future disrupts the present with grinders of steam and rivets of fire and no one around except the sky and the ground bare beauty of thought in fields of yellow.

Swingo Regular

SWINGO

Swingo Bold

SWINGO

Swingo

Samy Halim
2002

Furby Light

FURBY

buckets and spoons dug trenches of thought into hard luck stories where cars ignore the laybys and whys because in clanking madness the hissing fury controls no past no future disrupts the present with grinders of steam and rivets of fire and no one around except the sky and the ground

Furby Regular

FURBY

buckets and spoons dug trenches of thought into hard luck stories where cars ignore the laybys and whys because in clanking madness the hissing fury controls no past no future disrupts the present with grinders of steam and rivets of fire and no one around except the sky and the ground

Furby Bold

FURBY

buckets and spoons dug trenches of thought into hard luck stories where cars ignore the laybys and whys because in clanking madness the hissing fury controls no past no future disrupts the present with grinders of steam and rivets of fire and no one around except the sky and the ground

Furby

Jonathan Nicol
2003

746   www.unionfonts.com

AMP Light

abcdeFghijklmnopqrstuvwxyz0123456789
ABCDEFGHIJKLMNOPQRSTUVWXYZ@E$%&

AMP Regular

abcdeFghijklmnopqrstuvwxyz0123456789
ABCDEFGHIJKLMNOPQRSTUVWXYZ@E$%&

AMP Bold

abcdeFghijklmnopqrstuvwxyz0123456789
ABCDEFGHIJKLMNOPQRSTUVWXYZ@E$%&

AMP Outline

abcdeFghijklmnopqrstuvwxyz0123456789
ABCDEFGHIJKLMNOPQRSTUVWXYZ@E$%&

Eva Normal

Eva Normal Italic

Eva Bold

Eva Bold Italic

EVA EVA EVA EVA

IXTAN

Ixtan Light

abcdefghijklmnopqrstuvwxyz
ABCDEFGHIJKLMNOPQRSTUVWXYZ

Ixtan Light Italic

abcdefghijklmnopqrstuvwxyz
ABCDEFGHIJKLMNOPQRSTUVWXYZ

Ixtan Medium

abcdefghijklmnopqrstuvwxyz
ABCDEFGHIJKLMNOPQRSTUVWXYZ

Ixtan Medium Italic

abcdefghijklmnopqrstuvwxyz
ABCDEFGHIJKLMNOPQRSTUVWXYZ

Ixtan Bold

abcdefghijklmnopqrstuvwxyz
ABCDEFGHIJKLMNOPQRSTUVWXYZ

Ixtan Bold Italic

abcdefghijklmnopqrstuvwxyz
ABCDEFGHIJKLMNOPQRSTUVWXYZ

Dispose

Lee Fasciani
2003

'During recent years I have grown
to recognize and appreciate the
real subtleties in type design
and concentrate on text fonts'
- Lee Fasciani

Dispose

Dispose

Dispose

Dispose Light

buckets and spoons dug trenches of thought
into hard luck stories where cars ignore the
laybys and whys because in clanking
madness the hissing fury controls no past no
future disrupts the present with grinders of
steam and rivets of fire and no one around
except the sky and the ground bare beauty of
thought in fields of yellow.

Dispose Oblique

*buckets and spoons dug trenches of thought
into hard luck stories where cars ignore the
laybys and whys because in clanking
madness the hissing fury controls no past no
future disrupts the present with grinders of
steam and rivets of fire and no one around
except the sky and the ground bare beauty of
thought in fields of yellow.*

Dispose Light Oblique

*buckets and spoons dug trenches of thought
into hard luck stories where cars ignore the
laybys and whys because in clanking
madness the hissing fury controls no past no
future disrupts the present with grinders of
steam and rivets of fire and no one around
except the sky and the ground bare beauty of
thought in fields of yellow.*

Dispose Heavy

buckets and spoons dug trenches of thought
into hard luck stories where cars ignore the
laybys and whys because in clanking
madness the hissing fury controls no past no
future disrupts the present with grinders of
steam and rivets of fire and no one around
except the sky and the ground bare beauty of
thought in fields of yellow.

Dispose Regular

buckets and spoons dug trenches of thought
into hard luck stories where cars ignore the
laybys and whys because in clanking
madness the hissing fury controls no past no
future disrupts the present with grinders of
steam and rivets of fire and no one around
except the sky and the ground bare beauty of
thought in fields of yellow.

Dispose Heavy Oblique

*buckets and spoons dug trenches of thought
into hard luck stories where cars ignore the
laybys and whys because in clanking
madness the hissing fury controls no past no
future disrupts the present with grinders of
steam and rivets of fire and no one around
except the sky and the ground bare beauty of
thought in fields of yellow.*

Kanister Kanister

Kanister

Martin Fewell
2003

Kryptk Flash

abcdefghijklmnopqrstuvwxyz0123456789
ABCDEFGHIJKLMNOPQRSTUVWXYZ@£$%&

Kryptk Flash

Neil Summerour
2002

Designed for use in Macromedia Flash MX

ARE YOU IN

Are You In

Arjen Noordeman
2003

CharifaSans

abcdefghijklmnopqrstuvwxyz0123456789
ABCDEFGHIJKLMNOPQRSTUVWXYZ@£$%&

Charifa Sans

Heiko Hoos
2003

Union Fonts

Ether Normal

Ether

buckets and spoons dug trenches of thought into hard luck stories where cars ignore the laybys and whys because in clanking madness the hissing fury controls no past no future disrupts the present with grinders of steam and rivets of fire and no one around except the sky and the ground bare beauty of thought in fields of yellow.

Ether Normal Slant

Ether

buckets and spoons dug trenches of thought into hard luck stories where cars ignore the laybys and whys because in clanking madness the hissing fury controls no past no future disrupts the present with grinders of steam and rivets of fire and no one around except the sky and the ground bare beauty of thought in fields of yellow.

Ether Bold

Ether

buckets and spoons dug trenches of thought into hard luck stories where cars ignore the laybys and whys because in clanking madness the hissing fury controls no past no future disrupts the present with grinders of steam and rivets of fire and no one around except the sky and the ground bare beauty of thought in fields of yellow.

Ether Bold Slant

Ether

buckets and spoons dug trenches of thought into hard luck stories where cars ignore the laybys and whys because in clanking madness the hissing fury controls no past no future disrupts the present with grinders of steam and rivets of fire and no one around except the sky and the ground bare beauty of thought in fields of yellow.

Ether Connected Normal

Ether

buckets and spoons dug trenches of thought into hard luck stories where cars ignore the laybys and whys because in clanking madness the hissing fury controls no past no future disrupts the present with grinders of steam and rivets of fire and no one around except the sky and the ground bare beauty of thought in fields of yellow.

Ether Connected Slant

Ether

buckets and spoons dug trenches of thought into hard luck stories where cars ignore the laybys and whys because in clanking madness the hissing fury controls no past no future disrupts the present with grinders of steam and rivets of fire and no one around except the sky and the ground bare beauty of thought in fields of yellow.

Ether Connected Bold

Ether

buckets and spoons dug trenches of thought into hard luck stories where cars ignore the laybys and whys because in clanking madness the hissing fury controls no past no future disrupts the present with grinders of steam and rivets of fire and no one around except the sky and the ground bare beauty of thought in fields of yellow.

Ether Connected Bold Slant

Ether

buckets and spoons dug trenches of thought into hard luck stories where cars ignore the laybys and whys because in clanking madness the hissing fury controls no past no future disrupts the present with grinders of steam and rivets of fire and no one around except the sky and the ground bare beauty of thought in fields of yellow.

VLAD

Vlad Regular

ΛᏏႠᎴᎬᖴᏩᎻᏆᏆᏦᏞᎷᏂᎾᏢᏒᏃᎡᏕᎢᏌᏉᏯᏔᏗᎩᏃᎮᏏᎮᎥᎦᎨᎧᎨᎿᎨᎯᎧᎧ

Vlad Slant

ABCDEFGHIJKLMNΦPQRSTUVWXYZ812345678q

MEMORY

abcdefghijklmnopqrstuvwxyz0123456789

ABCDEFGHIJKLMNOPQRSTUVWXYZ@£$%&()

BARBAPAPA

System Extra Light

SYSTEM

System Light

SYSTEM

System Regular

SYSTEM

System Bold

SYSTEM

System Extra Bold

SYSTEM

System Extra Light Force

SYSTEM

System Light Force

SYSTEM

System Force

SYSTEM

System Bold Force

SYSTEM

System Extra Bold Force

SYSTEM

Vlad
Lee Fasciani
2003

Memory
Lee Fasciani
2003

Barbapapa
Samy Halim
2002

System
Lee Fasciani
2003

Union Fonts

cosmorton
cosmorton

Cosmorton

buckets and spoons dug trenches of thought into hard luck stories where cars ignore the laybys and whys because in clanking madness the hissing fury controls no past no future disrupts the present with grinders of steam and

Cosmorton Bold

buckets and spoons dug trenches of thought into hard luck stories where cars ignore the laybys and whys because in clanking madness the hissing fury controls no past no future disrupts the present with grinders of

EPOCH

Squirrel *Squirrel* Squirrel *Squirrel*

buckets and spoons dug trenches of thought into hard luck stories where cars ignore the laybys and whys because in clanking madness the hissing fury controls no past no future disrupts the present with grinders of steam and rivets of fire and no one around except the sky and the ground bare beauty of thought in fields of yellow.

EXHAUST LIGHT
EXHAUST REGULAR

buckets and spoons dug trenches of thought into hard luck stories where cars ignore the laybys and whys because in clanking madness the hissing fury controls no past no future disrupts the present with grinders of steam and rivets of fire and no one around except the sky and the ground bare beauty of thought in fields of yellow.

EXHAUST BOLD
EXHAUST BLACK

buckets and spoons dug trenches of thought into hard luck stories where cars ignore the laybys and whys because in clanking madness the hissing fury controls no past no future disrupts the present with grinders of steam and rivets of fire and no one around except the sky and the ground bare beauty of thought in fields of yellow.

Datastream Regular

DATASTREAM

Datastream Oblique

DATASTREAM

AIRBRAKE REGULAR
AIRBRAKE OBLIQUE

buckets and spoons dug trenches of thought into hard luck stories where cars ignore the laybys and whys because in clanking madness the hissing fury controls no past no future disrupts the present with grinders of steam and rivets of fire and no one around except the sky and the ground bare beauty of thought in fields of yellow.

AIRBRAKE ROUNDED
AIRBRAKE ROUNDED OBLIQUE

buckets and spoons dug trenches of thought into hard luck stories where cars ignore the laybys and whys because in clanking madness the hissing fury controls no past no future disrupts the present with grinders of steam and rivets of fire and no one around except the sky and the ground bare beauty of thought in fields of yellow.

Squirrel

Maurice van de Stouwe
2003

Exhaust

Martin Fewell
2003

Union Fonts

Datastream

Martin Fewell
2003

80's revival font

Airbrake

Martin Fewell
2002

Anarcharsis

Anarcharsis

ANARCHARSIS

ANARCHARSIS

Anarcharsis Regular

buckets and spoons dug trenches of thought into hard luck stories where cars ignore the laybys and whys because in clanking madness the hissing fury controls no past no future disrupts the present with grinders of steam and rivets of fire and no one around except the sky and the ground bare beauty of thought in fields of yellow.

Anarcharsis Bold

buckets and spoons dug trenches of thought into hard luck stories where cars ignore the laybys and whys because in clanking madness the hissing fury controls no past no future disrupts the present with grinders of steam and rivets of fire and no one around except the sky and the ground bare beauty of thought in fields of yellow.

Anarcharsis Mono

buckets and spoons dug trenches of thought into hard luck stories where cars ignore the laybys and whys because in clanking madness the hissing fury controls no past no future disrupts the present with grinders of steam and rivets of fire and no one around except the sky and the ground bare beauty of thought in fields of yellow.

Anarcharsis Mono Bold

buckets and spoons dug trenches of thought into hard luck stories where cars ignore the laybys and whys because in clanking madness the hissing fury controls no past no future disrupts the present with grinders of steam and rivets of fire and no one around except the sky and the ground bare beauty of thought in fields of yellow .

Anarcharsis Regular Caps

BUCKETS AND SPOONS DUG TRENCHES OF THOUGHT INTO HARD LUCK STORIES WHERE CARS IGNORE THE LAYBYS AND WHYS BECAUSE IN CLANKING MADNESS THE HISSING FURY CONTROLS NO PAST NO FUTURE DISRUPTS THE PRESENT WITH GRINDERS OF STEAM AND RIVETS OF FIRE AND NO ONE AROUND EXCEPT THE SKY AND THE GROUND BARE BEAUTY OF THOUGHT IN

Anarcharsis Bold Caps

BUCKETS AND SPOONS DUG TRENCHES OF THOUGHT INTO HARD LUCK STORIES WHERE CARS IGNORE THE LAYBYS AND WHYS BECAUSE IN CLANKING MADNESS THE HISSING FURY CONTROLS NO PAST NO FUTURE DISRUPTS THE PRESENT WITH GRINDERS OF STEAM AND RIVETS OF FIRE AND NO ONE AROUND EXCEPT THE SKY AND THE GROUND BARE BEAUTY OF THOUGHT IN

150 Regular

150 Inline

150 Outline

Digna Sans Light

DignaSans

Digna Sans Regular

DignaSans

Digna Sans Italic

DignaSans

Digna Sans Bold

DignaSans

Quarantine Regular

QUARANTINE

Quarantine Bold

QUARANTINE

Quarantine Padded

QUARANTINE

Quarantine Padded Bold

QUARANTINE

New Normal

New Inline

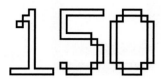

New Normal Script

New Outline

Union Fonts

Yumi

Neil Summerour
2003

Athens-based designer and
typographer Neil Summerour
began developing typefaces
in 1996. He is the co-principal
and senior designer of
interactive, design, and
advertising agency Genetic:ICG.

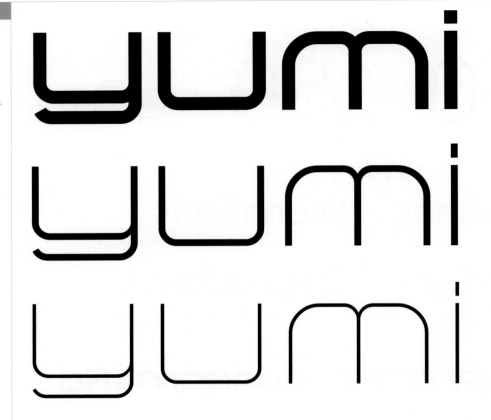

Yumi Ultra Light

buckets and spoons
dug trenches of
thought into hard luck
stories where cars
ignore the laybys and
whys because in
clanking madness the
hissing fury controls

Yumi Medium

buckets and spoons
dug trenches of
thought into hard luck
stories where cars
ignore the laybys and
whys because in
clanking madness the
hissing fury controls

Yumi Light

buckets and spoons
dug trenches of
thought into hard luck
stories where cars
ignore the laybys and
whys because in
clanking madness the
hissing fury controls

Yumi Bold

buckets and spoons
dug trenches of
thought into hard luck
stories where cars
ignore the laybys and
whys because in
clanking madness the
hissing fury controls

Yumi Normal

buckets and spoons
dug trenches of
thought into hard luck
stories where cars
ignore the laybys and
whys because in
clanking madness the
hissing fury controls

OKTOBER

ABCDEFGHIJKLMNOPQRSTUVWXYZ
0123456789@£$%^&*()+?

Oktober Slanted

OKTOBER

ABCDEFGHIJKLMNOPQRSTUVWXYZ
0123456789@£$%^&*()+?

NEW AMSTERDAM
NEW AMSTERDAM

ABCDEFGHIJKLMNOPQRSTUVWYZ
ABCDEFGHINJKLMONOPQRSTUVWYZ

YouWorkForThem

ThisIsTheTypefaceShowingFromYourFriendsAt:
http://www.youworkforthem.com

All our typefaces are available 24-7 on our website. Once you place an order, they are instantly ready for you to download and use!

6x7oct

YouWorkForThem
1998

12 Typestyles in family:
ExtraLight, Light, Regular, Bold,
ExtraBold, Black, ExtraLight
Alternate, Light Alternate,
Alternate, Bold Alternate,
ExtraBold Alternate, Black
Alternate.

6x7oct-Regular

ABCDEFGHIJKLMNOPQRSTUVWXYZabcd
efghijklmnopqrstuvwxyz123456789

6x7oct-Alternate

ABCDEFGHIJKLMNOPQRSTUVWXYZabCd
efghijklmnopqrstuvwxyz123456789

6x7oct-Light

ABCDEFGHIJKLM
NOPQRSTUVWXY
Zabcdefghijklm

6x7oct-LightAlternate

ABCDEFGHIJKLM
NOPQRSTUVWXY
ZabCdefghijklm

6x7oct-Bold

ABCDEFGHIJKLM
NOPQRSTUVWXY
Zabcdefghijklm

6x7oct-Bold Alternate

ABCDEFGHIJKLM
NOPQRSTUVWXY
ZabCdefghijklm

6x7oct-Black

ABCDEFGHIJKLM
NOPQRSTUVWXY
Zabcdefghijklm

6x7oct-BlackAlternate

ABCDEFGHIJKLM
NOPQRSTUVWXY
ZabCdefghijklm

Alloy

YouWorkForThem
1998

6 Typestyles in family:
ExtraLight, Light, Regular,
SemiBold, Bold, ExtraBold.

Alloy-Regular

ABCDEFGHIJKLMNOPQRSTUVWXYZabcde
fghijklmnopqrstuvwxyz1234567890!?&

Alloy-ExtraLight

ABCDEFGHIJKLMNOPQRSTUVWXYZabcd
efghijklmnopqrstuvwxyz1234567890!?

Alloy-ExtraBold

ABCDEFGHIJKLMNOPQRSTUVWXYZabcdefg
hijklmnopqrstuvwxyz1234567890!?&.,#$({

Alloy-Light

ABCDEFGHIJKLMN
OPQRSTUVWXYZa
bcdefghijklmnop

Alloy-SemiBold

ABCDEFGHIJKLMNO
PQRSTUVWXYZabc
defghijklmnopqrst

Alloy-Bold

ABCDEFGHIJKLMNO
PQRSTUVWXYZabc
defghijklmnopqrst

Blackgold

YouWorkForThem
2001

4 Typestyles in Family:
Light, Regular, Bold, ExtraBold.

Blackgold-Light

ABCDEFGHIJKLMNOPQRSTUVWXYZ
abcdefghijklmnopqrstuvwxyz1

Blackgold-Regular

ABCDEFGHIJKLMNOPQRSTUVWXYZ
abcdefghijklmnopqrstuvwxyz

Blackgold-Bold

ABCDEFGHIJKLMNOPQRSTUVWXYZ
abcdefghijklmnopqrstuvwxyz

Blackgold-ExtraBold

ABCDEFGHIJKLMNOPQRSTUVWXYZ
abcdefghijklmnopqrstuvwxyz

Blessed

YouWorkfForThem
2001

6 Typestyles in Family:
ExtraLight, Light, Regular,
SemiBold, Bold, Extra Bold.

Blessed-ExtraLight

ABCDEFGHIJKLMNOPQRSTUVWXYZabc
defghijklmnopqrstuvwxyz123456789

Blessed-Regular

ABCDEFGHIJKLMNOPQRSTUVWXYZabc
defghijklmnopqrstuvwxyz123456789

Blessed-ExtraBold

ABCDEFGHIJKLMNOPQRSTUVWXYZabcd
efghijklmnopqrstuvwxyz1234567890

Blessed-Light

ABCDEFGHIJKLMN
OPQRSTUVWXYZa
bcdefghijklmnop

Blessed-SemiBold

ABCDEFGHIJKLMNO
PQRSTUVWXYZab
cdefghijklmnopq

Blessed-Bold

ABCDEFGHIJKLMNO
PQRSTUVWXYZab
cdefghijklmnopq

info@youworkforthem.com

Caliper-Regular

ABCDEFGHIJKLMNOPQRSTUVWXYZabcd
efghijklmnopqrstuvwxyz123456789

YouWorkForThem
1998

8 Typestyles in family:
Alternate, ExtraWide, Light
Cubed, Regular, Regular Cubed,
Stairstep, Unicase, Wide.

Caliper-ExtraWide

ABCDEFGHIJKLMNOPQRSTUVWXY
zabcdefghijklmnopqrstuvwx

Caliper-Stairstep

ABCDEFGHIJKLMNOPQRSTUVWXYZabcdef
ghijklmnopqrstuvwxyz1234567890!?

Caliper-Wide

ABCDEFGHIJKL
MNOPQRSTUVW
XYZabcdefghi

Caliper-LightCubed

ABCDEFGHIJKLMN
OPQRSTUVWXYZa
bcdefghijklm

Caliper-Alternate

ABCDEFGHIJKLMN
OPQRSTUVWXYZa
bcdefghijkLm

Cam-Light

ABCDEFGHIJKLMNOPQRSTUVWXYZABC
DEFGHIJKLMNOPQRSTUVWXYZ1234567

YouWorkForThem
1997

8 Typestyles in family:
Light, Regular, Bold, ExtraBold,
Light Oblique, Oblique, Bold
Oblique, ExtraBold Oblique.

Cam-Regular

ABCDEFGHIJKLMNOPQRSTUVWXYZABC
DEFGHIJKLMNOPQRSTUVWXYZ1234567

Cam-ExtraBold

ABCDEFGHIJKLMNOPQRSTUVWXYZABC
DEFGHIJKLMNOPQRSTUVWXYZ1234567

Cam-Bold

ABCDEFGHIJKL
MNOPQRSTUVWX
YZABCDEFGHIJK

Cam-Oblique

ABCDEFGHIJKL
MNOPQRSTUVWX
YZABCDEFGHIJK

Cam-ExtraBoldOblique

ABCDEFGHIJKLM
NOPQRSTUVWXY
ZABCDEFGHIJKL

YouWorkForThem

Cinahand

YouWorkForThem
1998

5 Typestyles in family:
Light, Regular, Alternate Light,
Alternate Regular, Dingbats.

Cinahand-Light

ABCDEFGHIJKLMNOPQRSTUVWXYzabcdefghijklmnopqrstuv
wxyz1234567890!?$@#$%.^*()_+<œ®+©™

Cinahand-LightAlternate

ABCDEFGHIJKLMNOPQRSTUVWXYZabcdefghijklmnop
rstuvwxyz1234567890!?$@#$%^*() +<œ®+©™

Cinahand-Regular

ABCDEFGHIJKLMNOPQRSTUVWXYzabcdefghijklmnopqrstu
wxyz1234567890!?$@#$%.^*()_+<œ®+©™

Cinahand-Alternate

ABCDEFGHIJKLMNOPQRSTUVWXYzabcdefghijklmnop
rstuvwxz1234567890!?$@#$%^*() +<œ®+©™

CommunityService

YouWorkForThem
2002

7 Typestyles in family:
Thin, Light, Regular, Bold, Extra
Bold, Ultra Bold, Black.

CommunityService-Thin

ABCDEFGHIJKLMNOPQRSTUVWXYZabcd
efghijklmnopqrstuvwxyz123456789

CommunityService-Regular

ABCDEFGHIJKLMNOPQRSTUVWXYZabcd
efghijklmnopqrstuvwxyz123456789

CommunityService-Black

ABCDEFGHIJKLMNOPQRSTUVWXYZabc
defghijklmnopqrstuvwxyz1234567

CommunityService-Light

ABCDEFGHIJKLMNO
PQRSTUVWXYZab
cdefghijklmnopq

CommunityService-Bold

ABCDEFGHIJKLMNO
PQRSTUVWXYZab
cdefghijklmnopq

CommunityService-ExtraBold

ABCDEFGHIJKLMNO
PQRSTUVWXYZab
cdefghijklmnopq

Composite-Light

ABCDEFGHIJKLMNOPQRSTUVWXYZABCDEFGHIJKLMNO
PQRSTUVWXYZ1234567890!@#$%^&*[]_+<>?..

YouWorkForThem
1999

4 Typestyles in family:
Light, Regular, Bold, ExtraBold.

Composite-Regular

ABCDEFGHIJKLMNOPQRSTUVWXYZABCDEFGHIJKLMNO
PQRSTUVWXYZ1234567890!@#$%^&*[]_+<>?..

Composite-Bold

ABCDEFGHIJKLMNOPQRSTUVWXYZABCDEFGHIJKLMNO
PQRSTUVWXYZ1234567890!?0!@#$%^&*[]_+<>?..

Composite-ExtraBold

ABCDEFGHIJKLMNOPQRSTUVWXYZABCDEFGHIJKLMNO
PQRSTUVWXYZ1234567890!?0!@#$%^&*[]_+<>?..

Crossover-ExtraLight

ABCDEFGHIJKLMNOPQRSTUVWXYZabcdef
ghijklmnopqrstuvwxyz1234567890!?

YouWorkForThem
1999

12 Typestyles in family:
ExtraLight, Light, Regular, Bold,
ExtraBold, ExtraLight Oblique,
Light Oblique, Oblique, Bold
Oblique, ExtraBold Oblique.

Crossover-Regular

ABCDEFGHIJKLMNOPQRSTUVWXYZabcdef
ghijklmnopqrstuvwxyz1234567890!?

Crossover-Black

ABCDEFGHIJKLMNOPQRSTUVWXYZabcdef
ghijklmnopqrstuvwxyz1234567890!?

Crossover-Light

ABCDEFGHIJKLMN
OPQRSTUVWXYZa
bcdefghijklmno

Crossover-Oblique

ABCDEFGHIJKLMN
OPQRSTUVWXYZa
bcdefghijklmno

Crossover-BoldOblique

ABCDEFGHIJKLMN
OPQRSTUVWXYZa
bcdefghijklmno

YouWorkForThem

YouWorkForThem
2002

5 Typestyles in family:
ExtraLight, Light, Regular, Bold, and ExtraBold.

Enam-ExtraLight
ABCDEFGHIJKLMNOPQRSTUVWXYZabcdef
ghijklmnopqrstuvwxyz1234567890!?&@

Enam-Regular
ABCDEFGHIJKLMNOPQRSTUVWXYZabcdefghij
klmnopqrstuvwxyz1234567890!?&@#$%^*[

Enam-ExtraBold
ABCDEFGHIJKLMNOPQRSTUVWXYZabcdefghijkl
mnopqrstuvwxyz1234567890!?&@#$%^*[]_+‹

Enam-Light
ABCDEFGHIJKLMNOPQRSTUV
WXYZabcdefghijklmnopqrs

Enam-Bold
ABCDEFGHIJKL
MNOPQRSTUV

YouWorkForThem
1999

10 Typestyles in family:
Thin, ExtraLight, UltraLight, Light, Regular, SemiBold, DemiBold, Bold, ExtraBold, UltraBold.

Formation-Thin
ABCDEFGHIJKLMNOPQRST
UVWXYZabcdefghijklmnopqrstu

Formation-UltraBold
ABCDEFGHIJKLMNOPQRSTU
VWXYZabcdefghijklmnopqrstu

Formation-ExtraLight
ABCDEFGHIJ
KLMNOPQRST
UVWXYZabcdef

Formation-Light
ABCDEFGHIJK
LMNOPQRSTU
VWXYZabcdefg

Formation-DemiBold
ABCDEFGHIJK
LMNOPQRSTU
VWXYZabcdefg

Formation-SemiBold
ABCDEFGHIJK
LMNOPQRSTU
VWXYZabcdefg

Formation-Bold
ABCDEFGHIJK
LMNOPQRSTU
VWXYZabcdefg

Formation-ExtraBold
ABCDEFGHIJK
LMNOPQRSTU
VWXYZabcdefg

info@youworkforthem.com

Jute-Regular

ABCDEFGHIJKLMNOPQRSTUVWXYZabcdefghijklmnopqrstuvwxyz12
3456789O&$.;!@#%^*[[{+=\<™©®££¢¥§¶-†‡Øø¿?!¡ÀÁÄÂÃÈ

Jute-SemiBold

ABCDEFGHIJKLMNOPQRSTUVWXYZabcdefghijklmnopqrstuvwxyz12
3456789O&$.;!@#%^*[[{+=\<™©®££¢¥§¶-†‡Øø¿?!¡ÀÁÄÂÃÈ

Jute-Bold

ABCDEFGHIJKLMNOPQRSTUVWXYZabcdefghijklmnopqrstuvwxyz123
456789O&$.;!@#%^*[[{+=\<™©®££¢¥§¶-†‡Øø¿?!¡ÀÁÄÂÃÈÉÉÈ

Maetl-Light

ABCDEFGHIJKLMNOPQRSTUVWXY
Zabcdefghijklmnopqrstuvwxyz

YouWorkForThem
1999

8 Typestyles in family:
Light, Regular, Bold, ExtraBold
and Oblique versions of the
same weights.

Maetl-Regular

ABCDEFGHIJKLMNOPQRSTUVWXYZ
abcdefghijklmnopqrstuvwxyz12

Maetl-Bold

ABCDEFGHIJKLMNOPQRSTUVWXY
Zabcdefghijklmnopqrstuvwxyz

Maetl-ExtraBold

ABCDEFGHIJKLMNOPQRSTUVWXY
Zabcdefghijklmnopqrstuvwxyz

Maetl-LightOblique

ABCDEFGHIJK
LMNOPQRSTU
VWXYZabcdef

Maetl-Oblique

ABCDEFGHIJK
LMNOPQRSTUV
WXYZabcdefg

Maetl-ExtraBoldOblique

ABCDEFGHIJK
LMNOPQRSTU
VWXYZabcdef

Novum

YouWorkForThem
2002

4 Typestyles in family:
Light, Regular, Bold, ExtraBold.

Novum-Light

ABCDEFGHIJKLMNOPQRSTUVWXZ
YZABCDEFGHIJKLMNOPQRSTUV

Novum-Regular

ABCDEFGHIJKLMNOPQRSTUVWXZ
YZABCDEFGHIJKLMNOPQRSTUV

Novum-Bold

ABCDEFGHIJKLMNOPQRSTUVWXZ
YZABCDEFGHIJKLMNOPQRSTUV

Novum-ExtraBold

ABCDEFGHIJKLMNOPQRSTUVWXZ
YZABCDEFGHIJKLMNOPQRSTUV

OneCross

YouWorkForThem
2002

7 Typestyles in family:
Light, Regular, SemiBold, Bold,
ExtraBold, UltraBold, Black.

OneCross-Light

ABCDEFGHIJKLMNOPQRSTUVWXYZabcdef
ghijklmnopqrstuvwxyz1234567890!?&

OneCross-Bold

ABCDEFGHIJKLMNOPQRSTUVWXYZabcde
fghijklmnopqrstuvwxyz1234567890!?

OneCross-Black

ABCDEFGHIJKLMNOPQRSTUVWXYZabcd
efghijklmnopqrstuvwxyz1234567890

OneCross-Right

ABCDEFGHIJKLMNOP
QRSTUVWXYZabcde
fghijklmnopqrstuv

OneCross-SemiBold

ABCDEFGHIJKLMNOP
QRSTUVWXYZabcde
fghijklmnopqrstuv

OneCross-UltraBold

ABCDEFGHIJKLMNO
PQRSTUVWXYZabcd
efghijklmnopqrst

Overcross-Extra Light

ABCDEFGHIJKLMNOPQRSTUVWXYZabcd
efghijklmnopqrstuvwxyz1234567890

Overcross-Light

ABCDEFGHIJKLMNOPQRSTUVWXYZabcd
efghijklmnopqrstuvwxyz1234567890

Overcross-Regular

ABCDEFGHIJKLMNOPQRSTUVWXYZabcd
efghijklmnopqrstuvwxyz1234567890

Overcross-Semi-Bold

ABCDEFGHIJKLMNOPQRSTUVWXYZabcd
efghijklmnopqrstuvwxyz1234567890

Overcross

YouWorkForThem
1999

12 Typestyles in family:
Light, ExtraLight, Regular,
SemiBold, Bold, ExtraBold and
Oblique versions of the same
weights.

Pakt

YouWorkForThem
2001

10 Typestyles in family:
Regular, SemiBold, Bold,
ExtraBold, Black and Condensed
versions of the same weights.

YouWorkForThem

Pakt-Condensed

ABCDEFGHIJKLMNOPQRSTUVWXYZabcdefghijklmnopqrstuvwxyz1234567890&$.,:!@
#%^*[[{+=\<™©®£€¢¥§¶–†‡0ø¿?!iÀÁÂÃÄÅÆÉÈÊÊÍÌÎÏÒÓÔÕÖÙÚÛÜŇàáäâãÆëéèÊíìîïïö

Pakt-SemiBoldCondensed

ABCDEFGHIJKLMNOPQRSTUVWXYZabcdefghijklmnopqrstuvwxyz1234567890&$.,:!@#
%^*[[{+=\<™©®£€¢¥§¶–†‡0ø¿?!iÀÁÂÃÄÅÆÉÈÊÊÍÌÎÏÒÓÔÕÖÙÚÛÜŇàáäâãÆëéèÊíìîïïó

Pakt-BoldCondensed

ABCDEFGHIJKLMNOPQRSTUVWXYZabcdefghijklmnopqrstuvwxyz1234567890&$.,:!@#
%^*[[{+=\<™©®£€¢¥§¶–†‡0ø¿?!iÀÁÂÃÄÅÆÉÈÊÊÍÌÎÏÒÓÔÕÖÙÚÛÜŇàáäâãÆëéèÊíìîïïó

Pakt-BlackCondensed

ABCDEFGHIJKLMNOPQRSTUVWXYZabcdefghijklmnopqrstuvwxyz1234567890&$.,:!@~%^
*[[{+=\<™©®£€¢¥§¶–†‡0ø¿?!iÀÁÂÃÄÅÆÉÈÊÍÌÎÏÒÓÔÕÖÙÚÛÜŇàáäâãÆëéèÊíìîïó

Pakt

YouWorkForThem
2001

10 Typestyles in family:
Regular, SemiBold, Bold,
ExtraBold, Black and Condensed
versions of the same weights.

Pakt-Regular

ABCDEFGHIJKLMNOPQRSTUVWXYZabcdefghijklmnopqrstuvwx
yz1234567890&$.;!@#%^*[[{+=\<™©®£€¢¥§¶-†‡00¿?!ÌÁÄÂ

Pakt-SemiBold

ABCDEFGHIJKLMNOPQRSTUVWXYZabcdefghijklmnopqrstuvw
xyz1234567890&$.;!@#%^*[[{+=\<™©®£€¢¥§¶-†‡00¿?!ÌÀÁÄ

Pakt-ExtraBold

ABCDEFGHIJKLMNOPQRSTUVWXYZabcdefghijklmnopqrstuv
wxyz1234567890&$.;!@#%^*[[{+=\<™©®£€¢¥§¶-†‡00¿?!i

Pakt-Black

ABCDEFGHIJKLMNOPQRSTUVWXYZabcdefghijklmnopqrstuv
wxyz1234567890&$.;!@#%^*[[{+=\<™©®£€¢¥§¶-†‡00¿?!i

Praun

YouWorkForThem
1998

7 Typestyles in family:
Thin, ExtraLight, Light, Regular,
SemiBold, Bold, and ExtraBold.

Praun-Thin

ABCDEFGHIJKLMNOPQRSTUVWXYZabcdef
ghijklmnopqrstuvwxyz1234567890&$.;!

Praun-Regular

ABCDEFGHIJKLMNOPQRSTUVWXYZabcdefghij
klmnopqrstuvwxyz1234567890&$.;!@#%^*cc

Praun-ExraBold

ABCDEFGHIJKLMNOPQRSTUVWXYZabcdefghijklm
nopqrstuvwxyz1234567890&$.;!@#%^*ccc+=\<™©

Praun-ExtraLight

ABCDEFGHIJKLMNO
PQRSTUVWXYZabcd
efghijklmnopqrst

Praun-Light

ABCDEFGHIJKLMNOP
QRSTUVWXYZabcde
fghijklmnopqrstu

Praun-Bold

ABCDEFGHIJKLMNOPQ
RSTUVWXYZabcdefg
hijklmnopqrstuvwx

Proce55ing-Regular

ABCDEFGHIJKLMNOPQRSTUVWXYZabcdefghijkl
mnopqrstuvwxyz1234567890&$.;!@#%^*[[{+=

Proce55ing-Bold

ABCDEFGHIJKLMNOPQRSTUVWXYZabcdefghijklm
nopqrstuvwxyz1234567890&$.;!@#%^*[[{+=\<™

Pro55-Bold

ABCDEFGHIJKLMNOPQRSTUVWXYZabcdefghijklm
nopqrstuvwxyz1234567890&$.;!@#%^*[[{+=\<™

Proce55ing-Light

ABCDEFGHIJKLMNOP
QRSTUVWXYZabcdef
ghijklmnopqrstuvw

Pro55-Regular

ABCDEFGHIJKLMNOPQ
RSTUVWXYZabcdefg
hijklmnopqrstuvwxy

Pro55-Light

ABCDEFGHIJKLMNOP
QRSTUVWXYZabcdef
ghijklmnopqrstuvw

Proce55ing

YouWorkForThem
1998

6 Typestyles in family:
Light, Regular, Bold, Pro55-Light,
Pro55-Regular, Pro55-Bold.

Reversion-Thin

Reversion-ExtraBold

Reversion-RegularBroken

Reversion-SemiBold

Reversion-LightBroken

Reversion-Regular

Reversion

YouWorkForThem
1997

12 Typestyles in family:
Thin, ExtraLight, Light, Regular,
SemiBold, Bold, ExtraBold.
Includes a "Broken" Series with
Thin, ExtraLight, Light, Regular,
SemiBold versions also.

YouWorkForThem

YouWorkfForThem
1998

4 Type styles in family:
Light, Regular, Bold, Extra Bold

Selector-Light

ABCDEFGHIJKLMNOPQRSTUVWXYZab
cdefghijklmnopqrstuvwxyz12345

Selector-Regular

ABCDEFGHIJKLMNOPQRSTUVWXYZa
bcdefghijklmnopqrstuvwxyz1234

Selector-Bold

ABCDEFGHIJKLMNOPQRSTUVWXYZa
bcdefghijklmnopqrstuvwxyz1234

Selector-ExtraBold

ABCDEFGHIJKLMNOPQRSTUVWXYZa
bcdefghijklmnopqrstuvwxyz123

YouWorkfForThem
1999

8 Type styles in family:
Thin, Extra Light, Light, Regular,
Demi Bold, Bold, Extra Bold,
Black

Trisect-Thin

ABCDEFGHIJKLMNOPQRSTUVWXYZab
cdefghijklmnopqrstuvwxyz12345

Trisect-ExtraLight

ABCDEFGHIJKLMNOPQRSTUVWXYZab
cdefghijklmnopqrstuvwxyz12345

Trisect-Light

ABCDEFGHIJKLMNOPQRSTUVWXYZab
cdefghijklmnopqrstuvwxyz12345

Trisect-Regular

ABCDEFGHIJKLMNOPQRSTUVWXYZab
cdefghijklmnopqrstuvwxyz12345

info@youworkforthem.com

Trisect-DemiBold

ABCDEFGHIJKLMNOPQRSTUUWXYZabcd
efghijklmnopqrstuuwxyz123456789

Trisect-Bold

ABCDEFGHIJKLMNOPQRSTUUWXYZabcd
efghijklmnopqrstuuwxyz123456789

Trisect-ExtraBold

ABCDEFGHIJKLMNOPQRSTUUWXYZabcd
efghijklmnopqrstuuwxyz123456789

Trisect-Black

ABCDEFGHIJKLMNOPQRSTUUWXYZabcd
efghijklmnopqrstuuwxyz123456789

YouWorkForThem
1999

8 Typestyles in family:
Thin, ExtraLight, Light, Regular,
DemiBold, Bold, ExtraBold, Black.

Ultramagnetic-Light

ABCDEFGHIJKLMNOPQRSTUVWXYZabcdefghijklmno
pqrstuvwxyz1234567890&$.,;!@#%^*[({+=\<™©

Ultramagnetic-Regular

ABCDEFGHIJKLMNOPQRSTUVWXYZabcdefghijklmn
opqrstuvwxyz1234567890&$.,;!@#%^*[({+=\<™

Ultramagnetic-Bold

ABCDEFGHIJKLMNOPQRSTUVWXYZabcdefghijklmn
opqrstuvwxyz1234567890&$.,;!@#%^*[({+=\<™

Ultramagnetic-ExtraBold

ABCDEFGHIJKLMNOPQRSTUVWXYZabcdefghijkl
mnopqrstuvwxyz1234567890&$.,;!@#%^*[({+=

YouWorkForThem
1996

10 Typestyles in family:
Light, Regular, Bold, ExtraBold,
Black and Oblique versions of
the same weights.

YouWorkForThem

YouWorkForThem
1996

10 Typestyles in family:
Light, Regular, Bold, ExtraBold,
Black and Oblique versions of
the same weights.

Ultramagnetic-Black

ABCDEFGHIJKLMNOPQRSTUVWXYZabcdefghij
klmnopqrstuvwxyz1234567890&$.;!@#%^*[

Ultramagnetic-LightOblique

ABCDEFGHIJKLMNOPQRSTUVWXYZabcdefghijklmno
pqrstuvwxyz1234567890&$.;!@#%^*[({+=\‹™©

Ultramagnetic-Oblique

ABCDEFGHIJKLMNOPQRSTUVWXYZabcdefghijklmn
opqrstuvwxyz1234567890&$.;!@#%^*[({+=\‹™

Ultramagnetic-ExtraBoldOblique

ABCDEFGHIJKLMNOPQRSTUVWXYZabcdefghijkl
mnopqrstuvwxyz1234567890&$.;!@#%^*[({+=

Unfinished-Regular

ABCDEFGHIJKLMNOPQRSTUVWXYZabcdefgh
ijklmnopqrstuvwxyz1234567890&$.;!@#%^*
[({+=\‹™©®"£¢¥

Unfinished-SemiBold

ABCDEFGHIJKLMNOPQRSTUVWXYZabcdefghi
jklmnopqrstuvwxyz1234567890&$.;!@#%^*[
({+=\‹™©®"£¢¥

Unfinished-Bold

ABCDEFGHIJKLMNOPQRSTUVWXYZabcdefghi
jklmnopqrstuvwxyz1234567890&$.;!@#%^*[
({+=\‹™©®"£¢¥

Unfinished-Black

ABCDEFGHIJKLMNOPQRSTUVWXYZabcdefghi
jklmnopqrstuvwxyz1234567890&$.;!@#%^*[
({+=\‹™©®"£¢¥

Unisect-Light

ABCDEFGHIJKLMNOPQRSTUUWXYZabcdefghijkl
mnopqrstuuwxyz1234567890&$,;!a#×[[{+=2c

Unisect-Regular

ABCDEFGHIJKLMNOPQRSTUUWXYZabcdefghij
klmnopqrstuuwxyz1234567890&$,;!a#×[[{

Unisect-Bold

ABCDEFGHIJKLMNOPQRSTUUWXYZabcdefg
hijklmnopqrstuuwxyz1234567890&$,;!a

Unisect-ExtraBold

ABCDEFGHIJKLMNOPQRSTUUWXYZabcdefg
hijklmnopqrstuuwxyz1234567890&$,;!a

Unisect-Black

ABCDEFGHIJKLMNOPQRSTUUWXYZabcde
fghijklmnopqrstuuwxyz1234567890&

Unisect-LightOblique

ABCDEFGHIJKLMNOPQRSTUUWXYZabcdefghijkl
mnopqrstuuwxyz1234567890&$,;!a#×[[{+=2c

Unisect-BoldOblique

ABCDEFGHIJKLMNOPQRSTUUWXYZabcdefg
hijklmnopqrstuuwxyz1234567890&$,;!a

Unisect-BlackOblique

ABCDEFGHIJKLMNOPQRSTUUWXYZabcde
fghijklmnopqrstuuwxyz1234567890&

Unisect

YouWorkForThem
1999

10 Typestyles in family:
Light, Regular, Bold, ExtraBold,
Black and Oblique versions of
the same weights

YouWorkForThem

Essay:

Typocurious, and how to stay that way.

By Peter Bain

Your first reaction is probably amazement at how many typefaces there are. After further investigation, it dawns on you that there may be more to type and typography than just scrolling through a list of available fonts. The challenge of trying out all those styles beckons. You vow never to use Arial again...

With computers, type users can be players in a typographic culture, not just font fans. If this sounds impressive, that's because the opportunity is there. To provide you with maximum stimulation and nourishment, about 13 items were selected for the typographically curious. The introductory descriptions that follow are meant to inspire you to seek them out at bookstores, libraries, and on the shelves of typofriends. Advanced grasshoppers will want to join in the fun, comparing their own picks with these personal choices.

That popular eurostyle

Shopping for new furniture can be intimidating. You might want something with a modern look, but aren't sure where to start. You'll be relieved to know that typographic design does have its own modern masters. One name worth learning is that of Jan Tschichold, who championed the avant garde, only to become more conservative when his tastes changed. He recorded his formidable knowledge in various publications; his manual for moderns is a must-read.

Noticed that sans serif type is the height of fashion? The influence of so-called swiss design, or European-trained designers and teachers, encouraged this trend. In Basel, Emil Ruder formulated his rationale for going sans serif. His engagingly illustrated typographic manual continues to inspire. This is a useful stop on the way to grids and Joseph Müller-Brockmann.

Jan Tschichold. *Asymmetric Typography.* Trans. by Ruari McLean. New York: Reinhold Publishing; Toronto: Cooper & Beatty; and London: Faber, 1967.

Emil Ruder. *Typography: A Manual of Design.* Teufen AR, Switzerland: Arthur Niggli, 1967, 1st ed. Sulgen/Zurich, Switzerland: Verlag Niggli, 2001, 7th ed.

Seeking to become a better person?

Take a fulfilling path toward humility and greater attention to detail. Be led from the darkness of ignorance into the light of self-knowledge concerning careful line breaks, word spacing, and the differences between composition standards. Robert Bringhurst's *Elements of Typographic Style* is a commendable reference, yet your most humble compiler maintains a few quibbles. Accessible guidance for typographic seekers is available from Betty Binns, who mindfully explores the rhythms of body copy, and from Geoffrey Dowding, who heightens our awareness of both text and display type. These helpful gurus show why the fussy stuff really matters.

Betty Binns. *Better Type.* New York: Watson-Guptill, 1989.

Geoffrey Dowding. *Finer Points in the Spacing and Arrangement of Type.* London: Wace and Co., 1966. Vancouver: Hartley & Marks, revised edition, 1995.

Old school

Back in the day when display type could be expensive, you had an alternative. You could invent a new style or rework an existing one, hiring someone (or yourself) to draw the letters needed by hand. Handlettering artists developed insights into typographic shape and weight as valid today as they were in the heyday of vinyl LPs. Aspiring type designers now look to Fred Smeijers' *Counterpunch*, Walter Tracy's *Letters of Credit*, and Doyald Young's *Fonts and Logos*. But David Gates lays down a solid groove, deftly explaining aspects of letterform design others may not cover. In an expressive mode, Tommy Thompson plays through a range of scripts, improvising on past masters.

David Gates. *Lettering for Reproduction.* New York: Watson-Guptill, 1969.

Tommy Thompson. *Script Lettering for Artists.* (originally *The Script Letter*, 1955) New York: Dover Publications, 1965.

Breakthrough Eighties and Nineties hits

When some upstart Bay Area designers wanted to get noticed, they opted for the print version of college radio. They named their independent zine after their experiences crossing borders. Desktop publishing was beginning, so technology got thrown into the mix, too. The result was a magazine that had an explosive impact.

The first 32 issues of *Emigre* were in a large format that seems luxurious today. It was a powerful platform for presenting work from outside the mainstream of graphic design, and provided room for new criticism. *Emigre* had a similar interest in new approaches to typography and typeface design. If you've never had a chance to go through the back issues, you don't know what you're missing.

Emigre, since 1984.

Experimenting on the reader

Guinea pigs and readers have more in common than you might think. Any reader who isn't the originating designer becomes a kind of test subject, usually without suffering any adverse effects. But you may wonder just where the boundaries of legibility and readability fall. If you want to get a better understanding of these concepts, a tour of the typographic laboratory is in order. Herbert Spencer was an inquisitive, accomplished designer/editor/author who sought out typographic experimentation. While there are newer treatments of the psychology of reading, his book remains a key introduction to studies of reading.

Herbert Spencer. *The Visible Word.* New York: Hastings House and London: Lund Humphries, 1969.

An unexpected tour

There are fine books on the history of typefaces, charting when they were first cut or used, and what we still may not know. But the history and variety of letterforms is far deeper. Artists working with letters have been busy over the past two thousand years. Their efforts, whether cut in stone, worked into metal, woven in fabric, or written on vellum, can be astonishing. This is a tour going around the corners and down the side streets of letterforms, without neglecting familiar landmarks. The notes in these books, whether in the main text or following the pictures, are your expert commentary. Both Nicolete Gray and Jan Tschichold want to make sure that you appreciate the sights.

Nicolete Gray. *A History of Lettering: Creative Experiment and Letter Identity.* Boston: David R. Godine, 1986. London: Phaidon Press, 1986.

Jan Tschichold. *Treasury of Alphabets and Lettering.* New York: Reinhold, 1966; New York: Design Press, McGraw-Hill, 1992; and New York: W. W. Norton, 1995.

Essay questions

What is typography for, really? Why print something? What purposes does that serve? Gutenberg's invention of movable type changed Western society. Elizabeth Eisenstein's readable, scholarly account of the original demand for and effects of print offers a valuable perspective on this true paradigm shift. It will spur your thinking into the roles of electronic writing.

Robin Kinross takes a different tack, examining typography in the context of design and practice, with special attention to the past century. The story of how designers and typographers developed their ideas makes his book compelling. The reproductions are carefully captioned, adding a visual counterpart to the narrative. If you read both books, you're sure to be a hit at cocktail parties near campus.

Elizabeth Eisenstein. *The Printing Press as an Agent of Change.* London and New York: Cambridge University Press, 1979.

Robin Kinross. *Modern Typography: An essay in critical history.* London: Hyphen Press, 1992.

A few closing words

Blah, blah-blah blah, blah blah-ah, blah, bluh. Without words, type wouldn't be any fun; it wouldn't have much meaning, either. Language is the flip side of typography. How the two relate, and exploring the methods used in typography, are the subjects of Cal Swann's deceptively simple book. He covers everything from decision-making charts to linguistic theories of meaning in a clear, unpretentious way.

Cal Swann. *Language and Typography.* New York: Van Nostrand Reinhold, 1991.

Write on, and keep on typographing.

Peter Bain is principal of Incipit (www.incipit.com), a New York design studio whose practice is built upon letters. Projects undertaken for clients include custom typefaces, logotypes, handlettering, and typographic design. Bain has studied, specified, collected, curated, and lectured on typography, and still likes it.

Appendix A:
Character Reference Chart

This chart is for US keyboard layout; other countries may vary. This chart is intended for general reference. Individual font layouts may vary.

Character reference chart. Each cell shows the **character**, the Macintosh keystroke (top), and the Windows Alt-code (bottom).

A	B	C	D	E	F	G	H	I	J	K	L	M	N	O	P	Q	R	S
a A / A	**b** B / B	**c** C / C	**d** D / D	**e** E / E	**f** F / F	**g** G / G	**h** H / H	**i** I / I	**j** J / J	**k** K / K	**l** L / L	**m** M / M	**n** N / N	**o** O / O	**p** P / P	**q** Q / Q	**r** R / R	**s** S / S
t T / T	**u** U / U	**v** V / V	**w** W / W	**x** X / X	**y** Y / Y	**z** Z / Z	**A** Sh-A	**B** Sh-B	**C** Sh-C	**D** Sh-D	**E** Sh-E	**F** Sh-F	**G** Sh-G	**H** Sh-H	**I** Sh-I	**J** Sh-J	**K** Sh-K	**L** Sh-L
M Sh-M	**N** Sh-N	**O** Sh-O	**P** Sh-P	**Q** Sh-Q	**R** Sh-R	**S** Sh-S	**T** Sh-T	**U** Sh-U	**V** Sh-V	**W** Sh-W	**X** Sh-X	**Y** Sh-Y	**Z** Sh-Z	**1** 1	**2** 2	**3** 3	**4** 4	**5** 5
6 6	**7** 7	**8** 8	**9** 9	**0** 0	**!** Sh-1	**@** Sh-2	**#** Sh-3	**$** Sh-4	**%** Sh-5	**^** Sh-6	**&** Sh-7	***** Sh-8	**(** Sh-9	**)** Sh-0	**,** ,	**.** .	**;** ;	**:** Sh-;
- - / -	**/** / / /	**?** Sh-/	**'** '	**"** Sh-'	**¡** OP-1 / Alt-0161	**¿** Sh-Op-/ / Alt-0191	**–** Op-- / Alt-0173	**+** Sh-=	**≈** Op-x / Alt-0215	**÷** Op-/ / Alt-0247	**=** = / =	**±** Sh-Op-= / Alt-0177	**<** Sh-.	**>** Sh-,	**[** [	**]**]	**{** Sh-[	**}** Sh-]
' Op-] / Alt-0145	**'** Sh-Op-] / Alt-0146	**"** Op-[/ Alt-0147	**"** Sh-Op-[/ Alt-0148	**‹** Sh-Op-3 / Alt-0139	**›** Sh-Op-4 / Alt-0155	**«** Op-\ / Alt-0171	**»** Sh-Op-\ / Alt-0187	**‚** Sh-Op-0 / Alt-0130	**„** Sh-Op-W / Alt-0132	**—** Sh-` / Alt-0151	**** \ / \	**|** Sh-\	**_** Sh--	**…** Op-; / Alt-0133	**°** Sh-Op-8 / Alt-0176	**·** Sh-Op-9 / Alt-0183		**•** Op-8 / Alt-0149
ä Op-U A / Alt-0228	**â** Op-I A / Alt-0226	**á** Op-E A / Alt-0225	**à** Op-` A / Alt-0224	**ã** Op-N A / Alt-0227	**å** Op-A / Alt-0229	**ë** Op-U E / Alt-0235	**ê** Op-I E / Alt-0234	**é** Op-E E / Alt-0233	**è** Op-` E / Alt-0232	**ï** Op-U I / Alt-0239	**î** Op-I I / Alt-0238	**í** Op-E I / Alt-0237	**ì** Op-` I / Alt-0236	**ö** Op-U O / Alt-0246	**ô** Op-I O / Alt-0244	**ó** Op-E O / Alt-0243	**ò** Op-` O / Alt-0242	**õ** Op-N O / Alt-0245
ü Op-U U / Alt-0252	**û** Op-I U / Alt-0251	**ú** Op-E U / Alt-0250	**ù** Op-` U / Alt-0249	**Ä** Op-U Sh-A / Alt-0196	**Â** Op-I Sh-A / Alt-0194	**Á** Op-E Sh-A / Alt-0193	**À** Op-` Sh-A / Alt-0192	**Ã** Op-N Sh-A / Alt-0195	**Å** Sh-Op-A / Alt-0197	**Ë** Op-U Sh-E / Alt-0203	**Ê** Op-I Sh-E / Alt-0202	**É** Op-E Sh-E / Alt-0201	**È** Op-` Sh-E / Alt-0200	**Ï** Op-U Sh-I / Alt-0207	**Î** Op-I Sh-I / Alt-0206	**Í** Op-E Sh-I / Alt-0205	**Ì** Op-` Sh-I / Alt-0204	**Ö** Op-U Sh-O / Alt-0214
Ô Op-I Sh-O / Alt-0212	**Ó** Op-E Sh-O / Alt-0211	**Ò** Op-` Sh-O / Alt-0210	**Õ** Op-N Sh-O / Alt-0213	**Ü** Op-U Sh-U / Alt-0220	**Û** Op-I Sh-U / Alt-0219	**Ú** Op-E Sh-U / Alt-0218	**Ù** Sh-` Sh-U / Alt-0217	**ç** Op-C / Alt-0231	**Ç** Sh-Op-C / Alt-0199	**ñ** Op-N N / Alt-0241	**Ñ** Op-N Sh-N / Alt-0209	**ø** Op-O / Alt-0248	**Ø** Sh-Op-O / Alt-0216	**ß** Op-S / Alt-0223	**æ** Op-' / Alt-0230	**Æ** Sh-Op-' / Alt-0198	**œ** Op-Q / Alt-0156	**Œ** Sh-Op-Q / Alt-0140
ð Ctrl-B / Alt-0240	**Đ** Ctrl-A / Alt-0208	**ł** Ctrl-D	**Ł** Ctrl-C	**š** Ctrl-F / Alt-0154	**Š** Ctrl-E / Alt-0138	**ÿ** Op-U Y / Alt-0255	**ý** Ctrl-H / Alt-0253	**Ÿ** Op-U Sh-Y / Alt-0159	**Ý** Ctrl-G / Alt-0221	**ž** Ctrl-O	**Ž** Ctrl-N	**þ** Ctrl-L / Alt-0254	**Þ** Ctrl-K / Alt-0222	**ı** Sh-Op-B	**ª** Op-9 / Alt-0170	**º** Op-0 / Alt-0186	**fi** Sh-Op5	**fl** Sh-Op-6
¨ Sh-Op-U / Alt-0168	**ˆ** Sh-Op-I / Alt-0136	**´** Sh-Op-E / Alt-0180	**`**	**˜** Sh-Op-N / Alt-0152	**˚** Op-K	**¯** Sh-Op-, / Alt-0175	**ˇ** Sh-Op-.	Op-H	Sh-Op-G	**¸** Sh-Op-T / Alt-0184	**'** Sh-Op-Z	Sh-Op-X	**£** Op-3 / Alt-0163	**¥** Op-Y / Alt-0165	**ƒ** Op-F / Alt-0131	**¢** Op-4 / Alt-0162	**€** Sh-Op-2 / Alt-0164	**∞** Op-5
© Op-G / Alt-0169	**®** Op-R / Alt-0174	**π** Op-P	**™** Op-2 / Alt-0153	**⁄** Sh-Op-1	**‰** Sh-Op-R / Alt-0137	**µ** Op-M / Alt-0181	**§** Op-6 / Alt-0167	**†** Op-T / Alt-0134	**‡** Sh-Op-7 / Alt-0135	**¶** Op-7 / Alt-0182	**¦** Ctrl-[/ Alt-0166	**¹** Ctrl-W / Alt-0185	**²** Ctrl-Z / Alt-0178	**³** Ctrl-Y / Alt-0179	**¼** Ctrl-V / Alt-0188	**½** Ctrl-U / Alt-0189	**¾** Ctrl-X / Alt-0190	**** Sh-Op-K

US keyboard layout; other countries may vary. This chart is intended for general reference. Individual font layouts may vary.

 Characters generally not available in Windows.

 Characters generally not available in Macintosh OS.

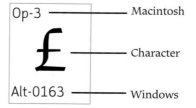

Op-3 — Macintosh
£ — Character
Alt-0163 — Windows

Appendix B:
Foundry Contacts

Atomic Media
PO Box 789
Tucson, AZ 85701 USA
http://atomicmedia.net
fonts@atomicmedia.net

Feliciano Type Foundry
Rua do Quelhas 20 R/C Dto.
1200-781 Lisboa, Portugal
TEL + 351 21 390 61 40
FAX + 351 21 394 07 04
http://www.secretonix.pt
ftfinfo@secretonix.pt

Galápagos Design Group, Inc.
256 Great Road, Suite 9
Littleton, MA 01460 USA
TEL 978-952-6200
FAX 978-952-6260
http://www.galapagosdesign.com
info@galapagosdesign.com

Holland Fonts
95 Bolsa Avenue
Mill Valley, CA 94941 USA
TEL 415-380-8303
FAX 415-398-6738
http://www.hollandfonts.com
info@hollandfonts.com

The Identikal Foundry
Studio 5, The Oasis Buildings
Empire Square
540 Holloway Road
London N7 6JN United Kingdom
TEL +44 (0) 20 7263 2129
FAX +44 (0) 20 7272 1521
http://www.identikal.com
info@identikal.com

ingoFonts
Kreitmayrstrasse 30/30a
86165 Augsburg, Germany
TEL 0049 821 72 93 55 0
FAX 0049 821 72 93 55 1
http://www.ingo-zimmermann.de
info@ingo-zimmermann.de

Jukebox
1116 North Spaulding Ave., Unit D
West Hollywood, CA 90046 USA
TEL 323-650-2740
http://www.JAWarts.com
jasonwalcott@earthlink.net

MVB Fonts
PO Box 6137
Albany, CA 94706 USA
TEL 510-525-4288
FAX 510-525-4289
http://www.mvbfonts.com
info@mvbfonts.com

Neufville Digital
Visualogik Technology & Design bv
PO Box 1953
5200 BZ 's-Hertogenbosch
The Netherlands
TEL +31 73 613 2747
FAX +31 73 614 7714
http://www.neufville.com
visualogik@neufville.com

Nick's Fonts
6 W. Deer Park Rd., Unit 203
Gaithersburg, MD 20877 USA
TEL 301-947-5428
FAX 419-793-7314
http://www.nicksfonts.com
himself@nicksfonts.com

No Bodoni Typography
1170 West Farwell Ave, Suite C
Chicago, IL 60626 USA
TEL 773-934-2647
http://www.nobodoni.com
support@nobodoni.com

Parkinson Type Design
6170 Broadway Terrace
Oakland, CA 94618 USA
http://www.typedesign.com
parkinson@typedesign.com

Mark Simonson Studio
1496 Raymond Avenue
St. Paul, MN 55108 USA
TEL 651-649-0553
http://www.ms-studio.com
mark@ms-studio.com

Sherwood Type Collection
PO Box 770
Buffalo, NY 14213 USA
TEL 716-885-4490
FAX 716-885-4482
http://www.sherwoodtype.com
sherwoodtype@p22.com

Storm Type Foundry
Spalova 23, 162 00 Praha 6
Czech Republic
TEL +420 2 3333 75 11
FAX +420 233 337 890
http://www.stormtype.com
mail@stormtype.com

Terminal Design, Inc.
125 Congress Street
Brooklyn, NY 11201 USA
TEL 718-246-7069
FAX 718-246-7085
http://www.terminaldesign.com
type@terminaldesign.com

Underware
Schouwburgstraat 2
2511 VA, Den Haag
The Netherlands
TEL +31 (0) 70 4278 117
FAX +31 (0) 70 4278 116
http://www.underware.nl
info@underware.nl

Union Fonts Ltd
Blackswan Court
69 Westgate Road
Newcastle upon Tyne
NE1 1SG United Kingdom
http://www.unionfonts.com
jim@unionfonts.com

YouWorkForThem
4274 Meghan Lane
Eagan, MN 55122 USA
TEL 651-452-9191
http://www.youworkforthem.com
info@youworkforthem.com

Appendix C:
Bonus Fonts CD

The 38 indie fonts listed here are included on an unlocked Bonus Fonts CD-ROM located in a sealed package in the back of this book. The fonts are licensed from each contributing foundry for use solely by the owner of this book, and may only be used in accordance with the terms set forth in the respective End User License Agreements (EULA). Any further re-distribution or transfer of the license to use this software is strictly prohibited. Please consult the individual "read me" files and/or EULA files located in each foundry's directory.

By breaking the sealed package containing this CD-ROM, you are agreeing to be bound by the terms of the license agreement and limited warranty set forth by each foundry. If you do not agree to the terms of said agreements, please do not use these fonts.

PostScript, TrueType, and/or OpenType formats are included or available for the Mac OS and/or Windows operating systems. Not all foundries provide fonts in all available formats/platforms on this CD-ROM.

P-Type Publications is not responsible for errors, omissions or technical problems inherent in the font software or in its accompanying documentation. Please contact the individual foundries for more information on licensing, upgrades or support.

Font Type Key
Mac PS = Macintosh PostScript
Mac TT = Macintosh TrueType
Win PS = Windows PostScript
Win TT = Windows TrueType
OT = OpenType (cross-platform)

Foundry	Mac Fonts	Win Fonts	Font Name
Atomic Media	Mac PS	Win PS	GENETICA
Atomic Media	Mac PS	Win PS	GENETICA BOLD
Feliciano	Mac PS	Win TT & PS	35-Landscape
Galápagos	Mac TT & PS	Win TT & PS	Nikki New Roman GD
Holland Fonts	Mac TT & PS	Win TT & PS	MaxMix
Holland Fonts	Mac TT & PS	Win TT & PS	Chip-1
Identikal	Mac PS	Win PS	ID-01 Left
Identikal	Mac PS	Win PS	ID-01 Right
ingoFonts	Mac TT & PS	Win TT & PS	Charpentier Renaissance
ingoFonts	Mac TT & PS	Win TT & PS	Deutsche Schrift Lettwong
ingoFonts	Mac TT & PS	Win TT & PS	Ergogum
ingoFonts	Mac TT & PS	Win TT & PS	Josef Normal
ingoFonts	Mac TT & PS	Win TT & PS	KLEX
Jukebox	Mac TT & PS	Win TT & PS	Fairy Tale JF
Jukebox	Mac TT & PS	Win TT & PS	WALCOTT GOTHIC-SUNSET
Mark Simonson	Mac TT	Win TT	Anonymous
Mark Simonson	Mac TT & PS	Win TT & PS	MOSTRA ONE REGULAR
Mark Simonson	Mac TT & PS	Win TT & PS	MOSTRA TWO REGULAR
Mark Simonson	Mac TT & PS	Win TT & PS	MOSTRA THREE REGULAR
Neufville	Mac TT & PS	Win TT & PS	Futura ND Medium
Neufville	Mac TT & PS	Win TT & PS	Futura ND Medium Oblique
Nick's Fonts	Mac TT & PS	Win TT & PS	Annabelle Matinee NF
No Bodoni	Mac PS	Win TT & PS	Claudium
Sherwood	Mac TT	Win TT	Founders

Foundry	Mac Fonts	PC Fonts	Font Name
Storm Type Foundry	Mac TT & PS	Win TT & PS	Lido
Storm Type Foundry	Mac TT & PS	Win TT & PS	*Lido Italic*
Storm Type Foundry	Mac TT & PS	Win TT & PS	**Lido Bold**
Storm Type Foundry	Mac TT & PS	Win TT & PS	***Lido Bold Italic***
Storm Type Foundry	Mac TT & PS	Win TT & PS	Lido Condensed
Storm Type Foundry	Mac TT & PS	Win TT & PS	**Lido Condensed Bold**
Storm Type Foundry	OT	OT	*Walbaum Text Italic OT*
Terminal	OT	OT	Rawlinson OT
Underware	Mac TT		Unibody-8 Roman
Underware	Mac TT		Unibody-8 Italic
Underware	Mac TT		UNIBODY-8 SC
Underware	Mac TT		**Unibody-8 Black**
Union Fonts	Mac TT	Win TT	HOT METAL
YouWorkForThem	Mac PS	Win TT	niblah regular

PostScript Type 1 was developed by Adobe Systems for use with PostScript output devices. In Mac OS, a Type 1 font consists of an outline font (printer font) and a bitmap font (screen font) that also carries the metrics data. In Windows, a Type 1 font also uses two files, one containing the outlines (.PFB), and one containing the printer font metrics (.PFM). Thousands of PostScript fonts have been developed for use with both Mac OS and Windows, although the same font files can not be used interchangeably on both platforms.

TrueType, developed by Apple and intended for use with Mac OS 7, was also adopted by Microsoft for use with Windows (.TTF). TrueType fonts consist of a single file used for both screen display and printing, eliminating the need for separate outline and bitmap fonts. TrueType font files also cannot be used interchangeably on both platforms.

OpenType, developed jointly by Adobe and Microsoft, is a font format designed to combine the best of TrueType and PostScript into a single format for use on both Macintosh and Windows platforms. OpenType allows for up to 65,000 glyphs and conditional letter combinations, with easier access to full expert set characters, facilitating multilingual and advanced typography. An OpenType font consists of one font file that can be installed on either the Mac OS or Windows, eliminating the need for a separate font file for each platform.

Appendix C

Index

The following is a combined index of both volumes of *Indie Fonts*. To differentiate between the two books, page numbers from this volume are listed in bold face.

Legal Information

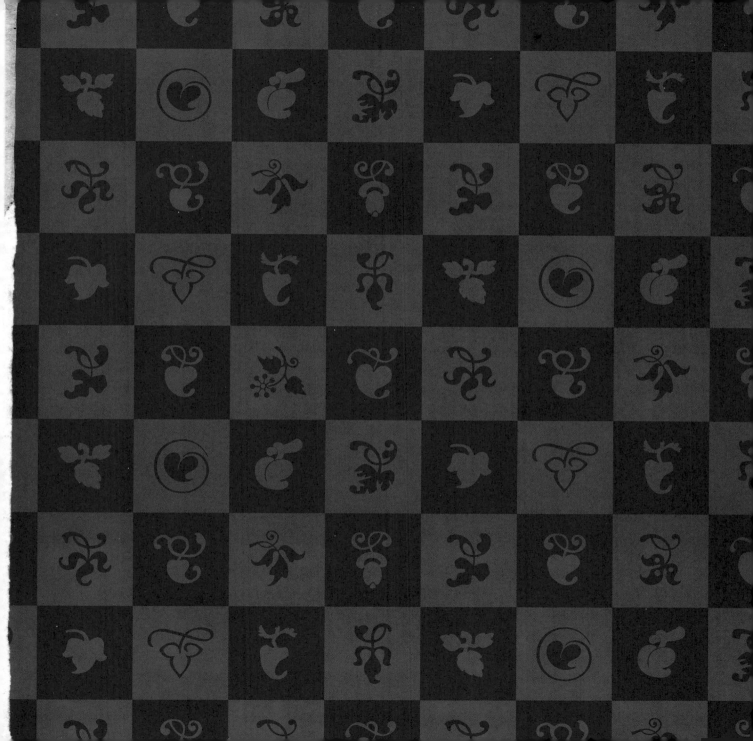